MW00619868

Shabbat

A COMPREHENSIVE DAILY HALACHA COMPANION FOR SEPHARDIM

ADAPTED FROM
השבת והלכותיה

WRITTEN BY HARAV
AHARON ZAKAY SHLITA

ROSH YESHIVA –
YESHIVAT OR YOM TOV
YERUSHALAYIM

AVICHAI SAMIMI

Copyright © 2021 by the author
Rabbi Avichai Samimi
Shabbatthesefer@gmail.com
ISBN 978-1-951125-23-3

All rights reserved.
No part of this book may be
reproduced in any form without
written permission of the
copyright holder.

Design & Print by:

315 4ᵀᴴ STREET • LAKEWOOD NJ 08701
732-475-0101 • MACHON@BPPRINTGROUP.COM

DEDICATED
IN THE LOVING MEMORY OF

בנימין בן אברהם הכהן ע"ה
Iraj Imanoel Z"L

We will never forget the lesson you've taught
us about love, family and happiness.
Your smiling face will remain forever in our hearts.

עטרת זקנים בני בנים
ותפארת בנים אבותם

The crown of elders is grandchildren,
And the splendor of children is their parents

(Mishlei/Proverbs 17:6)

WITH ALL OUR LOVE
Mazal Imanoel
(Devoted Wife)

Children & Grandchildren:
Babak & Negar (Ora) Imanoel
Erela, Eli & Edel

Bita & Benni Imani
Rafi, Michal, Gabi, Shira & David
First great-grandchild Judah

Bahareh & Saman Radparvar
Dalia, Daniel, Michael, Aviel and Benyamin

מוסדות
אור יום טוב

ע"ש הגאון יום טוב עוב ידיד הלוי זצ"ל
בראשות הרב אהרן זכאי שליט"א

רחוב גשר החיים 10,
ת.ד. 36669, ירושלים.
טל: 02-5389503
פקס: 02-5374658

INSTITUTIONS
OR YOM TOV
in memory of Hagao'n
Yom-Tov Yedid Halevi zt"l

Headed by HARAV
AHARON ZAKAI Shlita

10, Gesher Ha'Haim St.
P.O.B 36669, Jerusalem
Tel: 02-5389503
Fax: 02-5374658

ב"ה   ג' ספרו התורה

<u>מכתב ברכה</u>

שמחה לבי ויגל כבודי בראותי, שהאברך
היקר והנעלה הדין לצאת לאור ברבים
מהדורה של המקום והגירות התשובתית של אי טהו
לבבת רוחו לתרבות את ספרן דבבת והתוכחה
להבת הנעלבת, כדי שרבים ועוד יוכלו
את התלבת של הורין ולקיים ביינה
כאמור: אשרי מאמין, ובא אאהו ובוענו
בתלמתן עיד לשלום (שבת קיח.)

ותהיין אברבו לברך לך, יהי שיבה
לזרק של השואלין ולזבות את הרבים
ביתר שאת ויתר עוד, בהרייות אייתין
ונעשה לביאת בבן און!

בברכת התודה
אהרן זכאי

RABBI AHARON FELDMAN
421 YESHIVA LANE, Apt 3A, BALTIMORE, MD 21208
Tel.: 410-6539433 Fax: 410-6534694
Study: 410-4847200 Ext. 6050
E-mail: RAF@NIRC.EDU

Rosh Hayeshiva

Ner Israel Rabbinical College

ראש הישיבה

ישיבת נר ישראל

בס"ד שבט תשפ"א

LETTER OF BLESSING

A member of our Kollel, R. Avichai Samimi, has prepared a translation into English of the Laws of Shabbos for the Sepharadi community and has asked for my Haskama.

Unfortunately, I am unable to do this. Since this is a work of Halacha, this would require me to carefully go over every paragraph, something which time does not permit me to do. Let it suffice for me to say that the author is known to me and that his intention is *lesheym Shomayim,* to spread Torah among the Jewish people.

I extend my heartfelt *beracha* to him that he accomplish his goal of enhancing the observance of Shabbos among the Sepharadi public.

With deep respect,

Aharon Feldman

Rabbi Haim Benoliel
Rosh Yeshiva

מקדש מלך ירושלים
MIKDASH MELECH
JERUSALEM
ישיבת מגן אברהם
THE ALBERT J. BETESH YESHIVA

ב"ה

אבות מילין

18 Jan. '21

Dear Rabbi Avichai,

I was very pleased to see the manuscript of "Shabat" — the Sefer you intend to publish soon אי"ה.

As an outstanding יודע, you have been fulfilling the חיוב with dedication in the Kollel of Yeshiva Ner Israel; you now have the זכות of "לזכות" by making basic Halachot of Shabat available to many, including "new comers" — which is a great זכות הרבים וכו'.

May Hashem crown your efforts with success,

Sincerely,
Rabbi Haim Benoliel

Jerusalem Campus: 38 Ha'admor Milubavitch St. Jerusalem , Israel
U.S. Address: 1326 Ocean Parkway - Brooklyn, NY 11230
T: 732-370-6823 F: 347-214-8328
Website: www.mikdashmelechjerusalem.com Email: mmjerusalem@gmail.com

Rabbi Eliyahu Hakkakian
Director, Pardes Org.
409 Yeshiva Lane Apt. 2A
Baltimore   MD   21208

אליהו הכהן חקקיאן
רומ"'יר ק"'ק אהבת שלום
בלטימור, מרילנד
410-486-6508

June, 03 2021
כג סיון תשפ"א

I take joy and pride in seeing the fruit of labor of my dear *talmid* and friend, Rabbi Avichai Samimi , who worked tirelessly to translate and publish this essential *sefer*. Rabbi Samimi joined the *talmidim* of Ner Israel Yeshiva in the year 2012 and was quickly recognized for his passion in learning and teaching Torah. His diligence and organization, together with the value he assigns to seeking and following advice, have led to his exemplary progress. The idea and the undertaking to publish this *sefer*, **Shabbat**, manifest this passion and progress.

Over the years, numerous people have expressed the need and interest in an English guide on *Hilchot Shabbat* for Sephardim, a compendium which would cover different areas of *halacha* in simple and clear terms together with practical examples. This work which is a translation of the *sefer* השבת והלכותיה, authored by a leading Torah scholar, הרב אהרן זכאי, aims to address that need.

I extend my *bracha* to Rabbi Samimi and his supportive אשת חיל to continue to have success in all their holy endeavors and to be able to shine the light of Torah throughout the world and be blessed with *nachat, simcha* and *hatslacha*.

בברכת התורה ולומדיה
הצב"'י אליהו הכהן חקקיאן

ohr hamizrach congregation

RABBI ROUBEN ARIEH
3113 MARNAT ROAD
BALTIMORE, MARYLAND 21208
410-486-1529

6813 PARK HEIGHTS AVENUE
P.O. BOX 32201
BALTIMORE, MARYLAND 21282
410-764-6373

בס"ד

הובא לפני ספר שוקה בלב ע"י הלוגם שקח קוח בלשן צלילות
מספר יקח את מהרב אברהם בכב, ואאגי נחמד ונעים מעשיו מאפשי שקת
נרשראל הרב אבית סומח, ושלת הרבה לקחר חיגור בסף
שות לברות את הרבים כי שיוצו לן משפחות שראל היובה הדינא
של שגת קוח שברליהם רגיח לידא זא הדרך אשר ילנו בה ואת
רבים מאשא אלין הלבות שקת לתרות אשר עינו גבל לספר אם
לפי מה שראיין מתקלת תקראם לספר הלב שלול כתב היה טוב
גאין: ומותפסק אני שיצא תעולת הרב לכל הענינים בה ואונב לסני
שר בסם, ומי רלן טיברב לראות פרי טוב באפלו ונרברב וית
תבוא ספרים צלוים

אמן

קלוני ש/י/ל ס/י/ל

ACKNOWLEDGMENTS

"Hodu L'Hashem Ki Tov, Ki Le'olam Chasdo"- "Give thanks to the Lord for He is good, His Mercy is for all eternity." Hashem, you have only been good to me. I will never know or understand Your calculations that are store for me, but I am nothing compared to Your Greatness. My gratitude towards my Creator, the Holy One, the reason I live, is of no significance, but yet, You love me and have given me only the best in life. You support my every cell and molecule with Your Love. For every breath I breathe, may it only be to do Your Will. HaKadosh Baruch Hu, may it be Your Will to accept my constant gratitude, for Your Mercy is for all eternity. May it be Your Will that this Sefer serve as a source of Nachat to You and for us, as a nation, to become closer to You through the learning and the Mitzvot that we do. May we be Zocheh to keep the Shabbat in its entirety and to be able to serve You in Your Own home, speedily in our days, Amen.

It is my wish to express my utmost appreciation and gratitude to my father and mother who have held my hand and supported me througout my life. Role models who have molded, nurtured, and encouraged my decisions that have led me to the point in my life, to put this Sefer out. Giants who have shed tears for my success and who have literally stood beside me as I grew in my Yiddishkeit (so much so, that they called the Rosh Yeshiva on a Friday to make sure I get accepted to Yeshiva, only to drive out hundreds of miles that Sunday for my oral test, during which they waited for me to get accepted, only to drive back a few hours later.) They have shown me, by example, the worth of the Torah and how to carry my-self as a Ben-Torah, how sweet and beautiful the

Torah is And they have encouraged me to continue in all my endeavors. Dad and Mom, Mom and Dad, tears of happiness fill my eyes as I thank you and look back at the many years of my Torah learning you have supported, no matter how difficult that may have been. I hope that this Sefer, as many of my other accomplishments, shed a light of Nachat for you as I have nothing in this world that can thank you properly as I am unable to catch up. Please accept this Sefer as my "Thank you" to you for we have only grown and become closer through the power of Shabbat.

Ariella, Chaim Daniel, Elianna and Elinor Simcha- my appreciation for you goes far beyond words. The way you have supported me spiritually, physically and emotionally has only brought joy and happiness to my life. The amount of help you have displayed, in many different facets of my life, has only fueled my success, with much laughter and cheer. Our closeness has brought us to the greatest of heights, and I can't thank you all enough for always keeping me on track and on the road of accomplishment. From even the smallest of things that you've all done for me, to me, they will never go unnoticed for it is because of your warmth and character that has drawn me to a life of serving Hashem. Thank you!

I owe a tremendous amount of Hakarat Hatov to my dear Rav, HaRav Eliyahu Hakkakian who has shaped me, taught me, put up with me and never given up on me. The countless hours the Rav has put into me, no matter how late at night, is a testimony of how much the Rav has done for me. The Rav's display of investment, love and care makes me truly understand what it means that one's Rav is like a father and that a student is like a son. Rabbi Hakkakian, you have taught me Hashkafa, Halacha, Mussar, Torah and spirituality - the true essence of life, and you have given me an undeserved amount of guidance. The Rav was Shtark with me when I needed it most and soft with me when I had my troubles; kept

me in check and most of all, brought out my inner Kochot (not to mention making my Shidduch). I look up to the Rav for every decision I make in life and feel blessed to have the Rav as my Rebbi. I owe my success and whatever Torah I have to the Rav.

A big thank you goes out to one of the Chashuv Avreichei Kollel, R' Yechiel Schreck, who has put in a tremendous amount of time and effort to meticulously go over the Sefer, correct grammar and to make sure the sentence structure and translations make sense. He has gone over the Sefer, over a year span, and I thank him greatly for his hard work and dedication. I would also like to take the opportunity to thank another dear Chashuv Avreich, R' Zecharia Reisch, who as well has put in an enormous amount of time and diligence to go over the Sefer, to make sure everything is no less than perfect. I thank him as well for his utmost efforts. Hashem should bless you both to be Mezakeh the Rabim in both Ruchniyut and Gashmiyut.

Rav Meiliech Nussbaum, we did it! I cannot thank you enough for always being on top of me with such a gentle and professional demeanor. You always made me feel great about myself and my visions for the Sefer. You have supported my every decision and have only helped me bring it into reality. To work with someone with such Yirat Shamayim and excitement is no less than a Beracha from above. The Sefer looks and feels beautiful. I really am forever indebted to you and Machon for bearing with me, even when things had to be pushed off. You did a beautiful job, done with such precision and love. I look forward to continuing our relationship for many years to come.

"She girded her loins with vigor, and made strong her arms" (Mishlei 31,17). Malbim explains this Pasuk in depth to mean "If she decides on agricultural work outside the home, or

makes calculations and plans to acquire farmland- for this as well as for any far-ranging business venture, she "girds her loins" for her outside activity, while she "makes her arms strong" for her domestic duties. Chagit Sara, how beautifully you embody your Pasuk. As the backbone of our home, you have supported me, us, with a Torah life. You have supported us financially by working hard, day in and day out, to make sure I am able to learn in the Kollel for so many years. You have "girded your loins". You have brought two beautiful children into this world, our dearest children Nava Tehila and Aryeh, and you have supplied the "Torat Imecha" our family needs. You've created a warm and healthy home, filled with Simchat Ha'chayim and a comfortable environment for all of us to grow in, you have "made your arms strong". May Hashem bless you with Beracha "Ke'kochvai Ha'Shamayim La'rov". I am humbled by your dedication and love for our family. Behind any success I have is you, who fuels and encourages me to reach my potential. All my success is yours, it is all of your doings. This Sefer is in no way a "Thank You" for what you have and continue to provide for me, but please see it as a sense of pride from the fruit of your labor. It is no coincidence that your Pasuk is found in "Eshet Chayil".

O O O

o .... o

O O O

PREFACE

I am deeply grateful to HaKadosh Baruch Hu for enabling me to complete this Sefer and offer it to the growing public. This Sefer encompasses a rich selection of Halachot and Minhagim brought down from many different leading Poskim and Sefaradi Gedolim from the past few centuries. Adapted from the Sefer "Ha'Shabbat Ve'Hilchoteha", written by HaRav Aharon Zakay, Rosh Yeshivat Ohr Yom Tov in Yerushalayim, this Sefer is a comprehensive daily Halacha companion, made for the Sefaradi jury, in order to enhance one's understanding of the relevant Halachot and to learn and grow in one's Avodat Hashem. This compilation provides a concise yet thorough rendition of Hilchot Shabbat, one of the most practical aspects of Jewish life, with focus on the Halachah Le'Ma'aseh. After a mere eight years to put together, this Sefer was given careful attention to its design and format in order to provide an optimal learning experience for the reader, in order to finish learning the Halachot of Shabbat in the span of a year.

Shabbat is the crowned jewel and purpose of creation. It is the day that Hashem set aside and blessed, an eternal treaty between Hashem and the Jewish nation. By keeping Shabbat, we testify that Hashem is the Creator of the world and the Master of the universe. The Midrash says that Shabbat is the foundation of all the Mitzvot. Just as if the foundation of a house is damaged, it is bound to fall apart, so too, if a person is not careful in observing Shabbat properly, the other Mitzvot he performs is weakened. The Gemara in Shabbat 10b brings down that Hashem said to Moshe Rabenu, "I have a magnificent gift in my treasure house called Shabbat, and

I want to give it to the Jewish people. Go out and let them know that they are about to receive this magnificent gift." We see from here that Hashem calls Shabbat a gift. The Sages learn out that by keeping Shabbat, a person is cleansed from his spiritual impurity and is brought to the realm of Kedusha, holiness. Additionally, the reward for every single Mitzvah performed on Shabbat is equal to the reward of fulfilling all of the 613 Mitzvot in the Torah, what a gift!

The Apter Rav once said, "A gift is something you receive as a favor, not because you earned it." Hashem calls Shabbat a gift since He grants us this opportunity as an unearned favor. No matter how hard one works for Shabbat, both spiritually and physically, the Kedusha and benefit that is received through Shabbat outweighs all the efforts that one puts into it. Some of the benefits of Shabbat quoted throughout the Torah include:

"Anyone who has Oneg Shabbat, is given an inheritance, without any sorrows, and his heart's desires are granted to him. And Rebbi Shimon Bar Yochai says, "If all of Israel keeps two Shabbatot, they will be redeemed (from exile) right away" (Shabbat 119)

"Anyone who prays on Erev Shabbat and says "Vayechulu", two ministering angels that escort a person place their hands on his head and say, "Ve'sar Avonecha Ve'chatatechah Techupar" (Shabbat 119).

"Rebbi says, anyone who keeps one Shabbat in its entirety, the Torah considers it as though he has kept all the Shabbatot from the day Hakadosh Baruch Hu created his world until the resurrection of the dead," as it says "Ve'Shamru Bnei Yisrael Et Ha'Shabbat, La'assot Et ha'Shabbat Le'dorotam" (Mechilta 701, end of Parashah Alef)

"There are angels in Shamayim that are specifically there to look at the ones who are being Shomer the Shabbat and have Oneg in it, according to Halacha, and they (the angels) bless them (the ones who are being Shomer the Shabbat) while tens of thousands of other angels present answer Amen. The Beracha that they give is "Az Titanag Al Hashem", that in Olam Habbah, they will delight about Hashem Yitbarach since Shabbat is Me'en Olam Habbah." (Zohar Ha'Kadosh Parashat Pekudei)

The Torah promises us that anyone who keeps Shabbat according to Halacha will be Zocheh to Siyata Di'Shmaya and the Berachah of Hashem from the heavens that one's Parnassah will be taken care of during the week, to the point that it looks to him as though his job is taken care of from Above.

In addition, one who is Shomer Shabbat is Zocheh to Arichut Yamim (Ya'alzu Chassidim). The Chofetz Chaim brings down many stories where keeping Shabbat has saved many from great danger and dire situations. One who is Shomer the Shabbat, Shabbat is Shomer over him. Many stories are brought down of the benefits of preparing for Shabbat and the open miracles that were granted to those who did their best for Shabbat. (see Taanit 25a) The benefits that come from lighting Shabbat candles, eating hot food, Oneg Shabbat, etc. only bring Berachah, Simcha, salvation, Refuah and Shalom/Shalom Bayit to a person. The benefits of keeping Shabbat are endless. Shabbat is the source of all Berachah for the week; the more we invest in, the more will be invested into us. As the Rambam says, "On Shabbat, you come closer to Hashem by learning Torah, taking delight in Shabbat and honoring it."

As you indulge in this Sefer, you will begin and continue to discover the reasons of why we keep Shabbat, the holiness of Shabbat, how to enjoy and take delight in Shabbat and

how Shabbat is properly kept. You will taste the sweetness of what Shabbat is and how keeping Shabbat will draw you closer to HaKadosh Baruch Hu.

It is my hope that this Sefer will bring about a deeper appreciation for Shabbat and help the reader savor every moment of Shabbat. By learning the Halachot, one will be able to become avid in his connection to Hashem and bring down all the benefits Shabbat has to offer. In the Zechut of all of us learning and keeping Shabbat properly, may we all be Zocheh to "The day which will be completely a Shabbat and rest day for eternal life," and may we be Zocheh to rebuild the Bet Hamikdash, brick by brick, speedily in our days, Amen!

The reason why I named this Sefer "Shabbat", besides for the obvious reason of it consisting Hilchot Shabbat Kodesh, is due to its connection to my name as well. Since the Gematria of the word "Shabbat" (702) is the same as Avichai Bar Elazar Samimi (701 with the Kollel,) I felt that it would only feel appropriate to do as it is written in Sefarim, that one should allude his name into the Sefer. With Hashem's help, I was Zocheh to complete this Sefer after eight years, and it is my absolute pleasure to be able to share this Sefer with you in order to be "Li'lmod U'lelamed, Li'shmor Ve'la'asot" as one, and to be able to Mekarev both Kerovim and Rechokim, Le'avodato Yitbarach!

-Avichai Samimi

O O O

O O O

INDEX

Chapter 1

Chapter 2

Chapter 3

Chapter 4

Chapter 5

Chapter 44

Chapter 45

Chapter 46

Chapter 48

○ ○ ○

○ ○ ○

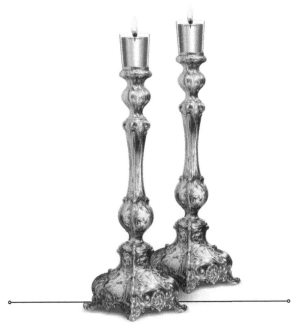

"WHEN I OBSERVE THE SHABBAT,
G-D WILL PROTECT ME;
A SIGN IT IS FOREVER AND EVER
BETWEEN HIM AND ME."

THIS MONTH'S LEARNING HAS BEEN DEDICATED FOR
the continued Hatzlacha, Bracha and Siyata Dishmaya of
Ha'Rav Aharon Zakay Shlita, Rosh Yeshivat Ohr Yom Tov
Yerushalayim and for the Hatzlacha, Bracha and Siyata
Dishmaya of the Rabbanim, Avreichei Kollel and Bachurim of
Yeshivat Ohr Yom Tov.

| Chapter 1 | The Laws Pertaining to Preparing for Shabbat |

1 *Shabbat* is the main sign and treaty that *HaKadosh Baruch Hu* gave to the *bnei Yisrael* so they know that *Hashem* took six days to create the heavens and earth, and rested on the seventh day. This is the secret to faith, to know that the world is renewed, and since He created it all, He is the owner of it all, and we are His servants. Therefore, we must do His will and serve Him with all of our body, soul, and assets because everything belongs to Him.

2 The *kedushah* of *Shabbat* is higher than any other *kedushah,* and its *berachot* are higher than any other *beracha*. As such, *Hashem* sanctified it and blessed it from the beginning of Creation. Like the *pasuk* says, "*Vayevarech Elokim et yom hashevi'i vaykadesh oto*", *Hashem* blessed the seventh day and sanctified it, making it the source of *beracha* for the rest of the days of the week. Accordingly, *bnei Yisrael* were commanded in seven *parshiyot* in the Torah (*Beshalach, Yitro, Mishpatim, Ki Tisa, Vayakhel, Emor* and *Va'etchanan*) to show that all seven days of the week are dependent on *Shabbat*. We also commemorate *Shabbat* every day when we say the *shir shel yom* by indicating that today is *rishon b'Shabbat, sheni b'Shabbat,* and so on for the rest of the week.

3 *Shabbat* is the basis for *emunah* in *HaKadosh Baruch Hu,* that He created His world in six days and on the seventh he rested and relaxed. As such, those who do not keep the *Shabbat* are lacking *emunah.* Therefore, our *chachamim* z"l all over Shas compare one who desecrates *Shabbat* to one who worships idols, and those who are *mechalel Shabbat* to heretics against the whole *Torah.* When the *nevi'im* rebuked *bnei Yisrael,* they specifically rebuked them about *chillul Shabbat,* such as when *Yeshaya* said (Yeshaya 56:2) *"Ashrei enosh ye'aseh zot u'ben adam yachzik bah, shomer Shabbat mechalelo, v'shomer yado me'asot kol ra",* meaning, the *zechut* of being *shomer Shabbat* will hold one back from doing evil.

Preparing for Shabbat Needs

4 One should wake up on Friday morning to prepare for the needs of *Shabbat.* Even if he has servants or maids, he should prepare something for *Shabbat* himself. One should not say "I will not tarnish my honor to prepare something," because it's specifically his honor and involvement that will further honor the *Shabbat.* Not only that, but the sweat one exudes in preparation of *Shabbat, HaKadosh Baruch Hu* comes and wipes all of his sins away, just like how tears wipe away sin. As such, one must burden himself very much for the honor of *Shabbat.*

Today's learning has been dedicated by the Author, for the continued Hatzlacha and Bracha of my dear son, Aryeh ben Chagit Sara.

∾ଓଉ
• Day 03 •
ଓଉଚ

∾ଓଉ
• ג' אלול •
ଓଉଚ

5 It is good to say "*Lichvod Shabbat kodesh*" about all things one buys for *Shabbat* so that the *kedushah* of *Shabbat* falls upon it. When one goes on Friday to buy what he needs for *Shabbat*, it is good to say that he's specifically buying for *Shabbat* so that he can fulfill the *mitzvah* of "*Ve'haya be'yom ha'shishi ve'hachino et asher yaviyu letaken shoresh mitzvah zu be'makom elyon, vihi noam…*". However, if he goes out on Thursday to buy his *Shabbat* needs, he should just say "*Hareini holech liknot l'chvod Shabbat letaken shoresh mitzvah zu be'makom elyon, vihi noam…*".

6 According to the Ari HaKadosh z"l, one should buy his *Shabbat* needs on Friday so the *kedushah* of *Shabbat* falls on them, but if one estimates that he won't have enough time to prepare, for example when the days are shorter and there are things that take longer to do, then he should buy his *Shabbat* needs on Thursday.

7 One should have no less than two cooked foods on *Shabbat*. If one regularly has two cooked meals during the week, he should add another cooked food on *Shabbat*, making it three cooked meals for *Shabbat*. It is good to be stringent and have fish by all three meals on *Shabbat*, but if one is unable due to monetary concerns or because he dislikes fish, he shouldn't eat fish because *Shabbat* was given for *oneg* and not for *tza'ar*.

Today's learning has been dedicated by Ezri and Tamar Azizi, Leilui Nishmat their dear Sabba Meir Dovid ben Yehoshua Heshel and their dear Baba Aziz ben Yechezkel, may their Neshamot have an Aliyah.

8 It is a *mitzvah* on *erev Shabbat* to taste a bit of each cooked food to make sure it came out well. Not only that, on *erev Shabbat Chazon* (the *Shabbat* before *Tisha B'av*) it is permissible to taste the cooked foods even if it has meat and fats because there is a *mitzvah* involved in tasting the cooked foods for the sake of *kavod Shabbat*. Nonetheless, one who is strict on himself will receive *beracha*.

Showering and Tevilah

9 It is a *mitzvah* for a person to wash his whole body with hot water on *erev Shabbat*, but if he can't wash his full body with hot water, he should at least wash his face, hands, and feet with hot water. It is also a *mitzvah* to wash his hair as well. It is a *mitzvah al pi hasod* to immerse in a *mikveh* on *erev Shabbat*.

○···○

10 One should be very careful to not come into a *chashash chillul Shabbat* as a result of doing the *mitzvah* of *tevilah*. *Be'avonotaynu ha'rabim*, many people are at fault with this particular aspect as they sit in the *mikveh* until *chashecha* during the winter when the days are short. Even if he did the *rechitzah* with permission, this might still lead people to an *issur* because sometimes, people comb their head at the end of the immersion, which constitutes a *melacha mehaTorah b'eShabbat*. Another problem is that people come to squeeze out the sponge that was filled with water after finishing the immersion. Therefore, it is befitting to whomever has *yirat Hashem* in his heart to hold back people from doing this, and from this one will merit many *zechutim*.

Today's learning has been dedicated for the continued Hatzlacha and Bracha of Dr. and Mrs. Moshe Barkhordar and family.

᠃᠂᠃
• Day 05 •
᠃᠂᠃

᠃᠂᠃
• ה' אלול •
᠃᠂᠃

11 The *mitzvah* of showering on *erev Shabbat* applies to women as well, but in the winter months when the days are short and the women don't have spare time, they may fulfill the *mitzvah* by washing their hands and face.

Haircuts and Nail Cutting

12 It is a *mitzvah* on *erev Shabbat* to cut one's hair (on his head) if it's too long, and he should have in mind that he is cutting his hair for *kavod Shabbat* when he cuts it. However, if he has a reason to cut his hair on any other day besides for *erev Shabbat*, he doesn't have to wait until *erev Shabbat* to cut it, but it is preferable to wait to as close to *erev Shabbat* as possible to cut one's hair.

○···○

Shabbat, but if one is unable to cut his nails every *erev Shabbat* because they don't grow quickly enough, he should cut his nails every second *erev Shabbat*. He must throw the cut nails into the toilet, and not deal with them *kele'achar yad* (perfunctorily) so that the nails won't scatter and be stomped upon. However, if the nails happen to fall on the ground, it's fine to sweep that area and throw the waste into the toilet or into the garbage.

13 It is a *mitzvah* to cut one's nails on *erev*

○○○

───────❧❀❧───────
Today's learning has been dedicated by Dara and Chana Abaei, for the continued Hatzlacha and Bracha of Mordechai Abaei, Daniel Aryeh Abaei and Akiva Abaei.

14 There are those that say one should not cut his nails in the normal order. Rather, he should start with the left hand and cut from the ring finger rightward, and then switch to the left hand and cut from the finger next to the thumb rightward. However, the Ari HaKadosh was not worried about this and cut his fingernails in the regular order. The *minhag* is to be lenient in this regard.

15 There are those who hold that one should not cut his nails or cut his hair on Thursday, since it takes three days for the nails or hair to regrow which will lead it to grow on *Shabbat*. The *minhag,* however, is that we are not worried about this, and if one, for whatever reason, can't cut his nails or hair on *erev Shabbat*, he may do so on Thursday.

16 There are those who have the custom to cut neither their nails nor hair on *Rosh Chodesh*, even if it falls out on *erev Shabbat*. The reason is that Rabbenu Yehudah HaChasid commanded that one should not cut his nails or hair on *Rosh Chodesh*. As such, in this case, they cut their nails and hair on Thursday instead. However, if one did not cut his nails or hair on Thursday and they become long or have ingrown into the skin, one has what to rely on to cut his nails on *Rosh Chodesh* that falls out on *erev Shabbat*, even though one follows Rabbenu Yehudah Hachasid because the *issur* is more stringent when the nails are long and growing into the skin.

Today's learning has been dedicated for the continued Hatzlacha and Bracha of Mr. and Mrs. Shmuel Nakhon and family.

17 After one cuts his nails or hair, he must wash *netilat yadayim*. This applies both to men and women, whether or not the nail is ingrown into the skin. Not only that, but if one bites his nails with his teeth, he must wash *netilat* *yadayim* as well. In a case where one did not cut his nails but had someone else cut them for him, he must still do *netilat yadayim*, but the person who cut the other's n ails doesn't need to wash.

Changing Clothing

18 One should make sure he has nice clothing for *Shabbat*. Any clothing one wore during the week is not fit to be worn on *Shabbat*, even if it's a robe. Therefore, the *minhag* is that one should change all of his clothing and his hat for *kavod Shabbat*, and if possible, it is good to have a separate *talit* for *Shabbat*.

19 If one finds himself alone at home or alone on the road, he should still wear *Shabbat* clothing because the purpose of the clothing is not for the people to look at, but rather it's for the honor of *Shabbat*.

О О О

Today's learning has been dedicated for the continued Hatzlacha and Bracha of Mr. and Mrs. Daniel Mahgerefteh and family.

20 There is no need to set aside a special set of shoes for *Shabbat*. Rather, it is befitting for one to polish and shine his shoes nicely for *kavod Shabbat*. Still, it is said regarding one who goes above and beyond to set aside a pair of shoes for *Shabbat* that blessing will come upon him.

21 *Shabbat* clothing must be worn on *erev Shabbat* so that one accepts the *Shabbat* upon himself in pleasant clothing, and one should not act like those who go to the bet hakenesset on Shabbat night in their everyday clothing and only change into their *Shabbat* clothing on *Shabbat* day.

22 Even a mourner must change out of his everyday clothing into his superior *Shabbat* clothing, and so is the *minhag* in *Yerushalayim* that a mourner changes into his *Shabbat* clothing.

23 It is the *minhag* of the Sefaradim to wear *Shabbat* clothing even on *Shabbat Chazon*, but there are those that have the tradition not to wear white clothing or special clothing like clothing of a *moed*.

Today's learning has been dedicated for the continued Hatzlacha and Bracha of Mr. and Mrs. Jason Tavakoli and family.

Avoiding Quarrel and Chozer Be'Teshuvah

24 As *minchah* of *erev Shabbat* approaches, it becomes a very dangerous time for dispute between a man and his wife, and between the attendants of the house. The *Sitrah Achrah* exerts itself very much to cause dispute, and thus the man should suppress his urges and avoid sparking up any disputes or hard feelings. Rather, he should do the opposite and ask for peace. In any house where a dispute occurred on *erev Shabbat*, whether it be before or during *Shabbat*, it is tried-and-true that there is evil in front of their faces, and they didn't come out clean that week.

○·····················○

25 Every *erev Shabbat*, one should look into his actions and turn to do *teshuvah* to fix all of the bad behaviors he expressed during the week because *erev Shabbat* is an inclusion of all the days of the week, just like *erev Rosh Chodesh* is the inclusion of the whole month. Another reason one should look into his actions is because *Shabbat* is an atonement for one's sins if he is *shomer* the *Shabbat* according to *halacha* which comes through *teshuvah*. Therefore, one should look into his actions and do *teshuvah* every *erev Shabbat* so that the *shemirah* of *Shabbat* can atone for the sins. Another reason is that he may be able to accept a *neshamah yeterah* from the *Makom Gavo'ah* (Hashem)

Today's learning has been dedicated for the continued Hatzlacha and Bracha of Rena Levy and family.

26 Close to the time of the *kenisah* of *Shabbat* (around half an hour before *shekiah*), one should ask his household in a soft voice, "*Asartem*? (Did you take *ma'aser*), *Aravtem*? (Did you make an *eruv*), *Hifrashtem challah*?" (did you do separate *challah*). He should also tell them, "*Hidliku et haner*" (light the candles). However, if he is accustomed to remove the *ma'aser* or make the *eruv* himself, or if he buys from a place that already took off *ma'aser* and *challah*, he doesn't have to ask his household these questions.

27 It is a *mitzvah* for a person to check his clothing on *erev Shabbat* close to the time of *chashecha* to make sure that there is nothing that would be forbidden to remove on *Shabbat*. It is also a *mitzvah* to check clothing that were specially set aside for *Shabbat*, because there is a chance that there is something *muktzah* inside, such as money that was placed inside on *motzeh Shabbat* or from when he wore that clothing to a *simcha*.

Today's learning has been dedicated for the continued Hatzlacha and Bracha of Michael Bardi and family.

Chapter 2

Doing Melachah and Traveling on Erev Shabbat

1 Whoever does *melachah* on *erev Shabbat* from *minchah* and onward will not see a source of *beracha* from that *melachah* he did. Even if he benefits from one area, he will lose out elsewhere. The *zman* of *issur* is the *zman* of *minchah ketanah*, which is two and a half *shaot zemaniyot* before *sheki'at hachama*.

2 The reason for the *issur* of *melachah* is because of *kavod Shabbat*, so that he should be free to pursue his needs for *Shabbat*. Therefore, it is permitted to prepare one's clothing or utensils for *Shabbat* the entire day, but if it's not for the use of *Shabbat*, even if he does it for no pay, it is forbidden.

However, if he prepares his friend's clothing for *Shabbat* without pay, it is permitted.

3 The *chachamim* said this only by *melachah gemurah*, but by negotiation it is permissible, and the custom is to permit it. Regardless, one should stop the negotiations before sunset so that he's able to prepare for *Shabbat*, immerse himself, and change his clothing; if our *chachamim* said that one should shorten his learning on *erev Shabbat* so that one can prepare for *Shabbat*, how much more so that one should shorten his negotiations for *kavod Shabbat*. The one that has trust in *Hashem, chesed* will encircle him.

Today's learning has been dedicated for the continued Hatzlacha and Bracha of Mr. and Mrs. Daniel Levy and family.

4 The *issur* of *melachah* only applies if he does the job permanently on a regular basis, but if he does the job temporarily by the hour, then it is permissible. Therefore, one is allowed to write a friendly letter. Not only that, there is also what to permit in writing a letter of negotiation, even though it will not cause him loss if he does not write the letter, and also to permit writing out his calculations and thinking about his expenses. Nonetheless, if one wants to write an invoice written in a daily pad into another pad, it is forbidden.

5 It is permissible for one to take notes for himself in learning. This stems from the fact that if he habituates himself in writing, even if he is not writing a *chiddush*, the fact that it's a devar mitzvah makes it permissible. However, it is forbidden to write for a friend in exchange for a reward. As such, a *sofer* of *sifrei Torah*, *tefillin* and *mezuzot* who works for wages should be careful not to write after the time of *minchah ketana,* but if the former was needed presently or for *Shabbat*, then it is permissible to write them.

Today's learning has been dedicated by Mr. David Saeidian, Leilui Nishmat Yitzchak ben Moshe, may his Neshama have an Aliyah.

6. The *issur* of doing *melachah* after *minchah ketana* is specifically when he does *melachah* for himself, but a paid worker that works for a home owner is allowed to work past the time of *Mincha ketana* as long as he goes to his house at a set time before *shekiah* with enough time to fill up a pitcher of water, roast a small fish and light the candles. In any event, all of this is *be'diavad* when there is no other choice, but *le'chatechilah*, the responsibility is on the worker to make a condition with the homeowner to only work until the time of *minchah ketana*.

Laundry on Erev Shabbat

7. Ezra Ha'Sofer made a *takanah* that one should launder his clothes on Thursday for *kavod Shabbat* rather than on *erev Shabbat* so that people would be able to tend to their *Shabbat* needs. If one launders his clothing on Wednesday, it is also considered to be for *kavod Shabbat* like Thursday, because one can be considered to be preparing for *Shabbat* as early as Wednesday, while Sunday, Monday and Tuesday are relevant to the week before.

However, if there is a necessity to launder on Sunday, Monday or Tuesday, it is permissible. If one forgot and didn't launder until *erev Shabbat*, one may do so.

8. In our times, it is the norm to launder clothing even on *erev Shabbat* because we use laundry machines, so the laundering doesn't interfere with the *Shabbat* preparations.

Today's learning has been dedicated by the Author, for the continued Hatzlacha and Bracha of my dear brother-in-law, Mashiach Asher ben Miriam.

Melachah by Non-Jews

9 It is permissible to ride a steamboat in which the captain and the crew workers are *non-Jews* even though they will continue to travel even on *Shabbat*. One should not restrict it due to the issur of *techumin*. However, one should refrain from riding a steamboat in which the captain and crew workers are Jews, even though they travel on *Shabbat*, because the travelers are beneficiaries of *melechet Shabbat,* and in our times there is no *pikuach nefesh* involved in this matter so there are no leniencies.

○..○

10 It is permissible to bring one's car to a non-Jewish mechanic on *erev Shabbat* as long as the workers are *non-Jews,* the car will be returned on Sunday, there is a set price-rate before the job has been started, and there is enough time to fix the car on *erev Shabbat* or *motza'e Shabbat* The reason is because he isn't telling the workers to work on *Shabbat*, and the worker is able to complete the job on *Erev Shabbat* or *motza'e Shabbat*. However, if one gave in the car on *erev Shabbat*, when time is limited, and there isn't enough time for the *non-Jew* to fix the entire problem unless he works on *Shabbat*, *le'chatechilah* one should not do so since he is telling the worker outright to work on *Shabbat*. In a time of need, there is room to be lenient, even if one pays for the work that was done on *Shabbat*. Nevertheless, our brothers, the Ashkenazim, are strict with regards to this issue.

Today's learning has been dedicated for the continued Hatzlacha and Bracha of Mr. and Mrs. Chatzkel Iny and family.

Traveling on Erev Shabbat

11 One should not travel on *erev Shabbat* more than three *parsaot* from the beginning of the day, which amounts to up to the third half of the day. The reason is so he will arrive to attain his necessities while the day is still great, and be able to prepare his needs for *seudat Shabbat*, whether he is going to someone else's house or his own house. This only applies to a situation where they are not aware that he is coming, but if they are aware, he may even travel a long distance. There are those that say if it is the norm in his destination to set up for the *Shabbat* meals with ample food, there is no need to be stringent on travel.

only to one traveling on foot. However, if one is traveling by car or by horse, we are accustomed to be lenient. In any event, one should *le'chatechilah* be aware to not travel close to evening time (even if they set up his meal for him), because sometimes people come to do *chilul Shabbat*, where they add onto to the cooked foods in their own home, and all the more so when there are guests coming over. There are also instances in which people travel and reach their homes quite literally at the time of *chashecha* and can fall to *chilul Shabbat*. Therefore, one should take all of these considerations to heart and not fall to the *yetzer* that tells him there is still time.

12 There are those who hold the above-mentioned case applies

○○○

Today's learning has been dedicated for the continued Hatzlacha and Bracha of Mr. and Mrs. Avner Shotz and family.

Chapter 3 — Kevi'at Seudah on Erev Shabbat

1 It is forbidden to have a big meal that is not the norm during the week because of *kavod Shabbat*, so that one can eat the *Shabbat* meals with an appetite. The *issur* applies throughout the whole day, including the morning. However, a meal which is the norm during the weekdays may be eaten the entire day, though it is a *mitzvah* to hold oneself back from eating from the beginning of the tenth hour of the day (about three *sha'ot zemaniyot* before *shekiat hachamah*). Nevertheless, if he started eating before this time, he doesn't need to stop eating once the tenth hour arrives.

himself up like he does during the week, but rather to quiet his hunger, is permitted, *le'chatechilah*, even after the tenth hour until the time of entering into *Shabbat*. There isn't even a *mitzvah* to hold oneself back in this regard. However, if one wants to be strict on himself, even in this situation, blessing will come upon him. In short, the *chacham* keeps an eye on his thoughts (i.e. that he is worried to make sure he eats the *seudat Shabbat* with an appetite), because the *kavod* of *Shabbat* is very great.

○○○

2 Eating a small amount of food, without making a set meal where one eats bread to fill

Today's learning has been dedicated for the continued Hatzlacha and Bracha of Mr. and Mrs. Eli Hakakian and family.

3 Even though one is permitted to drink anything during the whole day, nevertheless, it is a *mitzvah* to hold oneself back from drinking enough to reach a state of satiation from the tenth hour of the day and on so he will eat the *seudat Shabbat* with an appetite. Similarly, it is a *mitzvah* to hold oneself back from drinking alcoholic drinks, since drunkenness will likely lead him to void the *seudat Shabbat* completely.

4 *Chassidim* and *ansheh ma'aseh* are accustomed to not setting a meal in which they eat as they would during the week, even before the tenth hour, opting instead to lessen their eating even more. There are those that are stringent upon themselves from *chatzot hayom* and onwards, in which they only eat certain types of *mezonot* foods or fruits.

5 A *seudat mitzvah* that falls out on *erev Shabbat*, such as *seudat brit milah, pidyon haben* and *bar mitzvah*, may be made by the letter of the law even after the tenth hour of the day. However, one should advance it as much as possible. It is befitting, *le'chatechilah*, to make it before *chatzot hayom*, but, at the latest, it should be before the tenth hour of the day

Today's learning has been dedicated for the continued Hatzlacha and Bracha of Mr. and Mrs. Alen Reyhan and family.

6 It is the way of the *ansheh ma'aseh* to fast every *erev Shabbat* so they crave to eat at night. However, the *poskim* wrote that one should not fast on *erev Shabbat* so one doesn't go into the *Shabbat* while he is afflicted. However, if he knows that if he eats during the day, he won't be able to eat at night with an appetite, then it is a good custom to fast. This all applies to *talmideh chachamim* and *ansheh ma'aseh* whose actions are all *leshem shamayim* and who know how to restrain their appetite. Also, when they become hungry, they're able to focus their minds to eat for the sake of *mitzvat seudat Shabbat*. However, with regular people, there is what to worry that when they become hungry, they won't eat for the sake of *mitzvah*, but simply to fill up their stomachs. Therefore, it is preferable that they don't fast on *erev Shabbat*.

7 Any *ta'anit yachid* that does not have a set time, should not be done on *erev Shabbat*. However, if the time is on *erev Shabbat*, for example, the *ta'anit* for the year of his father's memory or *zayin be'Adar*, it is permitted to fast on *erev Shabbat*. However, one should not complete the fast until *tzet hakochavim*, keeping in mind at the beginning of the fast that he is fasting with the understanding that he won't finish the fast. However, by *Asarah Be'Tevet* that falls out on *erev Shabbat*, one must fast until *tzet hakochavim*. This would also apply to a *ta'anit chalom* since a *ta'anit chalom* is done to prevent the dangers of a bad dream, and we are worried that it might not come to prevent the dream if he doesn't fast until *tzet hakochavim*.

ооо

Today's learning has been dedicated for the continued Hatzlacha and Bracha of Mr. and Mrs. Rodney Hakimi and family.

Chapter 4 — Laws Pertaining to Shnayim Mikrah Ve'echad Targum

1 Every person is obligated to read the *parasha* with the *tzibur*. Meaning, every week he should read the weekly *Torah* portion in the form of *shnayim mikrah v'echad targum*. The *poskim* give an allusion to this concept in the abbreviation of the *pasuk* *"Ve'eleh shemot"*, which expands to *vechayav adam likro haparasha shnayim mikrah v'echad targum*. Whoever finishes the *parasha* with the *tzibur*, his days and years will be elongated. In our infinite sin, there are those that disregard this *mitzvah*, and it is befitting to rebuke them on this matter.

....

2 Rabeinu Ha'Ari z"l was very particular, according to Kabbalah, in the reading of *shnayim mikrah*. Therefore, even if one doesn't understand the translations well, it still behooves him to read *shnayim mikrah*.

Today's learning has been dedicated for the continued Hatzlacha and Bracha of Chaim ben Sarah.

ᴖᴖᴖ
• Day 20 •
ᴖᴖᴖ

ᴖᴖᴖ
• כ' אלול •
ᴖᴖᴖ

3 If one learned the parasha with the perush of Rashi, this is considered a targum. However, a yireh shamayim should read both the targum and the perush of Rashi, since the targum has an advantage because it was given on har Sinai, and it explains each and every word, while Rashi has an advantage since he explains the inyan, according to the midrashim of our chachamim z"l, more than the targum. It is quite evident that one cannot remove himself from the group of yireh shamayim, and therefore it is befitting for every person to learn perush Rashi, and he will see how much he will benefit from this. One should take it to heart that Rashi afflicted himself through Tary"ag (six hundred thirteen) fasts so that he can interpret these explanations. These include superb mysteries and deep secrets, and one needs to be privileged to understand the holy and pure perush of Rashi.

4 One must read the shnayim mikrah with the melody of the trups. However, one should be stringent in reading the targum without the melody. There is no source or secret at all for those who read the targum with the Trups. In fact, whoever adds the melody should retract from doing so. Nevertheless, if one did read the shnayim mikrah without the melody, he has fulfilled his obligation.

Today's learning has been dedicated for the continued Hatzlacha and Bracha of Mr. and Mrs. Dani Reihani and family.

5 One may start reading *shnayim mikrah* right after *minchah* on *Shabbat* after the *tzibur* read the first section from the *Torah* portion of the upcoming week because at this time it is considered as if one is reading with the *tzibur*. It is a *mitzvah min hamuvchar* to read *shnayim mikrah* on Friday. It is the custom of the Chassidim and the *ansheh ma'aseh* to read it on Friday morning after *shacharit* wrapped in their *talit* and *tefillin*. However, if *Rosh Chodesh* falls out on a Friday, one doesn't need to rebind his *tefillin* and should read wrapped only in his *tallit*.

"Do not eat bread on *Shabbat* until you finish reading the whole *parasha*." If he didn't read before the meal, he should read it afterwards before *minchah* because only then does the *tzibur* begin to read the next week's *parasha*. If he still hasn't read it by then, he has until Wednesday to read it since the first three days of the week are still associated with the *Shabbat* that passed. There are those who say that *bediavad,* one has until *Shemini Atzeret* to read since that is when the *tzibur* finishes reading the whole *Torah*.

6 If one didn't read *shnayim mikrah* on Friday, he should finish reading before the *Shabbat* day meal, in spirit of what Rebbi commanded his sons,

7 One who only has a minimal amount of free time and has difficulty reading *shnayim mikrah* on Friday or *Shabbat* day may rely on the *poskim* that allow one to read *shnayim mikrah* on *Shabbat* night.

Today's learning has been dedicated for the continued Hatzlacha and Bracha of Mr. and Mrs. Erieh Hadjyan and family.

8 The order for reading is first the *pasuk* twice and then the *targum*. This applies to every *pasuk* until the end of the *parasha*. This was the custom of the Ari z"l. All of this is according to Kabbalah, but if it is difficult for one to read it in this order, he should read the *parasha* twice and once he is done reading the *parasha* twice, he should then read the *targum*. This is permitted since there are those *poskim* who hold that even *le'chatechilah,* one is permitted to read the *parasha* twice and then the *targum*.

9 One should not read the *targum* first and then the *mikrah*, or read one *mikrah*, then the *targum* and then read the *mikrah* again. *Bediavad,* if one did read *shnayim mikrah* this way, he has fulfilled his obligation.

10 One who is pressed for time and doesn't have free time to read to himself the *shnayim mikrah* may read the whole *parasha* quietly on *Shabbat* while the *shaliach tzibur* is reading the *Torah pasuk* by *pasuk* once, and when he gets home, he should read it over again and then read the full targum.

Today's learning has been dedicated for the continued Hatzlacha and Bracha of Mr. and Mrs. Sion Bitton and family.

11 After one finishes reading the s*hnayim mikrah v'echad targum*, he should read the last *pasuk* with only the *mikrah* twice and not the *targum* (in addition to the reading of the *mikrah* twice), so that he should end with *mikrah*. Afterwards, he should read the *haftarah* of that *parasha*. However, if *Rosh Chodesh* falls out on that *Shabbat* or it is the week of *Parashat Shekalim, Zachor, Parah* or *Hachodesh*, he must read the *haftarah* of that week.

12 Whoever has a *sefer Torah* in one's house, if he's an expert in reading the *sefer Torah* with vocalization and its *trups*, he should read from the *sefer Torah* since it has more *kedushah*, and it is the main *mitzvah* of the *sefer Torah* to read from it.

13 *Shanyim mikrah* isn't done on *Yom Tov* since the whole *Torah* was already organized and read week by week, and whenever people already read the order of *parshiyot*, there's no need to go back and read it over again. Therefore, on *Shabbat Rosh Chodesh* or *Shekalim* etc. we only read only the actual *parasha* of the week.

Today's learning has been dedicated for the continued Hatzlacha and Bracha of Mr. and Mrs. Jamshid Sassoun and family.

14 It is forbidden to interrupt oneself in the middle of the *shnayim mikrah* reading for any reason. Rather, one should read the entire piece at once, as there is a just and hidden reason for it. If one is exceedingly thirsty, he may interrupt the *parasha* to drink with a *beracha* both before and after. According to Kabbalah, one should not interrupt in the middle of the reading even for *divrei Torah*.

15 The *shnayim mikrah* for *Parashat Vezot Ha'beracha* should be read on the day of *Hoshanah Rabah*, but in any event, if he read it on the day of *Shemini Atzeret*, he doesn't lose out on the *mitzvah*.

16 Women are exempt from reading *shnayim mikrah* since according to some *poskim*, *shnayim mikrah* is considered learning *Torah*, and women are exempt from learning *Torah*.

17 There are those that say that a *choleh*, one who has a *chash be'eiynav*, a *sumah,* and one who doesn't know how to read are exempt from reading s*hnayim mikrah,* and they don't need to hear it read by someone else. However, it is befitting for them to make an effort to hear it from others, or, in the case of the *choleh*, to finish the reading when he heals from his sickness.

Today's learning has been dedicated for the continued Hatzlacha and Bracha of Mr. and Mrs. Ovadia Yaakov Herzfeld and family.

∾෬ౚ
• Day 25 •
ౚ෬ಾ

∾෬ౚ
• כה' אלול •
ౚ෬ಾ

18 Someone who is mourning is allowed to read *shnayim mikrah* on the *Shabbat* that falls out in the days of his mourning, but he should not read the *perush Rashi* on the *parasha*.

19 A teacher that teaches children the *parashat hashavuah* does not need to go back and read *shnayim mikrah v'echad targum* since he already went and reviewed the *mikrah* with the children a few times; he only needs to read the *targum*. All of this is according to the letter of the law, but according to Kabbalah, he must read the *shnayim mikrah v'echad targum* on each and every *pasuk*, and each one is supposed to be read in order without interruption. Therefore, one should read to himself the *shnayim mikrah v'echad targum* again.

20 One who was *ones* and didn't read the *shnayim mikrah* for a specific week and the next week already came, and now he has two *parashiyot* to read, he should first read the *parasha* that came beforehand and then read the *parasha* of that week.

Today's learning has been dedicated for the continued Hatzlacha and Bracha of Eli ben Ora Imanoel.

Chapter 5
Kindling the Shabbat Candles

1 The lighting of the *Shabbat* candles is an obligation both for men or women. There must be lit candles in the house on *Shabbat*. However, women are responsible for the actual lighting more than the men, since women are generally at home and engaged in house work. Also, since *Adam HaRishon* was the *ner* of the world, as it says *"Ner Hashem nishmat adam"* and *Chava* caused him to die, the *mitzvah* of *ner* was given to women.

○··○

2 It is good for the husband to be involved in the fixing of the candles and wicks. If he wants to light in another room, he will have blessing come upon him, but he should not make a *beracha* when he lights in the other room.

○··○

3 It is a *mitzvah* to light the candles next to the table which one dines on so that one should make *kiddush* and eat in the candle light, fulfilling the rule of *oneg Shabbat*. However, if one would rather eat in the yard because of the weather or if one would like to eat elsewhere due to the fact that there are flies around, it is permissible to make *kiddush* and dine somewhere else since the candles were lit for *oneg* and not for *tza'ar*. This applies even if he cannot see the candles from where he is sitting.

○○○

Today's learning has been dedicated for the continued Hatzlacha and Bracha of Erela bat Ora Imanoel.

4 One reason for the lighting of the *Shabbat* candles is *shalom bayit*, since in a place where there are no candles, there is no peace, as one will walk and stumble in darkness. Another reason is *kavod Shabbat*, since the presence of light elevates the meal.

5 In a situation where one says *kiddush* and eats on the roof (or yard) so that the moonlight shines onto the table, one must still light *Shabbat* candles since both reasons of *shalom bayit* and *kavod Shabbat* apply.

Amount of Candles and What We May Light With

6 One is only obligated to light a single candle, but we are accustomed to light two candles, one representing *zachor* and one representing *shamor*.

There are those that are accustomed to light seven or even ten candles. The *chassidim* and the *ansheh ma'aseh* are accustomed to lighting seven candles corresponding to the seven *olim laTorah* and the seven days of the week. There are also those who light a candle for every child in the family.

7 One who is careful to set up the *Shabbat* candles well will merit having his children become *talmidei chachamim*.

As such, it's befitting for a woman to pray after lighting that she should merit having her sons become *talmidei chachamim* who illuminate the world with *Torah*, since *tefillah* is heard more at the time a *mitzvah* is being done. It is also good to give *tzedakah* before lighting the candles.

Today's learning has been dedicated for the continued Hatzlacha and Bracha of Edel bat Ora Imanoel.

8 It is a *mitzvah min hamuvchar* to light with olive oil. If one doesn't have olive oil, he should light with other oils that will continue to burn with wicks; if he doesn't have any oil, he can light with wax candles, paraffin, or anything similar. It is proper for the one lighting to have in mind during the *beracha* before the kindling to exempt the turning on of any electricity afterwards.

9 When one is pressed for time or is in a place where it is not possible to get oil or wax candles, it's possible to fulfill one's obligation by turning on electric lights and making a *beracha* on the "kindling" of the light.

10 There are those who say it's better for one to wait to turn on the lights in the house only after the women have lit the *Shabbat* candles. In any event, the world is accustomed to turn on the lights before and only then light the *Shabbat* candles as we are not *makpid* to turn off the lights before one lights the candles. One should not deviate from their *minhag*.

11 The *beracha* on the *hadlakat hanerot* is "Baruch atah H-shem, Elokainu Melech Ha'olam, asher kidishanu bemitzvotav vetzivanu lehadlikner shel Shabbat". The *beracha* must be said before the kindling. It's a great *mitzvah* to publicize the fact that one must bless before the kindling. However, our brothers, the Ashkenazim, are accustomed to making the *beracha* after the kindling.

Today's learning has been dedicated by Yitzchak Saeidian, Leilui Nishmat Devorah bat Yisrael, may her Neshama have an Aliyah.

12 There is no need according to *din* for the husband to stand next to his wife during the candle lighting so that he should hear the *beracha* of *hadlakat nerot*.

○·····················○

13 It is a *segulah* for a woman who is having a hard time raising her children or doesn't have children at all to say after the candle lighting the *haftarah* of the first day of *Rosh Hashanah*. It's also good for her to understand what she is saying and to say it with *kavanah*.

The Accepting of Shabbat During Candle Lighting

14 The acceptance of *Shabbat* is not dependent on lighting the candles. Therefore, it is permitted for a woman to do *melachah* after the candle lighting as long as she is sure that it's not *shekiayh* yet. However, it is better for a woman to make a condition for herself that she won't accept *Shabbat* upon herself with the lighting of the candles; it's enough for her to make a condition once a year. Nonetheless, if she forgot and didn't make a condition, she is allowed to do essential *melachot* after the lighting, and certainly to pray *minchah*.

Today's learning has been dedicated for the continued Hatzlacha and Bracha of Yosef Chaim, Ezri, Aviel, Binyamin and Sara Azizi and family.

THIS MONTH'S LEARNING HAS BEEN DEDICATED
by the Author, for the Hatzlacha of everyone who got
me to this point and has supported me with open hands.
Hashem should give you back a million fold, Amen!

15 A woman whose *tevilah* fell out on the night of *Shabbat* should do all of her preparations (cutting the nails, washing, shampooing etc) while it is still daytime and then light the candles and go to the *mikveh*, as long as the lighting is done after *plag haminchah* (an hour and a quarter before *shekiayh*). She may still do *melachah* after the candle lighting, but it's good to make a condition that she will not accept *Shabbat* by this candle lighting. If she left the house early before *plag haminchah,* and the time for candle lighting approached, her husband should light the candles with a *beracha*.

16 A woman who lit *Shabbat* candles and became thirsty afterwards is allowed to drink until *shekiayh*.

17 A man who lit candles is allowed to do *melachah* and pray *minchah* after the lighting without making any conditions, because it's the *da'at* of the man to accept *Shabbat* on himself when he says the words *"Bo'i Kallah."* Still, it's better to make a condition once a year. If either a man or woman accepted the *Shabbat* upon oneself earlier in the day, he or she is allowed to tell a person who didn't accept *Shabbat* to do a *melachah* for him or her as long as it is not *shekiayh* yet.

18 It is befitting and correct *le'chatechilah* for women to wear their *Shabbat* clothing prior to the candle lighting. In any event, if she is worried that if she goes to put on her *Shabbat* clothing, the time for candle lighting will pass, she should light the candles first and then put on her clothing for *Shabbat*.

The Time for Hadlakah

19 It is the *minhag* of the Sefaradim and the *Edut HaMizrach* to light the candles ten to thirty minutes before *shekiayh*. There are those who claim that the custom in *Yerushalayim* to light forty minutes before *shekiayh*, as printed in the calendars, has no basis, and it's fitting to withdraw from *melachah* and light the candles twenty minutes before *shekiayh*.

20 One should not light the candles before *plag haminchah*, an hour and a quarter before *shekiayh*, because it will not be recognizable that he is lighting for *kavod Shabbat*. If for any reason, the woman pushed off the lighting, and she knows that it's not *shekiayh* yet, she may light with a *beracha*; if she is unsure, she should not enter into a *safek chillul Shabbat*, and it's better to stay in the dark rather than be *mechalel Shabbat*. If the husband sees that the time is approaching to light and the wife is late and won't be able to light the candles on time, he should light the candles himself with a *beracha*, even if she will protest.

Today's learning has been dedicated for the continued Hatzlacha and Bracha of Oshra, Yaakov, Sheyna, Adina, Shira and Uri Barkhordar and family.

The Place for Candle Lighting

21 One must light the candles in an area where they won't be moved but where they will still be used. One should not light the candles in one place and move them to another after they were lit. In any event, when needed, for example where the candles were lit on the table and now the table is needed, it's permissible to move the candles onto a tall shelf because it's evident that one is doing this for *kavod Shabbat*. Similarly, if a woman is sick, one may bring the candles to her to make a *beracha* and then place them in a proper place.

22 Since the essential *mitzvah* of lighting *Shabbat* candles is to light them in the place where one eats, our brothers, the Ashkenazim, have a custom to place the *Shabbat* candles on the table they eat on. In any event, even amongst the Ashkenazim, there are those who are not accustomed to leaving the candles on the table because it could lead to problems with extinguishing and *muktzeh*. The Zohar HaKadosh says one should not place the candles on the table, and should instead place them west of the table.

23 A woman who is in confinement is allowed to light the candles with a *beracha* in her house even if she is still seeing blood. This rule also applies to any woman who is in her *niddah* period.

Today's learning has been dedicated for the continued Hatzlacha and Bracha of Mr. and Mrs. Eli Levaddin and family.

24 A *kallah* who is lighting in her house for the first time is not allowed to recite *shehechiyanu* because there is a prohibition against reciting a *beracha* that is unnecessary.

Those Obligated and Exempt from Candle Lighting

25 A blind woman can still light the *Shabbat* candles with a *beracha*. In any event, if she has a husband that can see, it's better for him to light with a *beracha* instead of her.

⸰...⸰

26 A single daughter that relies on her father's table for food doesn't have so much of an obligation to light *Shabbat* candles. If she wants to be strict on herself and light the candles in her room, she is forbidden to make a *beracha* on the lighting. Instead, she should listen to the *beracha* from her mother lighting in the dining room, and once she answers *amen* she can go ahead and light in her room without a *beracha*.

27 A *kallah* who is staying by her in-laws may light candles in the room she is sleeping in with a *beracha*, while her mother-in-law should make the *beracha* on the candles in the dining room. The daughter or the *kallah* should be particular about bringing her own candles from home since the candles must belong to her when lighting. If they didn't, the parents may give the candles as a total gift. Moreover, the candles must also be large enough that when she returns to her room to go to sleep, they are still lit so that she may enjoy their light.

ooo

Today's learning has been dedicated for the continued Hatzlacha and Bracha of Mr. and Mrs. Sharon Fakheri and family.

28 One who eats at a parent's house or at a friend's house etc, on *Shabbat* night and will return home after the meal to sleep shouldn't light candles if leaving before *plag haminchah*. (If one would like to light before *plag*, one shouldn't say a *beracha*.) However, if one leaves his house after *plag haminchah*, the woman of the household should light the candles with a *beracha* in her own home and then leave. One needs to make sure that the candles are large and that they will stay lit until he returns home so that he has an opportunity to bask in the light of the candles. One should also taste a food item such as a cake or fruit so that he derives enjoyment from the light.

○···○

29 Families that stay in a rest home or in a hotel where they will be eating in a public dining room and sleeping in a room set aside for them should light the candles in the room in which they are sleeping; also, the candles must be long enough so that they will still be lit upon their return. One of the women should also light candles in the dining room with a *beracha* and then go to her room and light candles for herself without a *beracha*.

○···○

30 *Bachurei yeshiva* who live in the dorm rooms where a few *bachurim* all sleep in the same room should have one person in the room light the candles with a *beracha* and the others should hear and be *yotzeh yedeh chovatam*. The candles must be long enough so that they will still be lit upon their return.

○○○

Today's learning has been dedicated for the continued Hatzlacha and Bracha of Rabbi and Mrs. Avraham Levichaim and family.

ᑽᕦᑾ
• Day 35 •
ᑽᕦᑾ

ᑽᕦᑾ
• ו' תשרי •
ᑽᕦᑾ

31 One who is married but is alone in the house for *Shabbat* because his wife is in the hospital or he is traveling by himself must light *Shabbat* candles with a *beracha* in the place he is residing, even if his wife will be lighting candles herself as well. If a married woman is in the hospital or the recovery room, if she will eat in her room, she should light candles there with a *beracha* even if her husband lit candles at home. However, if others came beforehand and lit candles in her room, she shouldn't light there with a *beracha*. If the management of the building is against her lighting in the room, she should light with a *beracha* in the dining room if she will be eating there; however, if others came beforehand and lit candles in the dining room, she shouldn't light there with a *beracha*.

32 One who is unmarried or his wife can't light candles for whatever reason must light the *Shabbat* candles with a *beracha*. Even if he has an older single daughter that lives with him in the house, it's better that he light rather than his daughter.

Today's learning has been dedicated by the Author, for the continued Hatzlacha and Bracha of my dear Rebbi, Rav Shragi Neuberger and family.

Amount of Candles

33 A woman who is accustomed to lighting two candles and wishes to add more candles may not add more if her husband will complain about it.

34 Some women have the custom to light one candle for every child born into the family. If the husband's house had no such custom, the woman may not force her husband to buy candles from his own money to do so. In any event, since the *Shabbat* candles are for *shalom bayit,* it is good for the husband to give permission to his wife to continue her family custom.

35 A woman who is accustomed to lighting a certain number of *Shabbat* candles may not lessen the number of candles she lights. In a time of monetary need (for example, if she will be exact in her other *Shabbat* spending), she should do a *hatarat nedarim* in front of three people. This would also apply if she wants to add candles.

36 A woman who is accustomed to lighting long candles and would like to light smaller candles in the summer so that they should be lit only at the time of the *Shabbat seudah* (since it's not possible to stay in the room for a long period of time while the windows are closed) and she will complete the missing light by adding more small candles, is allowed to because the candles should be lit for *oneg* and not for *tza'ar.*

37 If one had a wife that was accustomed to lighting a candle per child born into the family, and his wife passed away and he married a widow, the second wife doesn't have to light the same amount of candles as the first wife lit, but rather she may go according to the regular custom of lighting candles.

Today's learning has been dedicated for the continued Hatzlacha and Bracha of Savta Parvin Samimi and family.

She Forgot to Light

38 A woman who forgot to light *Shabbat* candles, and her husband also forgot, there are those that say she must add an extra candle from now on to whatever she usually lights. If she keeps forgetting, she must keep adding an extra candle every time. The reason for adding more candles is a penalty so that she is more careful with *kavod Shabbat*. Therefore, if there were unforeseen circumstances and she didn't light, for example she was in a place where she couldn't light or she didn't have money to buy candles, she doesn't need to add candles because it is not befitting to fine her because she was *anusa*. Similarly, if one of the *Shabbat* candles went out, she doesn't need to add any. When the husband forgot to light candles (in a case where the obligation falls on him like when his wife isn't home) the wife doesn't need to add an extra candle from now on.

39 In our times, where the light is on in our houses, there is no need to fine the woman by adding an extra candle if she forgot beforehand; rather she may continue lighting the same way she used to light until now.

Today's learning has been dedicated by the Author, for the continued Hatzlacha and Bracha of my dear Rebbi, Rav Chaim Kosman and family.

The Way of Lighting and the Amount of Time

40 One who lights the candles must light the candle until most of the wick catches fire. This is done so that the flame may rise nicely right after removing one's hand, like how it was done by the lighting of the *menorah*.

....

41 One should light the candles or leave the oil in a way that the candles will remain lit at least until the end of the nighttime meal. However, there is no need to leave enough oil so that the candles remain lit the whole *Shabbat* until *motza'e Shabbat*. Those that do this are over on the *issur* of *ba'al tashchit* and one must nullify this custom. This is considered *ba'al tashchit* because the light is not useful during the day (unlike the *bet hakenesset* where the light increases the *kavod* of the *bet hakenesset*) since at home once doesn't get any enjoyment from the light during the day.

The Respect for Candles and their Purpose

42 One should not do anything next to the *Shabbat* candles that causes a *bizayon*. Therefore, one should not change a baby's diaper or stand unclothed in the room where the candles are lit because of *bizui mitzvah*. It goes without saying that one should not relieve himself or leave anything dirty in front of the candles.

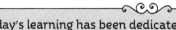

Today's learning has been dedicated by the Author, for the continued Hatzlacha and Bracha of my dear Rebbi, Rav Ezra Neuberger and family.

THIS CHAG'S LEARNING HAS BEEN DEDICATED
by Mr. and Mrs. Yitzchak and Orna Attar, for the
Hatzlacha and Bracha of the Attar family. May they merit
to see much Nachat from their children and live a true
Torah life.

43 If a *Shabbat* candle went out, that same candle or the extra oil may be used for one's needs after *Shabbat*. It is befitting to be as strict if possible and not throw out the candles along with the rest of the garbage; rather the candles should be disposed of in a proper manner or burned during the week in an honorable way.

Bet Hakenesset and Yom Tov

44 There are places that are accustomed to have the *shamash* of the *bet hakenesset* light candles before *Shabbat* without a *beracha*, and after about half an hour the *chazzan* comes and makes a *beracha* on the candles. This custom should be nullified immediately, and since the *amei ha'aretz* that are not versed in *halachah* have this *minhag*, it is a *mitzvah* to stop it.

45 It is also a *mitzvah* to light candles on *Yom Tov* and the *beracha* is "Baruch atah…le'hadlik ner shel yom tov." Although some women are accustomed to say *shehechiyanu* for the lighting of the *Yom Tov* candles, there is no real foundation in *halachah* for this *minhag* and it is right to stop it. Instead, women should have in mind to be *yotzeh yedeh chovatan* of *shehechiyanu* in the *kiddush* of *Yom Tov* like the *takanah* of the *chachamim*.

Chapter 6 — Tefillat Minchah on Erev Shabbat and Kabbalat Shabbat

1 One must add from the chol to *Shabbat* and accomplishes this by separating from doing *melachah* on *erev Shabbat*, before the time of *ben hashemashot* (which is before *sheki'at hachamah*). There is no specific time from the *Torah* for *tosefet Shabbat*; rather the principle is to create a separation from *melachah* while it is still surely day, and to stop at least five or ten minutes before *shekiayh* (one must make sure his clock is exact). However, it is befitting and correct to separate from *melachah* twenty minutes before *sheki'at hachamah*, because this way one fulfills his *chovah* according to all *posekim*.

○ .... ○

2 Despite the fact that it's befitting to separate oneself from doing *melachah* twenty minutes before *shekiayh*, one may accept *Shabbat* even before that on condition that it's done after *plag haminchah*, which is an hour and fifteen minutes before *sheki'at hachamah*. If he attempts to accept *Shabbat* before this, it doesn't work.

Today's learning has been dedicated for the continued Hatzlacha and Bracha of my dear brother in law, Avraham Shimon ben Mashiach Asher.

3 The acceptance of Shabbat is not dependent upon the lighting of the candles. From the ikar hadin, the Shulchan Aruch is in safek if the answering of barechu is considered as an acceptance of Shabbat. In places where they are accustomed to say Mizmor Shir Leyom HaShabbat, that is considered an acceptance of Shabbat. In any event, since in our times we are accustomed to say "Lecha Dodi", it is considered an acceptance of Shabbat when we say "Bo'i kallah Shabbat Malketah", and one is prohibited in doing melachah even if the sun didn't yet set. The Ar"i HaKadosh also holds that by saying the words "Bo'i kallah" one accepts the Shabbat.

4 If the majority of the kahal accepted Shabbat upon themselves, the minority are pulled along with them and are prohibited in doing melachah as well. In a town where there are many bateh kenessiyot, even if most of the people pray in one bet hakenesset and accept Shabbat upon themselves, the congregants who pray in the other bateh kenessiyot do not get pulled along with them. If one regularly prays in a specific bet hakenesset but was not present when that bet hakenesset accepted the Shabbat upon themselves, he doesn't have to follow them; if most of the town did not yet accept Shabbat, he is permitted in doing melachah.

Today's learning has been dedicated by Mr. and Mrs. Yaakov Attar, for the continued Hatzlacha and Bracha of the Attar family.

5 One who delayed praying *minchah* on *erev Shabbat* until after the *kahal* accepted the *Shabbat* upon themselves should not pray in the *bet hakenesset*; rather, he should go outside that *bet hakenesset* and pray *minchah shel chol*. This applies if he did not accept the *Shabbat* with them, but if he answered and accepted the *Shabbat* with them he may no longer pray *minchah shel chol*. Rather, he should pray *arvit shel Shabbat* twice (two *Amidot*).

6 If one comes into the *bet hakenesset* and finds the *tzibur* standing to accept the *Shabbat* upon themselves, he should start praying *minchah*. Even though the *tzibur* is accepting the *Shabbat* upon themselves while he is praying, nevertheless, it is still *mutar* because he started davening *beheter*. This applies even if he clearly knows that he won't finish his *minchah* before the *tzibur* accepts the *Shabbat*. In any event, it is preferable that he stands outside the *bet hakenesset*, and pray there.

7 One who is entering a *bet hakenesset* on *erev Shabbat* to pray *minchah*, and before he enters he hears the *shaliach tzibur* of another *minyan* say "Barechu et Hashem HaMevorach," should not answer "Baruch Hashem HaMevorach leolam va'ed." Answering would disqualify him from praying *minchah* because he initiates *kodesh* by answering the "*barechu*"; once he creates *kodesh* he may not turn it back to *chol* as there is no exception to this. Nonetheless, if he answered *barechu* anyways, he should not pray, but rather he should pray *arvit shel Shabbat* twice.

Today's learning has been dedicated for the continued Hatzlacha and Bracha of Rabbi and Mrs. Ari Bensoussan and family.

8. If one is praying by the *Kotel HaMa'aravi* or in a *bet hakenesset* that has many *minyanim* consecutively, and he prayed *arvit* before sunset (after *pelag haminchah*), he is allowed to answer *Kedusha* or any *amen* in the *shaliach tzibur's* repetition of the *amidah*, whether it is *chol* or *Shabbat*.

shaliach tzibur had the same *kavanah* to be *motzi* him as well, he is *yotzei yedeh chovah* for making up the missed *minchah*. However, this only applies to an individual; if the *shaliach tzibur* himself was *ones* and missed *minchah*, he may rely on *birkat me'ein sheva* to make up for his missed *minchah*.

9. If one was *ones* and didn't pray *minchah* on *erev Shabbat*, he may not rely on the *birkat me'en sheva* that the *shaliach tzibur* says and to have *kavanah* to be *yotzeh yedeh chovah* instead of making up for the lost *minchah*. Rather, he should pray the *arvit shel Shabbat* twice. *Bediavad,,* if he had *kavanah* to be *yotzeh yedeh chovah* and the

10. One must be meticulous to not delay saying *"Bo'i Kallah"* in the *Lecha Dodi* prayer, in which we accept the *Shabbat* upon ourselves, later than *sheki'at hachamah*. Therefore, if it's just before *sheki'at hachamah*, the *tzibur* should not wait even for an *adam gadol*, so as to save the *mitzvah* of *kabbalat Shabbat* before *sheki'at hachamah*.

Today's learning has been dedicated by Mr. David Saeidian, Leilui Nishmat Sara Eshrat bat Zebulon, may her Neshama have an Aliyah.

THIS CHAG'S LEARNING HAS BEEN DEDICATED
by Dr. and Mrs. Menachem Radparvar, for the
continued Hatzlacha and Bracha of the Radparvar
Family.

Chapter 7 **The Order of Tefilat Arvit of Shabbat**

1 We advance the *tefillah* of *arvit* on *leil Shabbat* more so than we do on regular days. After *plag haminchah* one may light candles, accept the *Shabbat* upon himself in the *tefillah* of *arvit*, and eat right away. Nowadays, the majority of *kehilot* are accustomed to accept the *Shabbat* upon themselves close to *sheki'at hachamah* like the custom of Rabeinu Ar"i z"l, and pray *arvit* afterwards.

2 Many holy *kehilot* in *Yerushalayim* have the custom to accept the *Shabbat* close to *sheki'at hachamah*, then say *Shir Hashirim* until nightfall, and only after that start praying *arvit*. One who says *Shir Hashirim* with proper *kavanah* saves himself from the *din* of *Gehenom* because Shlomo Hamelech established 117 *pesukim* opposite the 117 hours that man is judged every week in *Gehenom*. One must be careful not to interrupt by speaking during the reading of *Shir Hashirim* so that he will not, God forbid, undercut or create a separation in the holy *tevot* of the *sodei sodot*.

3 One should wear nice clothing for *Shabbat* and rejoice in its arrival as if one were running out to greet a king or a *chattan* and *kallah*. Rebbe Chanina would wrap himself on *erev Shabbat* and stand and say, "*Bo'u venimtzah likrat Shabbat Malketah*," and Rebbe Yanai would say "*Boee Kallah, Boee Kallah*."

4 There are those that are accustomed, *al pi Kabbalah*, to turn their faces to the west at the time of *kabbalat Shabbat* even though they turn their backs to the *Aron Kodesh*. There is no issue with this because the *sefer Torah* in the *Aron Hakodesh* is ten *tefachim* above ground level.

5 While saying *Boee Kallah*, it is customary to turn one's face to their right while saying *Boee Kallah* the first time. After this, one should turn his face to the left while saying *Boee Kallah* the second time. Finally, one stands erect towards the west and says *Boee Kallah* and then adds *Shabbat* Malketa. There's reason and support for this custom and it's therefore fitting to do.

6 Closing one's eyes at the time of *kabbalat Shabbat* is essential and has *sod* to it. Therefore, one should be careful to do this; only those that are compelled to say *kabbalat Shabbat* from the *siddur* are allowed to open their eyes to look in their *siddur*. One should not protest them in regard to this.

7 It is customary to say the perek of "*Bameh Madlikin*", and the Sefaradim are accustomed to say it before *tefillat arvit*. However, there are three different customs regarding when to say it. Some have the custom to say it before *kabbalat Shabbat*, while others have the custom to say it after *kabbalat Shabbat* or after *Mizmor Shir Leyom HaShabbat*. Every individual should follow the *minhag* of his place.

○ ○ ○

Today's learning has been dedicated for the continued Hatzlacha and Bracha of Rabbi and Mrs. Strouse and family.

8 There are those that have the custom to skip "*Bameh Madlikin*" on *Yom Tov* that falls out on *erev Shabbat* because one is not able to say "Isartem" (one of the three things we ask on *erev Shabbat*). Similarly, on *Yom Tov* we are only preoccupied in cooking and kindling (not a full-scale *Shabbat* preparation). Therefore, preparations for *Shabbat* are completed before sunset and there is no need to be as cautious like the other, regular *aravei Shabbatot*. Similarly, there are those that don't say "*Bameh Madlikin*" on *erev Shabbat* of *Chanukah* because it mentions the *pasul* oils which are not allowed to be lit on *Shabbat* but are allowed to be used for *Chanukah* candles. However, every individual should follow the *minhag* of his place. The custom in *Yerushalayim* is to refrain from saying "*Bameh Madlikin*" on these days. Also, we don't say it on *Yom Kippur* that falls out on *Shabbat*, *Shabbat chol hamoed*, *Yom Tov* that falls out on *erev Shabbat*, and in the house of a mourner. Those who do say it in the house of a mourner have what to rely on.

9 "*Mizmor shir leyom* Ha*Shabbat*," must be said while standing. The words "*Hashem malach geut lavesh*," according to *posekim*, are a *remez* since the letters of "*geut lavesh*" match the words "*goel Shabbat*." Similarly, the *posekim* wrote about the recitation of "*V'Shameru*," that if *Yisrael* keeps two *Shabbatot* consecutively we will merit the redemption. It is in this merit that they established the recitation of this *mizmor*.

OOO

Today's learning has been dedicated for the continued Hatzlacha and Bracha of Moshe ben Miriam.

10 The reason for not saying the *pasuk* of "*Vehu Rachum*" before the *tefilah* of *arvit shel Shabbat* is according to the *sod* that one should not say it. Moreover, there are three angels- *Mashchit*, *Af* and *Cheima* that control the *reshaim* with *yesurei Gehenom*, but they don't have *reshut* on *Shabbat* and therefore don't control the *reshaim* on *Shabbat*. Since these three angels are hinted to in the *pasuk* of "*Vehu Rachum*," we don't recite it on *Shabbat*.

11 By *arvit shel Shabbat*, it is the custom of the *chasidei Bet El* in *Yerushalayim ir hakodesh* to say the "*Leshem Yechud*," then "*Shavatenu Kabel*," then *kadish*, then *Barechu et Hashem*, and then the *berachot* of Keriyat Shemah of *arvit*. *Al pi Kabbalah*, one should stand for the *kadish* and the Barechu before *arvit*

for with this he is accepting upon himself *tosefet Shabbat*. There is a *kabbalah* that when *bnei Yisrael* down here say "*Barechu*" on *leil Shabbat*, a *bat kol* comes from the Heavenly academy to say "*Ashreichem am kadosh sheatem mevarchim lematah kedei shetitbarechu lema'alah.*"

12 In the *beracha* of *hashkiveinu*, one does not conclude the *beracha* with "*Shomer et amo Yisrael*," but rather he concludes with "*Hapores sukkat shalom aleinu*, etc." If one erred and concluded with "*Shomer et amo Yisrael*," and he remembered within the time frame of *toch kedei dibur* (the time it takes to say "*Shalom aleicha Rebbe*") he can correct it and say "*Hapores*, etc." However, if *toch kedei dibur* already elapsed he shouldn't say it or go back to repeat it.

Today's learning has been dedicated by Alen and Arielle Reyhan, Leilui Nishmat Netanel ben Yakov, may his Neshama have an Aliyah.

The Saying of Vayechulu

13 In the *amidah* of *arvit shel Shabbat* we say "*Vayechulu hashamayim veha'aretz...*" Our Rabbis said in the Talmud, "Anyone who prays on *erev Shabbat* and says '*Vayechulu*,' the *pasuk* says about him that it is as if he made a partnership with *HaKadosh Baruch Hu* in *Ma'aseh Bereishit.*" Furthermore, our Rabbis said, "Anyone who prays on *Erev Shabbat* and says '*Vayechulu*,' the two *malachei hasharet* that escort a person, take their hands and place it on his head and say to him, '*Vesar avonecha vechatotecha techufar.*'" Therefore, one should concentrate on *teshuvah* before saying "*Vayechulu*" because the atonement comes through doing *teshuvah.*

14 After the amidah the *tzibur* goes back and recites "*Vayechulu*" out loud while standing. The reason for this is because when *Yom Tov* falls out on *Shabbat* we don't say "*Vayechulu*" in the *amidah* (because we say "*Ata bichartanu*") and instead we must say it together after the *amidah.* Because of this, they made the *takana* that we should recite it every *Shabbat.* Another reason for saying "*Vayechulu*" aloud after the amidah is to be *yotzeh* those who don't know how to say it. According to the *chachamei Kabbalah,* one must say it three times (the third time being in *kiddush*) irrespective of the aforementioned reasons.

○○○

Today's learning has been dedicated for the continued Hatzlacha and Bracha of Rabbi and Mrs. Yisroel Meir Rubinfeld and family.

15 When the congregation repeats "Vayechulu" after the amidah, they should not add the words "Yom Hashishi" like we do by *kiddush*, but rather they should begin with "Vayechulu Hashamayim." It is only by *kiddush* that we add "Yom Hashishi," in order to complete the count of the 72 Tevot, which does not apply by *tefilah*.

16 Although it is best to recite "*Vayechulu*" together with a *tzibur*, even an individual praying in his home should repeat "*Vayechulu*" after his amidah. The same applies to an individual who prayed in the *bet hakenesset,* but did not finish the amidah before the *kahal* recited "*Vayechulu*" together. Certainly, according to the Kabbalah in which there is a *sod* reason to say "*Vayechulu*" three times, one should repeat "*Vayechulu*" individually.

17 If one made a mistake and began the *tefilat chol amidah* and then remembered in the middle of one of the *berachot* that it is *Shabbat*, he should finish that *beracha* and start the *beracha* for *Shabbat*. It doesn't matter if he remembered in the middle of *atah chonen* or any other *beracha* of the *amidah*. This *halacha* also applies to *shacharit* and *minchah* of *Shabbat* as well. However, if he made a mistake during the *mussaf amidah* he should stop, even in the middle of a *beracha*, and start *tikanta Shabbat*. Every person should be exceptionally careful to not make mistakes in the *Shabbat* prayers because it's not a good sign and causes an unnecessary *beracha* to be made. Therefore, it's good to always pray from the *siddur* and to concentrate fully on praying properly

○○○

Today's learning has been dedicated for the continued Hatzlacha and Bracha of Rabbi and Mrs. Salem and family.

THIS CHAG'S LEARNING HAS BEEN DEDICATED
y Baroch and Yehudit Laleh, in honor of their son
Gavriel David Laleh.

18 Only the *shaliach tzibur* recites *birkat me'ein sheva*, not the individual. *Birkat me'ein sheva* was instituted as a result of the different dangers that were present in the *batei kenessiyot* that used to be in the fields. In order to make sure that everyone had enough time to finish their *amidah* and not be left alone to walk home, the Rabbis instituted that the *shaliach tzibur* recite *birkat me'ein sheva* after the *amidah*. Even nowadays this *takanah* is still in place. This is the simple explanation, but there is also a reason *al pi hasod* to recite *birkat me'ein sheva* that it is like repeating the *amidah*.

19 There are places that have the custom to recite *birkat me'ein sheva* with the *shaliach tzibur* (albet without the *beracha* in the beginning and end because the *beracha* was only instituted for the *shaliach tzibur* and is therefore prohibited for the *tzibur* to say) from "*magen avot bidvaro*" until "*zecher lema'aseh bereishit.*" There are also some places that the *tzibur* only says excerpts from the *beracha*. Each individual should act according to the *minhag* of his place.

20 A place in which the *tzibur* has the custom to recite *birkat me'ein sheva* in a nice melody together with the *shaliach tzibur* while only the *shaliach tzibur* recites the first and last *beracha* should not discontinue this custom. On the contrary, this *minhag* is founded from *Hararei kodesh* as it prevents the *tzibur* from conversing during *birkat me'ein sheva.*

THIS CHAG'S LEARNING HAS BEEN DEDICATED
by Shirin Azizi, Leilui Nishmat Batyah bat
Mordechai, may her Neshama have an Aliyah.

21 One does not say *birkat me'ein sheva* in the house of a *chattan* or an *avel* because it is not a scenario (like above in *halachah* 18) in which they will be left behind in danger. In any event, in *Yerushalayim ir Hakodesh* they have the custom to recite the *birkat me'ein sheva* in the house of a *chattan* or *avel* because the *beracha* is very holy, and the house has the status of a home that is *maleh sefarim*.

22 If there is an apartment building 20 stories or higher, and on *leil Shabbat* they form a *minyan* in one of the upper apartments to pray instead of their regular *bet hakenesset*, they must recite *birkat me'ein sheva* because they have a set *minyan* there every *leil Shabbat*. If there is a *sefer Torah* present, then certainly *birkat me'ein sheva* should be said.

23 If *leil Pesach* falls out on *Shabbat*, the *shaliach tzibur* should not say *birkat me'ein sheva* because *Pesach* night is *leil shimurim* which precludes the issue of *mazikim* for which *birkat me'ein sheva* was established.

24 The *shaliach tzibur* should not kneel or bow down in the first or last *beracha* of *birkat me'ein sheva*, but we should not rebuke him if he does. It's proper to inform him afterwards that it's not in accordance with the law to do this.

25 It is prohibited to speak at the time we recite *Vayechulu* or while the *shaliach tzibur* recites *birkat me'ein sheva*.

THIS CHAG'S LEARNING HAS BEEN DEDICATED
by the Author, for the continued Hatzlacha and
Bracha of my dear sister, Elinor Simcha bat
Rivka Chaya.

26 There was a *chassid* that saw another *chassid* dead (in a dream) and noticed his face had turned green. When he asked him why his face had turned green the *chassid* replied, "It's because I used to speak during *Vayechulu* while the *tzibur* would recite it, as well as during *birkat me'ein sheva* and *Kadish*." If this was said regarding *birkat me'ein sheva*, how much more so is the severity of speaking during *tefillah* that is *kavuah* when it's prohibited to speak.

27 If one made a mistake in the *tefilah* of *arvit* and prayed the *tefilah* of chol instead of *Shabbat*, or if one didn't pray *arvit* at all but heard the *shaliach tzibur* recite *Birkat Me'ein Sheva* from beginning to end, he is *yotzeh yede chovato*. He is only *yotzeh* if he recited it with the *shaliach tzibur* word for word and had the intention of being *yotzeh yede chovato*. However, if he did not say it with the *shaliach tzibur* he is not *yotzeh*.

28 After *tefilat arvit*, it is the custom in *Yerushalayim* to recite the song of "*Yigdal Elokim Chai*," but in *bet E-l* they do not say it. Also, in the places that have the custom to recite this song, it's generally not recited on *leil Yom Tov*. This custom is special for *Shabbat* because *Shabbat* is the testimony to the creation of the world through the Creator's words, and to His oneness that should be blessed; this song of the 13 Central Principles include these testimonies. In any event, in the Western *kehilot* they say them in *leil Yom Tov* as well.

1 It is a *mitzvat aseh* from the *Torah* to sanctify the *Shabbat* verbally, as it is written "*Zachor et yom HaShabbat lekadesho*," by mentioning it with praise and *kiddush*. According to the *soferim*, this declaration should be done over a cup of wine.

2 Our Rabbis learned from the *pasuk* of "*Zachor et yom HaShabbat lekadesho*" that one mentions *Shabbat* when it commences and we learn from here that it is a *mitzvah* to sanctify the *Shabbat* as soon as possible on *leil Shabbat*. Therefore, one should immediately make *kiddush* when he comes home from the *bet Hakenesset*, and after he should eat his *seudat Shabbat*. However, if one doesn't have an appetite to eat he may delay making *kiddush* until he becomes hungry. This applies only if it won't interfere with the *shalom bayit*. Similarly, if one has hungry guests he must prioritize them.

3 Women are obligated in the *kiddush* both by night and by day, even though *kiddush* is a time-bound *mitzvah*. The reason is because the two words of keeping *Shabbat*, "*Zachor*" and "*Shamor*" are juxtaposed because they were said simultaneously. The *Zachor* aspect signifies the proactive *mitzvat Shabbat* of *kiddush* and the *Shamor* aspect signifies the abstention of *melachah* side of *mitzvat Shabbat*. Just as women are prohibited from performing *melachah* on *Shabbat*, women are equally obligated on the proactive *mitzvah* of *Zachor*.

Today's learning has been dedicated for the continued Hatzlacha and Bracha of Tiferet Rochel bat Nahid Naomi.

4 Women may fulfill the obligation of *kiddush* for men. However, because of *tziniyut*, it's befitting to be *machmir le'chatechilah* that women should not recite for men. This stringency is only in a case where the men are not from her household.

○···○

5 A woman may recite *kiddush* for a man even if she had already heard or recited it for herself because of the principle "*Kol Yisrael areivim ze lazeh.*"

○···○

6 A *kattan* who has not yet turned thirteen years and one day old may not recite the *kiddush* for men or women. Because his obligation in *kiddush* is only Rabbinic (*M'din chinuch*) he cannot fulfill their obligation which is from the *Torah*. He can't fulfill their obligation even if the man or woman already prayed *arvit*. Even if the boy is thirteen years and one day old but it's not known for certain that he has grown two hairs, he's still considered a *kattan*. However, in a pressing situation if he's thirteen years and one day old but has not been checked for two hairs, he may recite *kiddush* for a woman after she has prayed *arvit*. In the event of a pressing situation, if he is under the age of thirteen, the *kattan* should recite the *kiddush* and the woman should repeat it after him word for word.

Today's learning has been dedicated for the continued Hatzlacha and Bracha of Rabbi and Mrs. Emanuel Goldfeiz and family.

7 One who regularly recites *kiddush* on the wine for himself may give the honor of reciting *kiddush* to someone else. This is not considered a *neder* that one would need a *hatarah* from. Rather, he's permitted to give the honor to someone else to recite the *kiddush* provided that he listens intently and has in mind to be *yotzeh yedeh chovah*.

8 One who recites *kiddush* must have the intent to be *yotzeh yedeh chovah* for the people listening as well. Similarly, those who are listening must also concentrate on being *yotzeh yedeh chovah* with him. Therefore, before the *ba'al habayit* recites *kiddush* he should remind those in his household to have in mind to be *yotzeh*. One should not answer *Baruch hu ubaruch shemo* to a *beracha* in which someone else is reciting for him to be *yotzeh yedeh chovah*. However, *bediavad*, if one did mistakenly answer *Baruch hu ubaruch shemo*, he is still *yotzeh yedeh chovah* and need not repeat *kiddush*.

9 If one cannot hear the *kiddush*, be it from his own trouble hearing or from the *ba'al habayit* reciting *kiddush* not speaking clearly, he may quietly say the *kiddush* to himself while looking at the cup of wine that the *kiddush* is being recited over. In this instance, because he has made the *beracha* for himself, he should not answer *amen* to the *ba'al habayit* since that would make a *hefsek* between his *beracha* and drinking the *kiddush* wine.

○ ○ ○

Today's learning has been dedicated for the continued Hatzlacha and Bracha of Rabbi and Mrs. Yisrael Klapholtz and family.

10 Before one recites the kiddush, the lechem mishneh must be placed on the table with a covering both on top and below as a tribute to the mun which was "delivered" in a box, so to speak, with a layer of dew on top and a layer of dew underneath it. Another reason for covering the challah is to spare it embarrassment while we recite the kiddush first.

11 After one makes kiddush, he may take off the challah covering. However, it's better to leave the challah covered until the beracha of hamotzi, when he should place both hands on the challah and recite the beracha.

Seder Kiddush

12 The seder of kiddush set by the Arizal is printed in the siddur. When one returns home, he should exclaim excitedly, "Shabbat Shalom!" If one's mother is present, he should kiss her hand. While reciting "Shalom Aleichem," one should not say Mimelech malchei hamelachim rather one should say Melech malchei hamlachim (with one mem). One should also say "Betzeitchem leshalom" (with the letter bet at the beginning of the word). The intention with this is to follow what we say in Barchuni leshalom, that is, when they leave they should be blessed and not that we are pushing them out, chalilah.

13 If there is chalilah a fight or any arguments in the house, it's accepted from a big Rav that one should not say "Betzeitchem leshalom" on leil Shabbat.

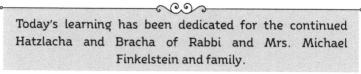

Today's learning has been dedicated for the continued Hatzlacha and Bracha of Rabbi and Mrs. Michael Finkelstein and family.

∽◎∾
• Day 57 •
∾◎〜

∽◎∾
• כח' תשרי •
∾◎〜

14 If one is not able to place his table on the north side of his dining room, his candles on the south side on *erev Shabbat*, and also does not have *hadas*, he should not say the words "*Asader lidroma menarta disetima...*" which is found in the *piyut* "*Azamer bishevachin.*" This is simply because he has not performed what those words declare and reciting them would suggest that he lied. However, he does not have to skip the verse entirely, but rather he can change "*Asader*" to "*Asderu.*" This makes the verse apply to *klal Yisrael* in general, that they set their tables in the north, candles in the south, and have a cup of wine and *hadas* on the table for *Shabbat*.

15 How does one make the *beracha*? He should take the cup, which holds at least a quarter *lug* (86 grams, which is the numerical value of the word "*kos*") of wine, and he should clean the inside and rinse the outside before filling it with wine. He should then pick up the cup in his right hand and hold it exclusively in his right hand at least a *tefach* (8 cm) above the table. While standing, he should recite the *parasha* of "*Vayechulu*" until "*Asher barah Elokim la'asot,*" recite *birkat hagefen* and *birkat kiddush*, and then drink the equivalent of a *maleh lugmav*, which is a quarter *revi'it* (44 grams). All those listening should taste the wine to show affection for the *mitzvah*.

Today's learning has been dedicated for the continued Hatzlacha and Bracha of Chana bat Ariella.

16 Al pi Kabbalah, the kiddush cup should be passed to the one reciting it with two hands. The mekadesh should also use both hands to receive it and then hold it exclusively with his right hand parallel to his chest. He should hold the cup with his fingers pointing upwards while they are around the perimeter of the cup. He should not hold the cup in his palm nor on his fingers while they are flat, rather they should be pointing upwards. Before reciting the kiddush, water should be mixed in with the wine already in the cup to fill it. It's best that the person adding the water should pour it three times with his right hand. Finally, the mekadesh should gaze into the cup of wine, for there is a deep sod and much kavannah to this.

○···○

17 Before the kiddush one should recite the paragraph of "Mizmor ledavid Hashem ro'ee." Afterwards, he recites "Yom hashishi, vayechulu hashamayim veha'aretz..." Al pi sod, there is significance as to why we add these two words Yom hashishi to Vayechulu. The rashei tevot of "Yom hashishi vayechulu hashamayim," spell the name Hava"ya. One must concentrate intently on the kiddush and reflect on teshuvah because with the recitation of Vayechulu we are testifying that Hashem created heaven and earth and rested on Shabbat. Since a rasha is disqualified from testimony, one must reflect on teshuvah in order to be fit for testimony. Al pi Kabbalah, one must recite kiddush of leil Shabbat while standing. This is the minhag of the Sefaradim and even some Ashkenazim have this minhag as well.

○○○

Today's learning has been dedicated for the continued Hatzlacha and Bracha of Rabbi and Mrs. Ani and family.

18 Once the *mekadesh* recites "*Vayechulu hashamayim...*," he should say "*Savri meranan*" to which the listeners reply, "*Lechayim!*" Even if one recites *kiddush* alone, he should still say *Savri meranan* because there is *sod* and *kavannah* to this practice. He then continues with *birkat "Borei peri hagafen"* and *birkat "Asher kidishanu bemitzvotav veratzah vanu...,*" and then sits to drink the wine.

Drinking the Wine

19 *Me'ikur hadin*, one must drink a *melo lugmav* which is one quarter of a *revi'it* (44 grams) from the *kiddush* wine. However, the *mitzvah min hamuvchar* is to drink a full *revi'it* (86 grams).

20 One should take no longer to drink the *kiddush* wine than the average time it takes to drink a *revi'it*, which amounts to two gulps. At the very least, one must not drink it slower than the time of *achilas pras* (4-5 minutes).

Today's learning has been dedicated for the continued Hatzlacha and Bracha of Rabbi and Mrs. Eisig and family.

THIS MONTH'S LEARNING HAS BEEN DEDCIATED
for the Hatzlacha and Bracha of the donor and
Klal Yisrael.

21 Le'chatechilah, the mekadesh should personally drink more than half of a *revi'it*. However, if he is unable to drink it himself, he may give it to another member of the meal to drink the prescribed amount. Before he passes it, the mekadesh must first taste some wine and only then give it to another to drink. *Al pi sod*, when the mekadesh gives the wine to another to drink it's best to give it to another man instead of a woman. *Bediavad*, the members of the meal are *yotzeh yedeh chovah* if they drank at least a total of *rov revi'it*, as long as they finished it within the time frame of *k'dei achilat pras*.

22 The most preferable way to accomplish this *mitzvah* is for every member of the meal to taste a bit of the *kiddush* wine, even though the mekadesh already drank the full amount necessary.

23 It is best for the mekadesh to drink the *kiddush* wine from the *kiddush* cup itself as opposed to pouring into a secondary cup to drink from. Nowadays because the mekadesh drinks from the *kiddush* cup directly, one need not worry that it is contaminated. In any event, it is a good idea for the mekadesh to pour some *kiddush* wine into a second cup, drink from the *kiddush* cup, and then proceed to pour from the second cup for the other members of the meal. However, he must make sure that the *kiddush* cup has a *rov revi'it* of wine left for him to drink. If there is not, he must drink a *rov revi'it* from the second cup before pouring for them.

24 If the woman of the household is impure, we may be lenient in her drinking following her husband and then passing along to the other members of the meal. However, if they have the custom to pour wine into individual cups for each person, he should pour the individual cups for all and his wife should receive one of those.

25 On *leil Shabbat*, if those at the meal did not hear the *mekadesh* recite the *beracha* of *"Boreh peri hagefen,"* and instead only heard the *beracha* of *"Asher Kkdishanu bemitzvotav veratzah banu..."* they are still *yotzeh* yedeh *chovatam* since the *chovah* of *kiddush* for *Shabbat* is only dependent on the *beracha* of *"Asher Kidishanu."* However, for *kiddush shel yom*, the *beracha* of *"Boreh peri hagefen,"* is the essential part of *kiddush*, and therefore if one did not hear this *beracha* on *Shabbat* day it's as if he didn't hear *kiddush* at all.

26 It is the custom amongst the entire Jewish nation to give a special *beracha* to children on *leil Shabbat*. Parents are allowed to bless their children with *birkat kohanim* so long as they place their right hand or both hands together on the child's head. One need not object to this practice for there is no *nesiat kapayim* or the intent to fulfill the *mitzvah* of *birkat kohanim*.

Today's learning has been dedicated for the continued Hatzlacha and Bracha of Rabbi and Mrs. Dovid Zargari and family.

27 If one recited the kiddush but dropped the cup of wine before he drank, he should refill the cup and recite only the beracha of Boreh peri hagefen, again without repeating the beracha of mekadesh HaShabbat. However, if he had intended with his original beracha to drink more wine in addition to the kiddush cup, he doesn't have to repeat Boreh peri hagefen,, and rather he should drink immediately from another cup. He should not make a beracha and drink from another cup only if he did not make a hefsek dibbur with things that do not concern kiddush.

The Kiddush Cup

28 The cup for kiddush must have at least a revi'it lug of wine. This measurement is 86 grams, the numerical value of the word "kos". Some follow a stricter measurement and use a cup that holds 137 grams. Those who have the custom to follow the opinion of the Chazon Ish Zt"l, are stricter still and use a cup that holds 150 grams, which is the numerical value of "kos hagun."

29 One must clean the inside and rinse the outside of the kiddush cup, for both sides of the cup must be clean. However, if the cup is already clean it doesn't need to be rinsed and cleaned. If the cup was covered with cloth on both sides, it's kosher for kiddush and considered as if he cleaned and rinsed it. Al pi Kabbalah it's customary to clean and rinse the cup even if it was clean and clear.

Today's learning has been dedicated for the continued Hatzlacha and Bracha of Rabbi and Mrs. Yoel Bursztyn and family.

30 One must fill the *kiddush* cup. One may not make *kiddush* on a cup that is broken or has a faulty rim, and there also should not be a fault in the base of the cup. In a pressing situation, when one does not have another cup, he may make *kiddush* with it.

31 If the cup is cracked or punctured in the bottom, it's *pasul* even *bediavad* to be used for *kiddush* if it cannot hold a *revi'it* of a *lug*. *Le'chatechilah*, one should not make *kiddush* on a cup that is cracked even if the wine does not leak from the crack.

32 *Le'chatechilah*, one should be stringent not to use a disposable paper cup to recite *kiddush*. In a pressing situation where he has no other cup he may recite *kiddush* with such a cup.

33 One should choose a nice cup for *kiddush*. Those who do *mehadrin* choose a silver cup because of the concept of *"Ze Keli veanvehu,"* for the *kavod* of the *Shechinah*, calling it a cup of *beracha*.

Today's learning has been dedicated for the continued Hatzlacha and Bracha of Rabbi and Mrs. Netanel Gralla and family.

34 One should not make *kiddush* on a blemished cup by drinking from a cup of wine that another already drank from. Even if another took a small taste from that cup, it becomes flawed for *kiddush*. In a pressing situation, where one doesn't have any other flawless wine (and doesn't have any other way to fix it, as we shall see later on) it is permitted to use the flawed wine.

35 One who drank from the cup through a hollow reed (such as a straw and the like) has not made the cup flawed *min hadin* because it can be fixed by adding some more wine or water to the cup. However, one should not be lenient in this matter.

36 One can fix a flawed cup of wine by adding to it wine from the bottle or some water as long as the water doesn't weaken the strength of the wine.

37 One cannot add water even if one drank the *kiddush* wine from a pitcher, bottle, or small barrel. However, if he drank from a large barrel, one need not be *makpid*. However, there are some that are stringent in the case of drinking from a large barrel. Therefore, *le'chatechilah* it is best to observe this view and not drink from the tap of a large barrel.

Today's learning has been dedicated for the continued Hatzlacha and Bracha of Mr. and Mrs. Yehoshua Soleimania and family.

38 If one has leftover wine in his cup and wants to return it to the bottle, he should first add some wine from the bottle into the cup, and only afterwards pour it all back into the bottle. By doing this he keeps the wine in the bottle befitting for a *beracha*. He may only do this if there is more wine in the bottle than in the cup.

○..○

39 One should fill the *kiddush* cup with wine to the brim. However, if he is worried that filling it to the brim will cause some wine to spill and be wasted, he may leave some room at top of the cup, as it's still considered full. No matter the case, the *kiddush* cup must be filled with a minimum of a *revi'it*.

40 It is brought down in the *Talmud* that the *chachamim* would make an *itur* (crown) for the cup. There were those that crowned the cup with *talmidim*, meaning that the *talmidim* would gather around the *rebbe* at the time of the *beracha*, and there were also those that would actually crown the cup by placing filled cups around the *kiddush* cup for it's honor and adornment. Even though we don't have the custom to make an *itur*, in any event one shouldn't do the opposite. Therefore, one should not place empty utensils on the table around the cup at the time of *beracha*. The *gedolim* were very careful with this.

Today's learning has been dedicated for the continued Hatzlacha and Bracha of Rabbi and Mrs. Aryeh Yudin and family.

Types of Wine

41 It is a *mitzvah min hamuvchar* to choose a good wine for *kiddush*. *Le'chatechilah* *kiddush* should be recited on red wine. However, if one does not have red wine, or the red wine isn't *meshubach*, one may recite *kiddush* on white wine.

42 We do not make *kiddush* on wine that contracted a bad smell from a dirty bottle or the like. Even if the wine were to maintain its taste and smell enough that we would recite "*Boreh peri hagefen*," since this wine is *pasul* for use on the *mizbeach* because of "*Hikrivuhu na lefachtecha*," it is also *pasul* for *kiddush*.

43 If the wine has started to smell like vinegar but the taste remains, the wine may be used for *kiddush*. However, if the taste has changed to vinegar, even if it still smells of wine, it may not be used for *kiddush* since taste is the determining factor. It is the *mitzvah min haamuvchar* to use a good wine to make *kiddush* on, and also the wine should have a pleasant smell.

44 It is permitted to make *kiddush* on wine that is *mevushal* or that contains sugar or honey as a sweetener. According to the Rambam though, one should not make *kiddush* on such wine. If possible, one should use a wine with which he may be *yotzeh yedeh chovah* in accordance with the Rambam, and be particular that the other wine he chooses should be sweet and tasty.

Today's learning has been dedicated by Eli and Alinor Zobdeh, for the continued Hatzlacha and Bracha of the Zobdeh Family.

45 Grape juice that is *mevushal* is *kosher* for *kiddush* just like wine that is *mevushal*. Similarly, raisins that were cooked and then pressed for wine are also *kosher* for *kiddush*.

46 Our *minhag* is that pasteurized wines and grape juices are fit for *kiddush* use *le'chatechilah*.

47 It is permissible to make *kiddush* on new grape juice or on wine that is less than forty days old. The *Shulchan Aruch* writes that one may squeeze a cluster of grapes (while it is still day) and make *kiddush* on it. As well, sparkling wine is *kosher* for *kiddush*. In any event, the best way of fulfilling the *mitzvah* is to make *kiddush* on wine that is at least forty days old.

48 One may make *kiddush* over raisin wine provided that there was still moisture in the raisins before they were soaked for wine. If the raisins were completely dried to the extent that even pressing and squeezing them would not yield juice, one may not use this liquid for *kiddush* nor recite the *beracha* of "*Boreh peri hagefen.*"

Today's learning has been dedicated for the continued Hatzlacha and Bracha of Rabbi and Mrs. Aryeh Cohen and family.

49 Even small raisins that do not contain grape pips inside are considered full-fledged regular wine in regard to reciting "*Boreh peri hagefen*" and *kiddush*.

○..○

50 The production of *kiddush* raisin wine entails soaking them in water for three days. However, if one crushed the raisins, then placed them in the water for less than three days, and then squeezed them for wine, he may still use it for *kiddush*. Also, if one cooked the raisins or placed them in hot water, it is considered wine even if it wasn't placed in water for three days.

The Amount of Water in Wine

51 In raisin wine, the raisins must be the main ingredient over the water within. Therefore, the amount of water may not be more than the amount of the raisins after they grew.

○..○

52 When buying wines sold in stores, one must be careful that the wine is acceptable according to the Sepharadim in that the dominant ingredient is wine. Otherwise, one can not use it for *kiddush* nor recite "*Boreh peri hagefen*" on it. Therefore, one should not rely on different *hechsherim* for wine unless they have the reputation of also following the Sepharadi standard regarding *kiddush* and "*Boreh peri hagefen*."

○○○

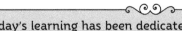

Today's learning has been dedicated by Ariel Afrah, Leilui Nishmat Michael Dovid ben Moshe and for the Hatzlacha of Ariel ben Homa and Yarden Miriam bat Elham.

∾ॐॐ
• Day 69 •
ॐॐૐ

∾ॐॐ
• י' חשוון •
ॐॐૐ

53 According to *Maran Shulchan Aruch*, if Sepharadi *bachurim* learn in an Ashkenazi *yeshiva* in which they make *kiddush* on wine that is mostly water, the Sepharadi *bachurim* should not make the *kiddush* on that wine. However, they are still *yotzeh yedeh chovatam* of *kiddush* for it is no worse than being *yotzeh kiddush* with alcohol of the *medina*. After all, the Ashkenazi *bachurim* are simply following what their Rebbeim *paskin* according to the *Rema*, and one should not protest this for peace is paramount.

54 We do not make *kiddush* on wine that was left uncovered overnight, even if it has not changed in taste or smell. *Le'chatechilah*, one should be *makpid* to make sure the wine is not left uncovered for even a short period of time. However, if the wine was left uncovered in a cupboard or a fridge, one may still recite *kiddush* over it even if it was left there for a long time provided it does not have a bad taste or smell.

55 If wine left uncovered was mixed with covered wine, this mixture may be used for *kiddush* as long as sixty percent of the mixture is that of the covered wine.

56 If one found his pitcher of wine uncovered, but a family member told him that it was covered the night before at an unknown time by an unknown person, one is allowed to recite *kiddush* over this wine because it's merely a *safek derabanan* and *safek derabanan lehakel*.

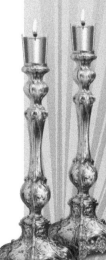

Today's learning has been dedicated by the Author, for the continued Hatzlacha and Bracha of my dear brother-in-law, Yehoshua Gamliel ben Yehudis Sheindel.

57 If, *bediavad,* one did recite *kiddush* over wine that was left uncovered, he is *yotzeh yedeh chovah* and need not recite a second *kiddush.* This *halachah* applies only to the *kiddush* of *leil Shabbat* because during the night *kiddush* one recites the *beracha* with *hazkarat Hashem* that he should not repeat. However, *kiddush* of *Shabbat* day, where there is no mention of *hazkarat Hashem umalchut,* one must recite a second *kiddush.* This should be over another wine if available, and he should make a *hefsek* between the two *kiddushin;* alternatively, he may recite *kiddush* over the bread.

58 Sefaradi *bachurim* learning in an Ashkenazi *yeshiva* that hear *kiddush* or *havdalah* in the Ashkenazi accent and pronunciation, or conversely, Ashkenazi *bachurim* that hear *kiddush* or *havdalah* in a Sephardi accent and pronunciation, are *yotzeh yedeh chovatam.* (This *halacha* applies specifically by *kiddush* and *havdalah.* However, by the reading of *Parashat Zachor* or *Parashat Parah* which is a *mitzvah* from the *Torah,* it is proper to hear the reading of the *parasha* according to the *minhag* of his father.)

Today's learning has been dedicated for the continued Hatzlacha and Bracha of Rabbi and Mrs. Eli Storch and family.

One Without Wine

∼७७∼
• Day 71 •
९७७∽

∼७७∼
• יב׳ חשוון •
९७७∽

59 One who finds himself without wine for *kiddush* on *leil Shabbat* should recite it over the bread. The procedure is as follows: he washes his hands and recites the *beracha* "*Al netilat nadayim*," places his hands on the *mapah* that is covering the bread and recites "Yom Hashishi Vayechulu Hashamayim... Asher Bara Elokim La'asot." He then uncovers the bread, places his hands on the *lechem mishneh* and recites the *beracha* of Hamotzi (instead of Boreh Peri Hagefen). When he finishes the *beracha* of Hamotzi he covers the bread one more, places his hands on the covered bread and recites Birkat *kiddush* of "Asher Bachar Banu...Mekadesh HaShabbat," at which point he cuts the bread and eats it.

60 One who does not have wine or bread to recite *kiddush* over on *leil Shabbat* may not recite *kiddush* over another food. Rather, he should eat without *kiddush* as he is *ones*. It is best to have *kavanah* to be *yotzeh yedeh chovah* of *kiddush* from the Torah during the *tefilah* of *leil Shabbat*.

∘·····································∘

61 A *choleh* that cannot eat or drink, but is fed through infusions, is exempt from *kiddush* because this is not considered "eating." When he is able to pray, he should have *kavanah* to be *yotzeh yedeh chovah* of *kiddush* from the Torah during the *tefilah* of *leil Shabbat*.

Today's learning has been dedicated by Shlomo Golfeiz, in honor of his wife Oshra Golfeiz and the success of the Golfeiz family.

62 If one did not make kiddush on leil Shabbat, whether on purpose or by accident, he may make it up the whole next day and say the whole kiddush of leil Shabbat except for "Vayechulu."

Kiddush in a Place of Seudah

63 One must recite kiddush with a seudah because the pasuk says "Vekarata laShabbbat oneg" and our sages explain this to mean that the calling of Shabbat (the kiddush) should be in a place of oneg (the seudah). Therefore, if one made kiddush on wine but did not have a seudah with it, he is not yotzeh the chovah of kiddush. He is also not yotzeh yedeh chovato if he subsequently had the seudah somewhere else. Therefore, if his meal is in another place, he repeats kiddush there.

64 One who hears kiddush from a friend or from a neighbor nearby but has no intention of eating there is prohibited to taste anything because he is not yotzeh yedeh chova of kiddush. However, if one is in his own house with the table set in front of him and hears the kiddush from his neighbor, and both have the correct intentions of being yotzeh kiddush for/with each other, he is yotzeh the chovah of kiddush because he is making a seudah in the place he heard the kiddush.

Today's learning has been dedicated for the continued Hatzlacha and Bracha of Rabbi and Mrs. Yisrael Kaminetzky and family.

65 If one made *kiddush* having in mind to eat in one corner but then ate in a different corner, even if it is a large hall, he should not repeat *kiddush*. However, le'chatechilah one should not change his place from one corner to another. If he intended before he recited *kiddush* to eat his *seudah* in another corner, he can change places even le'chatechilah.

66 If one made *kiddush* in one room, he should not change his place to another room, even if this was his intention prior to *kiddush*. bediavad, even if one changed his location from one house to another house, or from the house to the courtyard, as long he intended beforehand to move he need not repeat *kiddush*. If he didn't intend to move but he can still see his original location, he need not repeat *kiddush*. If he can't, he must then recite *kiddush* again.

67 One may recite *kiddush* for others even if he does not eat with them. However, he may not taste with them if he did not make *kiddush* in his house where he will eat his *seudah*. Even by *kiddush* of *Shabbat* day he may do this. Nonetheless, it is best that he drinks a *revi'it* of wine in the daytime *kiddush* with the intention that it be the *kiddush* in a place of *seudah*.

Today's learning has been dedicated for the continued Hatzlacha and Bracha of Moshe ben Yechezkel and family.

68 If one eats a *kezayit* of bread (30 grams) after reciting *kiddush*, this is considered as having made *kiddush* in a place of *seudah* and he may then eat his *seudah* somewhere else. Therefore, if one has a *kezayit* of cake from the five major grains, this too works to be *yotzeh* the *chovah* of *kiddush* in a place of *seudah*. Even if he only drank a *revi'it* of wine from the *kiddush* cup, he is *yotzeh* the *chovah* of *kiddush* in a place of *seudah*. However, some disagree with the *din* of the cake and do not consider it to constitute a *seudah*. Therefore, one should be *machmir* for this opinion by the night *kiddush* because it stems from the *Torah*.

69 Because *kiddush* requires a *seudah*, *Maran* wrote in the *Shulchan Aruch* that it is best not to recite *kiddush* in the *bet hakenesset* because nowadays no one eats a *seudah* in the rooms adjacent to the *bet hakenesset*. nIn any event, if a *bet kenneset* has the custom to recite *kiddush* on *leil Shabbat*, one should not stop this practice because there are *amei ha'aretz* that do not make *kiddush* in their own home but will be *yotzeh yedeh chovah* of *kiddush* from the *Torah* with the *kiddush* in the *bet kenesset*.

Today's learning has been dedicated by Yosef Chaim Azizi, in honor of his wife Aviva and children Adina and Eliyahu.

Wine Touched by a Gentile

70 Wine of a gentile is prohibited in both drinking and benefit. This *din* also applies to the wine of a Jew that a gentile touched. This prohibition does not have any *heter* at all, and the punishment for this transgression is very great as one uproots his *neshamah* and loses his portion in *olam habah*.

71 The prohibition of benefiting from wine touched by a gentile is limited to gentiles that worship *avoda zara*. However, gentiles that do not worship *avodah zara*, for example *Yishmaelim* that don't have idols, do not render wine prohibited from benefit, but rather only from drinking; *Yishmaelim* believe in the singularity of G-d and do not worship idols or the like.

72 A non-observant Jew (*mumar*) whom is *mechalel Shabbat* publicly that touches the wine may prohibit the wine. If he is *mechalel Shabbat* because of monetary hardship and is *moreh heter* for himself, but he still recites *kiddush* and *havdalah* and prays on *Shabbat*, *bediavad* the wine is not prohibited. However, if he is *mechalel Shabbat* irrespective of monetary hardship and does not recite *kiddush* or *havdalah* or pray on *Shabbat*, one should be *machmir* to not use wine which he touched.

O O O

Today's learning has been dedicated for the continued Hatzlacha and Bracha of Rabbi and Mrs. Baruch Amiri and family.

73 A *mumar* who is *mechalel Shabbat* publicly with contempt, even if he does so for personal gain, renders the wine that he touches unfit for consumption like that touched by a *Yishmaeli*. However, wine touched by this *mumar* is not prohibited in benefit like that which is touched by an idol worshipper. However, if this *mumar* merely picked up the closed bottle of wine, it's still permitted. If he poured the wine from the bottle, the poured wine becomes prohibited but the wine left in the bottle is still *muttar* since the wine poured by a *Yishmaeli* or a *mumar mechalel Shabbat* in public is not connected to the wine which remains in the bottle.

○ .... ○

74 If one is a guest by people who are *mechalel Shabbat*, or if one *chalila* has *mechalelei Shabbat* in his family, he should boil out some of the wine on *erev Shabbat*. With this he will make it *yayin mevushal* which will not be made forbidden through their touch. It's also best for him to pray from the depths of his heart to the *Boreh Olam* to awaken in them the spirit from above and that they do *teshuva shelemah*.

Today's learning has been dedicated for the continued Hatzlacha and Bracha of Mr. Pedram Soleimania and family.

1 One must eat in the place of *kiddush* right away. One should not even wait for a short time. Therefore, after *kiddush* one should immediately wash his hands for the *seudah* from a vessel that is not punctured. Before he washes his hands he should say *Mizmor ledavid Hashem roee lo echsar....* become it consists of fifty seven words corresponding to *za"n* so that he won't lack his sustenance and his *mazon nefesh*. One must wash his hands standing by all of the three *Shabbat* meals.

2 Those who are accustomed to eating fish between *kiddush* and *netilat yadayim*, should nullify their custom since they are making a *beracha* that is unnecessary because foods that are a part of the *seudah* are covered by the *beracha* of *hamotzi*.

3 *Le'chatechilah,* one should be careful not to leave outside between *kiddush* and the *seudah* even if he will return to eat in the place of *kiddush*. In any event, if he went outside to wash his hands for the *seudah* or to relieve himself, there is no *chashash* because it is for the need of the *seudah*. Therefore, one should not doubt the *pashut minhag* of going to wash one's hands for the *seudah* even if he is changing his location or if he is unable to see the original location that he made *kiddush* in since it is for the sake of the *seudah*.

Today's learning has been dedicated for the continued Hatzlacha and Bracha of Rabbi and Rebbetzin Netanel Louie and family.

Cutting of the Bread

4 One should cut two loaves of bread (called *lechem mishne*) by holding both loaves in his hands and cutting the bottom loaf. One should not begin to slice the bread until he finishes the *beracha* of *hamotzi* so that the *beracha* be made on two whole loaves.

⚬..⚬

5 *Al pi Kabbalah*, one should place twelve breads on the table, six on the right of the table and six on the left in the shape of two circles. That is, he should place three loaves in a circle on the right and place three loaves on top of that, and so too for the left hand side. If he doesn't have twelve loaves, he should place four loaves on each side with two on top of another two on each side of the table. However, if he has only three loaves, he should only place two on the table. So too if he has five or six, he should only place four. When he wants to make the *beracha* he should take the top two middle loaves (when there are twelve loaves) and stick the bottoms of the two loaves together with the tops of the loaves, one facing the right and one facing the left, and make *hamotzi*. When he is done making the *beracha* he should cut a *kezayit* from the bread facing the right and have a taste of it. He should then cut a *kabetza* and give it to his wife, and after that cut for the rest of the guests.

○○○

Today's learning has been dedicated for the continued Hatzlacha and Bracha of Rabbi and Mrs. Yonah Gidanian and family.

6 It is permitted for one to be *machmir* and place twelve loaves on his table according to Kabbalah, even if his father was not accustomed to doing so, and there is no *ga'ava* in doing this. However, if one is dining with his father it is not right to be *machmir* more than his father to place twelve loaves because it's not respectful to the father. Particularly, this is only *chassidut* according to the Ar"i z"l and the world is not accustomed to doing this.

7 If there is an *adam gadol* dining at one's table, one should not give to him before he gives to his wife. Rather, after he tasted the bread, he should first give to his wife and only after give to the *adam gadol* and the rest of the guests.

8 It is a *mitzvah* to cut a large slice of bread that will be enough for one for the whole meal. This will not make him look like a *ra'avtan* since he doesn't do this during the week, as it's quite evident that he is doing it for the love of *seudat Shabbat*. In any event, the cutting of the large slice should only be done after he cut a *kezayit* for himself and a *kebetza* for his wife.

9 The *mesubim* are not allowed to taste from the bread until the cutter tasted his bread first. If there is however in front of each guest a *lechem mishne*, they are allowed to eat even if the cutter hasn't tasted from his bread yet.

Today's learning has been dedicated by Mr. and Mrs. Meir Hakimi, Leilui Nishmat Malka bat Moshe, may her Neshama have an Aliyah.

10 The one who cut the bread should not give the piece of bread into the hand of the other diners since bread is only given to the hand of *avelim* (during the week) because it says "*Parsa Zion beyadehah*," corresponding to the piece of bread (*paroset hamotzi*) that is given to an *avel* during his mourning. Rather the cutter should place the bread in front of each and every guest and they will take it and eat it. Also, one should not throw the bread in front of them since this is considered a shame to the *mitzvah,* and it also isn't respectful to the one receiving the bread.

Lechem Mishne

11 If one does not have a second loaf of bread for *lechem mishne*, he is able to borrow a *lechem mishne* and return it to it's owner after the *beracha* and the cutting of the loaf of bread since both breads don't have to necessarily be his. Similarly, one is also permitted to take a frozen piece of bread from the fridge for *lechem mishne*, even if it isn't fit to be eaten at that moment.

12 If the bread wanted to be used for *lechem mishne* is in a plastic bag, it is correct *le'chatechilah* to take it out of the plastic bag during the *beracha*. Sliced bread that is in a plastic bag is not considered *lechem mishne*.

OOO

Today's learning has been dedicated for the continued Hatzlacha and Bracha of Mr. Avichai Kheradyar and family.

13 One should be *makpid* in taking at least a *kezayit* for each loaf when choosing the *lechem mishne.*

---

14 Bread that was burnt at the time of baking should not be eaten before looking for another piece of bread. If he is unable to find another piece of bread, he may use the burnt bread as *lechem mishne.* One should take off the burnt part only after he says *hamotzi* so that the bread be full at the time of *beracha.* However, if the bread is only slightly burnt, so that when you take off the burnt area it still looks whole, it is permissible to take off the burnt area before the *beracha.*

---

15 If one has only one loaf and doesn't have another piece of bread to add to the *lechem mishne,* he should not split his piece into two separate pieces for *lechem mishne.* He should rather make the *beracha* on that one whole piece he has. If he can, he should add a piece of cake to the bread while making the *beracha* so that in a pressing time he can be *mekayem* the *mitzvah* of *lechem mishne.* If he doesn't have a whole piece of cake, he should take a piece of bread and add it to the whole piece he has and make a *beracha* on both of them. If he doesn't even have a whole piece of bread, he should take two pieces of bread and make a *beracha* on them so that there will be a differentiation between *Shabbat* and *chol* where he only makes *hamotzi* on one piece of bread. This is all in a pressing situation, but *le'chatechilah* one should be *makpid* in taking two fully whole pieces of bread for the *beracha.*

Today's learning has been dedicated for the continued Hatzlacha and Bracha of Mr. and Mrs. Jerry Levine and family.

16 If one has only one full loaf, he may add a full *matzah* to the *lechem mishne*. He should be *makpid* that the *matzah* not be cracked or broken. Similarly, he may add sweet *challah* to the *lechem mishne*.

○·······································○

17 If one has only one full loaf, he may add dairy bread to it (for ex. it was kneaded with milk or the such) for the *seudah* of which meat is being eaten at, but he should cut the bread that is not dairy. After he cuts the bread, he should remove the dairy bread from the table so that one should not come to make a mistake and eat the dairy bread.

○·······································○

18 *Le'chatechilah* one should eat the amount of a *kezayit* from the *lechem mishne*. In any event, if there are many people present at the table and there isn't enough bread for everyone to get a *kezayit* from the *lechem mishne*, or if because of health reasons one needs to eat from another bread, it is enough that he tastes less than a *kezayit* of the *lechem mishne* and finish eating his *kezayit* from another bread. It is a *hidur* if the other bread is next to the *lechem mishne* at the time of cutting.

○·······································○

19 Women are also obligated in *lechem mishne*. Therefore, if a woman eats alone, she must bless on two loaves. When the *ba'al habayit* makes a *beracha* on the bread, he should keep in mind the women so they will be *yotzeh yedeh chovah,* and the women should also keep in mind that the *ba'al habayit* is keeping them in mind for the *chiyuv* of *lechem mishne*.

―――――∽ଓଓ∾―――――

Today's learning has been dedicated for the continued Hatzlacha and Bracha of Rena Levy and family.

20 The *seudah* of *leil Shabbat* and *seudat shacharit* need to be made specifically with bread. *Le'chatechilah* one should eat more than a *kabetza* (60 grams). If it is hard for one to eat that much bread, it would be good enough if he ate a *kezayit* (about 30 grams) by itself. When he eats only a *kezayit*, he should wash his hands without a *beracha*.

Eating the Seudah

21 It is a *mitzvah* to eat fish in each of the three meals of *Shabbat*, even if it is a small amount. One should increase in meat, wine, and choice-fruits according to his capabilities. In any event, if eating will cause him harm (for ex. he is sick or the like) and he isn't able to eat even a *kezayit* of bread, he is exempt from eating the *Shabbat seudah* since the *seudah* is given for *oneg* and not *sa'ar*.

22 If *Rosh Chodesh* falls out on *Shabbat*, one should make one extra dish compared to what one regularly makes since there is a *mitzvah* to increase in the *seudah* of *Rosh Chodesh*. It is written in the *Talmud Yerushalmi* that if *Rosh Chodesh* falls out on *Shabbat*, one must make a *seudat Rosh Chodesh* on Sunday. Even though we are not accustomed to this, one who is careful in this will see blessing come upon him.

Today's learning has been dedicated for the health and success of the donor's families and all of Klal Yisrael.

23 Anyone not able to be *mekayem* the *seudah* of *leil Shabbat* should push off the *seudah* for the next day. That is, he should have three meals the next day. This applies only if he makes *kiddush* at night and eats right after the *kiddush* a *kezayit* of one of the five grains or drinks a *revi'it* of wine so that it is considered a *kiddush* in a place of *seudah*. One must however put in his utmost effort to make sure one makes the *seudah* at the right times.

24 One must be careful not to put anything of dishonor on the table since the *malachei Elyon* look at the table. Also, when one places fruits on the table, he should place the fruits in a presentable manner even if he is sitting alone by the table.

25 It is better to have a meal of vegetables and be in harmony with one's wife and children and to respect the *Shabbat* than argue with one's wife and children.

26 It is good to learn the first four *perakim* of *mishnayot masechet Shabbat* at the table on *leil Shabbat* and to finish the rest during the day. However if it is hard to learn on *leil Shabbat*, he should learn at least one *perek*. It is good to say *divrei Torah* to the people in his house on *leil Shabbat* on the *parashat hashavua*.

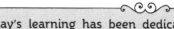

Today's learning has been dedicated for the continued Hatzlacha and Bracha of Mr. and Mrs. Elazar Levin and family.

27 A pleasant custom is to decorate the *Shabbat* table with flowers and roses. Our sages explained that the rose is *metukenet* for *Shabbatot* and *Yamim Tovim*. Also one should decorate the table with flowers and roses for *minei besamim* so that one can make a *berachat hareiach* on them and complete the hundred-count of *berachot* on *Shabbat*.

Songs on Shabbat

28 A pleasant custom is to sing songs of praise to *Hashem Yitbarach* during *Seudat Shabbat*.

∘⋯⋯⋯⋯⋯⋯⋯⋯⋯∘

29 It is permissible for the *ba'al* to sing with his wife, who is a *nidah* at the time, *zemirot Shabbat*. However, the one who is strict with this will see blessing come upon him. If there are guests present at the table, the women may not sing in front of them since it is forbidden for them to hear the voice of their singing. If the women sing anyways and go against *halachah*, one should look into a *sefer* and distract himself from the voice of their singing so he doesn't get pleasure from it. He may also sing louder than them so that he won't hear their singing. Similarly, a *bachur* who is sitting at his table with his parents and siblings should do the same if he hears women singing and is unable to stop them. This also applies if he hears his neighbors singing from his house.

ooo

Today's learning has been dedicated for the continued Hatzlacha and Bracha of Mr. and Mrs. Amir Yeghaneh and family.

30 They were accustomed in a number of *kehillot Yisrael* to sing *Tzur Mishelo Achalnu* before *birkhat hamazon*. One should not be doubtful in saying it before *birkhat hamazon* because of the *chashash* of being *yotzeh birkhat hamazon* by the *Torah* with this *pizmon* and thus saying a *safek beracha levatala*. Rather one is permitted in singing this *pizmon* even *le'chatechilah* before *birkhat hamazon*.

31 We are accustomed to covering the knife during *birkhat hamazon* but by *Shabbat* and *Yom Tov* we are not accustomed to doing this. *Al pi Kabbalah* it is better to fully cover the knife during *birkhat hamazon* even by *Yom Tov*.

32 In the *birkhat hamazon* one says *Retzeh Vehachalitzenu* (the meaning of *Vehachalitzenu* is *Vezarizenu* to say we should be *zariz* or agile in your *mitzvot*). If one forgot and didn't say *Retzeh* and finished saying *ohelh Yerushalayim*, he should say *Baruch Ata Ado-nai Elokenu Melech Ha'olam Asher Natan Shabbatot Lemenuchah Leamo Yisrael Be'ahava Leot V'lebrit, Baruch Ata Ado-nai Mekadesh HaShabbat*. If he didn't remember and went on to the fourth *beracha* and said *Baruch Ata Ado-nai Elokeni Melech Haolam* and suddenly remembered, he should finish it with *Asher Natan Shabbat*ot etc. but if he only remembered it as he was saying *La'ad*, he should go back to the beginning of the *birkhat hamazon*. This also applies to women as well. Also, at the last *Harachaman* we say *Migdol* and not *Magdil* like the rest of the days of the week.

○○○

Today's learning has been dedicated for the continued Hatzlacha and Bracha of Yaffa bat Yechezkel and family.

∾◌∾
• Day 87 •
∾◌∾

∾◌∾
• כח' חשוון •
∾◌∾

33 One who is *safek* if he said *Retzeh Vehachalitzenu* in the *birkhat hamazon* does not have to go back and say *birkhat hamazon* again.

⚬···⚬

34 One may leave the fruits that he brought to the table for Seudat *Shabbat* until after *birkhat hamazon* so that one may make a *beracha* on these fruits both before and after so that he may complete the hundred-count of *berachot*. One should not be worried about the *issur* of saying a *beracha* that is not needed. It is good to instruct the members of the household to bring the fruits only after *Birkhat Hamazon*.

⚬···⚬

35 It is permitted for one to stay awake one *leil Shabbat* and learn the throughout whole night. One should not make it forbidden because of *bitul oneg Shabbat* as long as it does not bother him and the lack of sleep will not make him *ones*. If it doesn't bother him, he should have *oneg* from his learning.

⎯⎯⎯⎯⎯⎯ ∾◌∾ ⎯⎯⎯⎯⎯⎯
Today's learning has been dedicated for the continued Hatzlacha and Bracha of Mr. and Mrs. David Fink and family.

Chapter 10 — Eating and Drinking Before Shacharit and Before Mussaf

1 Those who are accustomed to wake up early in the morning to say *bakashot* and taste some cake or sweets before *alot hashachar*, one should not protest them. In any event, the *tzenuim* hold themselves back and don't taste so that they may hold of *divrei Hazohar* which says it is strongly forbidden to taste anything before *tefillah* even if it is before *alot hashachar*.

2 It is forbidden to eat and drink before *tefilats hacharit* because it says "*Lo Tochelu Al Hadam*". The *chachamim* expounded from this that one should not eat before he prays for his blood. In any event, one may drink water before *tefillah*. Similarly, it is permissible to drink coffee or tea, with sugar, before *tefillah*, even on *Shabbat*, since the *chovah* of *kiddush* has not been *chal* yet.

Today's learning has been dedicated for the continued Hatzlacha and Bracha of Shayan Davatgar and family.

TODAY'S LEARNING HAS BEEN DEDICATED
by Ezra and Meshy Ebriani, for the complete
Refuah of Yaakov Coby ben Nofar Meshy.

• Day 89 •

• א' כסלו •

3 A woman who prays *tefillat shacharit* every day is allowed to drink coffee or tea before *tefillat shacharit* since she hasn't prayed yet and the *din* of the *chov* of *kiddush* was not *chal* on her like that of a man. However, if she doesn't pray *shacharit* daily, she may not taste anything before *kiddush*. In any event, a woman who is lenient in drinking before *kiddush*, even if she doesn't pray every day (except if she is weaning and the like) has what to rely on. A woman whose husband comes back late from shul and it is hard for her to wait without eating anything may make *kiddush* to herself on grape juice or white beer (doesn't have to be wine) and she may then eat *mezonot*.

4 It is permitted to give a *kattan* that didn't reach the age of *bar mitzvah* cake and milk before he goes to shul to pray *shacharit*, whether it be *Shabbat* or *chol*.

5 It is permitted for a *shaliach tzibur* to swallow raw eggs before *tefillat shacharit* on *Shabbat* day so that he may touch up his voice so that it will be clear for the *tzibur* to hear. Before he eats he should say *Shehakol Nihiyeh Bidevaro* but after he eats he should not make a *beracha acharonah*. He should also be careful not to heat up the egg a bit in a *kli sheni* because there is a *chashash* of an *issur sekilah*. It is proper that the one drinking coffee or tea mixed with milk (like by a person who is weak) or one eating raw eggs first say all of the *birkhot hashachar*, start to prepare for the *zemirot* before *baruch she'amar*, and then drink the raw eggs.

6 It is permitted to make *kiddush* before *tefillat mussaf* and eat fruits or even a *kabetza* (fifty-six grams). However, more than this is prohibited.

○·······························○

7 One who is weak and is unable to make *kiddush* on wine between *tefillat shacharit* and *tefillat mussaf* can be lenient and have an *achilat aray*, which is bread in the amount of less than a *kabetza*. However, by fruits he may have plenty even without *kiddush*. If he has the ability to make *kiddush*, it seems that he may make *kiddush*, eat, go back and make another *kiddush* after *mussaf,* and have *seudat shacharit*. Similarly, by a *shaliach tzibur* who reads from the *Torah*, there is what to be lenient on occasionally that he may have an *achilat aray* before the *Torah* reading even without *kiddush* if he is unable to make *kiddush*.

Today's learning has been dedicated by the Azizi Family, Leilui Nishmat, Ezra Aziz ben Yechezkel, may his Neshama have an Aliyah.

Chapter 11 — Tefillah on Shabbat Morning and the Torah Reading

1 We have a practice to increase the amount of *zemirot* we sing over the course of *Shabbat*, each according to his custom. Nevertheless, one should not prolong his singing so much that he can't eat his meal before the sixth hour.

a tune. This passage is also a *segulah* for any *tzara* one might suffer, and it is proper to make a *neder* to recite *Nishmat Kol Chai* when he is saved from his *tzara* because this will help him.

2 After reciting *Shirat Hayam,* we recite the passage of *Nishmat Kol Chai,* which contains the topic of *Yetziat Mitzrayim,* justifying its placement next to the *Shira.* Another reason is because of the *Neshama Yetera* that man has. The praise of *Nishmat Kol Chai* is very precious to *Hashem,* and warrants being said with

3 If one forgot to say *Nishmat Kol Chai* and has already said *Yishtabach,* if he has not yet started the *beracha* of *Yotzer Ohr,* he should say *Nishmat* right there without finishing it. However, if he has begun the *beracha* of *Yotzer Ohr,* he should say *Nishmat* after *tefilah* until *Yishtabach.*

◯◯◯

Today's learning has been dedicated the Elyassian Family, Leilui Nishmat, my dear grandfather, Yechezkel ben Rebbi, may his Neshama have an Aliyah.

4 If one came late to Shul and needs to skip either *Pesukei De'zimrah* or *Nishmat Kol Chai* in order to catch up to the *tzibur*, it is better to skip *Nishmat Kol Chai* instead of *Pesukei Dezimrah.*

○·····································○

5 The *beracha* of *Yishtabach* contains thirteen words of praise. One should say these words patiently, with a tune, and have *kavanah* while saying them. One does not need to say them all in one breath and should not hurry while reciting them.

○·····································○

6 During the *beracha* of *Yotzer Ohr* on *Shabbat* one accepts the *kedusha* of *Tosefet Shabbat* in the *Olam Haberiyah,* since the whole order of *yotzer* is in the *beriyah*. Therefore, one must pause between the words "*Yotzer*" and "*Ohr*" so that it doesn't sound like "*Yitzror.*" In the passage of the *Alef-Bet* within the *Yotzer* for *Shabbat*, we recite "*E-l Adon Al Kol Hama'asim...*" instead of "*E-l Baruch Gadol De'ah,*" which is recited during the week. The *sod* to this is written in the Zohar Ha'Kadosh; therefore, it is proper for one to say each and every word carefully with full *kavannah*.

○·····································○

7 A man once explained that a certain *shamesh* of the *bet ha'kenesset* merited to go to *gan eden* after his passing simply because he would say the *berachot* in a pleasant voice in the *bet ha'kenesset*. Even though he was a simple man, he was brought to *gan eden* and honored because of this merit.

○ ○ ○

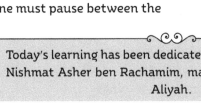

Today's learning has been dedicated by Dani Reihani, Leilui Nishmat Asher ben Rachamim, may his Neshama have an Aliyah.

8 In the *amidah* of *shacharit*, we say "*Yismach Moshe Be'matenat Chelko...*" This paragraph details the time when our forefathers were in Egypt, and *Moshe* saw that the burden placed upon his brothers had become heavier. In response, he asked *Pharaoh* to give them one day out of the week to rest, and when the request was granted by designating the seventh day as a day of rest, *Moshe* rejoiced. An alternative explanation to the prayer is based on the *pasuk* "*Lada'at Ki Ani Hashem Mekadishchem*", where *Ha'Kadosh Baruch Hu* said to *Moshe*, "I have a present in my *bet genizah* named *Shabbat*, and I ask of you to give it to *Yisrael* and announce it to them." *Yismach Moshe* is the realization of that gift.

Taking out the Sefer Torah

9 After *shacharit*, we take out the *sefer Torah* and read seven *aliyot*, with more being added if desired. It is proper not to add too many *olim* due to the issue of *tirchah* de'tziburah.

In any event, in a situation where there is worry that certain people may bear a grudge if they are not called up to the *Torah*, one may add many *olim*.

Today's learning has been dedicated for the continued Hatzlacha and Bracha of Yaakov Coby ben Yisrael Ezra.

10 Before taking out the sefer *Torah*, we say *"Ata Haraeta Lada'at...",* which contains eight *pesukim*, corresponding to the seven *olim* and the *maftir*. On *Yom Tov*, however, we add two more *pesukim* and start from *"Yehi Hashem Elokenu Imanu..."* During the week, we say only three *pesukim*, corresponding to the three *olim*. On *Shabbat*, we say *"Berich Shemeh De'marei Almah,"* which we do not say during the week.

The Olim to the Torah

11 Anyone can be called up to the *Torah* for one of the seven *aliyot*, even a minor who knows to Whom he is blessing. This applies only to the *Torah* reading on *Shabbat*, but on *Yom Tov* and on all other days, when there are less than seven *olim*, a minor may not be one of them. *Bediavad*, if a child already started saying the *beracha* and was only noticed after he started, there are grounds to rely on those that permit it.

12 A child who reached the age of *chinuch* (six years old) may be called up for both the middle or end *aliyot*, and certainly for *maftir*. He may also read his *aliyah* portion of the *Torah* by himself. However, in an area where there is an explicit custom not to give a child an *aliyah*, one should not be called for one.

O O O

Today's learning has been dedicated by the Author, for the Hatzlacha and Bracha of my dear brother-in-law, Michael ben Mashiach Asher.

13 A child may be called up for the *maftir* of *musafim* on the *moadim* or *Rosh Chodesh*, as well as for *parashat shekalim* and *parashat hachodesh*. However, he should not go up for *parashat zachor* and *parashat parah*, *le'chatechilah*. If he has already reached the *Torah*, he should not sit back down. The child then makes the *beracha,* but the *shaliach tzibur* should read the *pesukim* to fulfill the obligation for the *tzibur*.

....

14 A child should not be appointed as the *ba'al keriah* to read from the *Torah*. However, in a pressing situation where there is no other man who can read with the cantillations, the child is permitted to read.

....

15 Some communities have the custom to sell the *mitzvot* (such as *petichat hechal, aliyot le'Torah,* etc.) on *Shabbat* and *Yamim Tovim*. One should not protest this *minhag,* as it is a *davar mitzvah* all done for the sake of *Shamayim,* for the upkeep and betterment of the *bet ha'kenesset*. There is no concern of conducting business on *Shabbat* here since it is purely for the sake of the *Torah* and has become the custom throughout *Klal Yisrael*. During this time, the *tzibur* should not converse with each other and should instead read chapters of *Tehillim* or learn from a *sefer*.

....

16 One who goes up for an *aliyah* must read along quietly with the *shaliach tzibur,* as he does not fulfill his obligation if he merely listens while it is read. If he does not read along, there is concern that his *beracha* was made *le'vatala*.

Today's learning has been dedicated Leilui Nishmat HaRav Sheftel Meir ben Harav Naftali Ha'Levi Neuberger, may his Neshama have an Aliyah.

17 There is a custom to add extra *olim* to the *Torah* during a *simcha* in the *bet ha'kenesset*, during which each *oleh* goes up and reads the same portion that was already read. The root for this custom is in *Harareh Kodesh*. In any event, it is proper for the *chazan* who is reading the *Torah* to read three *pesukim* or more for each of the seven *olim* who go up to the *Torah*. This allows for each added *oleh* to have a reading of new *pesukim*. If even with all this, because of the amount of people going up for an *aliyah,* he must go back and repeat some of the *pesukim*, he may do so.

○·····························○

18 It is permitted to give an *aliyah* to one who shaves his face with a razor (which actively transgresses five *lavin* from the *Torah*), counting him as one of the seven *olim*. However, it is better to give him an *aliyah hosafa* instead of one from the main seven. One should reprimand him and bring him to rectify his deeds in a pleasant manner.

Laws Regarding Going up to the Torah

19 One must have the proper intentions when listening to the *berachot* of the *Torah* or the *maftir* and answer *"amen"* afterwards to help him reach the daily hundred-count of *berachot* on *Shabbat*. As such, it is a *mitzvah* for the *olim* to say the *beracha* in a loud voice so that the whole congregation can hear him and answer *"amen."* It is said about those who recite the *beracha* silently, *"Vechoteh Echad Ye'aved Tova Harbeh."*

○────────◦◦◦◦────────○

Today's learning has been dedicated Leilui Nishmat Rebbetzin Aviva bat Moreinu V'Rabbenu Ha'Rav Shmuel Yaakov Weisbord, may her Neshama have an Aliyah.

20 It is better for one not to say *"Emet Toratenu Hakedosha"* at the end of the *aliyah* before the latter *beracha*. However, if he is accustomed to saying it, others should not protest. The *pasuk* of *"Go'alenu,"* which people tend to say after the *haftarah* should not be prevented.

---

21 The custom of kissing the *oleh* after he finishes reading his portion is incorrect according to *halacha,* and it is a *mitzvah* to annul it in a careful and pleasant way in order for others to listen to him. However, the custom of kissing the hand of the *Rav,* one's father, or other direct relatives who must be given honor is a correct custom whose foundation stems from *Hararei Kodesh.*

22 There are places where it is customary for the *chatan bar mitzvah* to go up for the third *aliyah* and to say a *derashah* for the congregation after making the latter *beracha.* This custom has some basis, but at the time of the *derashah,* it is proper to close the *sefer Torah* and not merely cover it with a cloth. In any event, it is best for the congregation to agree, by their good will and without any argument, that going forward, the *chatan bar mitzvah* will give his *derashah* only after the conclusion of the *berachot* of the *haftarah,* like the custom of most *bateh kenessiyot* in *Yerushalayim.*

∾೧∾
• **Day 97** •
∾೧∾

∾೧∾
• ט' כסלו •
∾೧∾

Today's learning has been dedicated by the Khalili, Lavian, Ashorzadeh, Rahmanfar, Eshaghian and Shreiber families, Leilui Nishmat Malka bat Shlomo. Yehi Ratson that the merit of this holy Sefer stand for us and our children, so that the Torah should not cease from us, and may our home be filled with all the Blessings of the Torah.

∼✿∼
• Day 98 •
∽✿∾

∼✿∼
• י' כסלו •
∽✿∾

23 One should not be insistent on the different pronunciations in the *Torah* reading. As such, a Sepharadi who prays with Ashkenazim and hears their *Torah* reading in the Ashkenazi pronunciation and vice versa fulfills his obligation. In any event, for *parashat zachor* and *parashat parah,* whose obligations are from the *Torah*, it is proper for every person to hear the *Torah* reading according to the custom of his father.

○···○

24 The Sepharadi custom is to say *"Chazak U'baruch,"* after the *oleh* finishes his *Torah* portion, to which he answers back, *"Chazak Ve'amatzu."* There are some communities where it is customary for the *oleh* to wait by the *Torah* after his *aliyah* until the next *oleh* comes up to read the *Torah*. There those who are concerned that they will not be able to hear the *Torah* sufficiently while on the way back to their seat, so they wait until the next person finishes his *aliyah* and only then do they return to their seat. The current *minhag* is to wait by the *Torah* until the next *oleh* finishes his reading and *berachot* and only return to his seat after the *chazan* has given the *oleh* a *"Mi Sheberach."* This is a good and proper custom because it prevents any interference to those listening to the *Torah* when everyone says, *"Chazak U'baruch."*

○···○

25 It is better for a mourner who is within the twelve months over his father or mother to receive *aliyat maftir* than one of the *aliyot mashlim*, especially if the *maftir* is one of the *korbanot musafim* and certainly if it is *zachor* or *parah.*

Today's learning has been dedicated for the continued Hatzlacha and Bracha of Mr. and Mrs. Tzvi Odzer and family.

26 A mourner should not argue with his friend if the friend insists on going up for *maftir*. It is better for him not to go up if it will lead to controversy and argument, and through his silence, he will give his father more comfort than speaking and going up for *maftir*. Also, saying the *kaddish* that belongs to his friend does not count for him or cause any loss to his friend since the *kaddish* goes up for whichever *neshamah* it was meant for.

··

27 The custom is that a blind person who wants to go up to the

Torah on *Shabbat*, *Yamim Tovim*, or even on Monday or Thursday is not prevented from receiving an *aliyah*. (This is despite the fact that *Shulchan Aruch* (129:3) writes that a blind person should not go up to the *sefer Torah*.) However, this is on the condition that his faculties are still intact. If possible, it is better that he goes up for *maftir* if he knows how to read the *haftarah* in braille, or for an *aliyat mosifin*.

Today's learning has been dedicated Leilui Nishmat Tamara bat Morad Mordechai, may her Neshama have an Aliyah.

Haftarah

28 The *Haftarah* read from *Nach* is matched to the topic of the *parasha,* and it is at least twenty-one *pesukim* long unless that section of *Nach* is shorter. The reason we read a *haftarah* is because at one point in time, there was a government decree placed on *Bnei Yisrael* forbidding us from reading from the *Torah.* The Sages established that everyone should read from a portion of *Nach* that pertains to the *parasha* of the week. They read twenty-one *pesukim* to match the law pertaining to the reading of the *Torah,* which requires three *pesukim* for each of the seven *aliyot.* They would also make seven *berachot* on the *haftarah* correspondent to the seven *berachot* of the seven *olim.* Therefore, even after the decree was nullified and they reverted back to reading the *Torah* again, they maintained the reading of the *haftarah* only after the *Torah* reading. This is due to the fact that if only *Nach* was read [with a *beracha*] and not the *Torah,* then the *kavod* of *Torah* and *Nach* would become equivalent. Therefore, one must read the *Torah* first and only then read the *haftarah,* and through this, the people will see that the *Torah* is greater.

29 There is a beautifying aspect to the *mitzvah* of reading the *haftarah* from a *sefer* which was hand-written and holds the *kedushah* of a *klaf.* This applies even if it is merely a compilation of the *Shabbat haftarot* from the entire year and not a full *sefer Nach.* However, if there is no *sefer* like this, it is better to read the *haftarah* from a full printed *sefer Nach* rather than from printed *chumashim.*

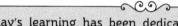

Today's learning has been dedicated for the continued Hatzlacha and Bracha of Mr. and Mrs. Yaakov Soleimania and family.

30 Every person in the congregation must read the *haftarah* by mouth and not rely on the *oleh* except for the *berachot* which one must hear and answer "*amen.*" The people must read it in a soft tone, and if they raise their voices while reading the *haftarah*, the *oleh* should knock on the *teva* lightly to remind them to lower their voices.

○······································○

31 There are some who go up for *maftir* to read the *haftarah* for their parents' memory and skip half the letters and swallow words to the point of incomprehension.
Even though the *kaddish* and *haftarah* will save his parents from the judgement of *Gehinnom*, which is why there is a custom to recite *kaddish* and read the *haftarah* on the *Shabbat* prior to their date of passing, doing these things will only work if he says them word for word and letter by letter. However, those who swallow the words or skip letters cause their parents *Nega* (*N"GA*) instead of *oneg* (*AN"G*). The absence of good brings about bad, and it is close to being a *beracha le'vatalah,* which will also cause the congregation to not fulfill their obligation. It is better that he takes the money that he used to buy the *haftarah* and instead give it to poor *talmidei chachamim* or decent human beings which will bring comfort to his parents' souls.

○······································○

32 The *oleh* for *maftir* should read the *haftarah* himself and not give it over to the *shaliach tzibur* to read. The same applies to the *berachot* of the *haftarah*. The *oleh* must recite the *berachot* of the *haftarah* and read it himself.

Today's learning has been dedicated for the continued Hatzlacha and Bracha of Mr. and Mrs. Elazar Aryeh and family.

33 When there is only one kohen present and he would like both aliyat kohen and maftir because he has an azkara, le'chatechilah one should not let him go up for both. Bediavad, if he already bought the aliyot and he would be pained if he doesn't go up for maftir, it is permissible for him to go up for both. There is also no need to be stringent and make the kohen leave the bet hakenesset so that they may call up a yisrael in the place of the kohen.

34 The custom to recite the pasuk of "Go'alenu Hashem tz'vakot shemo..." at the end of the haftarah need not be condemned because it is not considered a break between the haftarah and berachot. Rather, it is said merely to finish the haftarah off on a good note.

35 The one who went up for maftir must answer "amen" after Birkat Mekadesh Ha'Shabbat, the last beracha after the haftarah. Whoever does so is considered wise and praiseworthy, so this practice should be perpetuated.

36 It is permissible to place the sefer haftarot into the aron kodesh next to sifrei Torah. However, the rimonim of a sefer Torah should not be placed atop it. Instead, a special pair of rimonim should be made for the sefer Haftarot.

Today's learning has been dedicated for the continued Hatzlacha and Bracha of Sara bat Morvarid.

37 It has become the common practice to return the *sefer Torah* to the *aron kodesh,* following the reading, while it is open. This applies whether it is Monday, Thursday, *Shabbatot* or *Yamim Tovim,* and one should not change this custom.

some don't. Since the one reading the *Torah* was made *shaliach tzibur,* it is as if they made him a *shaliach* to escort the *sefer Torah* as well because overcrowding precludes everyone being able to escort it. One should be very meticulous in honoring the *Torah* as much as possible.

38 It is a *mitzvah* to escort the *sefer Torah* and kiss it. The *nekiyeh hada'at* in *Yerushalayim* would walk behind the *sefer Torah* when it was taken out and when it was returned. Sefaradim have the custom for the *shaliach tzibur* who read the *Torah* to carry it to the *teva* and return it back to the *aron hakodesh.* As for the rest of the congregation, some choose to escort it and

39 When returning the *sefer Torah* to its place, we have the practice to recite the *mizmor* of *"Havu L'Hashem Bneh E-lim."* We recite this *mizmor* because it was the one said by *matan Torah* as well as for the fact that the seven *berachot* of *tefilat Shabbat* were established corresponding to the seven *kolot* contained in this *mizmor.*

Today's learning has been dedicated for the continued Hatzlacha and Bracha of Rabbi and Rebbetzin Nissan Hakakian and Yeshivat Tiferet Torah.

Tefilat Mussaf

40 Every individual is obligated to pray *tefilat Mussaf*, whether there is a *minyan* or not.

41 The time for *tefilat Mussaf* is right after *tefilat Shacharit*, just like the *Korban Mussaf* which, *le'chatechilah*, immediately follows the *Korban Tamid*.

42 One should not delay in praying *tefilat Mussaf* past seven hours (one hour after *chatzot hayom*) into the day and in doing so one is called a violator. In any event, if he did not pray *tefilat Mussafin* before seventh hour, he should still say it because *bediavad* one can do so the whole day.

43 After the *kahal* has finished the *tefilat Lachash* of *Mussaf*, the *shaliach tzibur* repeats the *tefilah*. The merit of the *chazarah* is greater than the *tefilat Lachash*.

Today's learning has been dedicated by Shmuel and Reena Moinzadeh for continued Hatzlacha and Briut.

∽⟡∾
• Day 105 •
∽⟡∾

∽⟡∾
• יז' כסלו •
∽⟡∾

44 Women are exempt from *tefilat Mussaf*, but it is still good for them to listen to the *shaliach tzibur's* repetition. In any event, if they do pray *Mussaf*, one should not rebuke them since they have what to rely on.

○·······································○

45 There is a custom on *Shabbat* day, after the *tefilah*, to visit a *bet chatan* or *avi haben* where the people taste fruits and sweets after hearing *kiddush* from the *mekadesh* who drinks a *revi'it* of wine. Those who do this practice have what to rely on and one should not protest them. There are *poskim* who hold that since the *mekadesh* drank a *revi'it* of wine from the cup for *kiddush* to be *yotzeh yedeh chovatam*, it is considered a *kiddush* in a place of *seudah* even for those listening. Blessing will come upon the individuals who are *machmir* and don't taste anything. It is best to inform the *ba'al hasimchah* to set up enough cake for the *kahal* in a way that everyone can eat a *kezayit* which will definitely be a *kiddush* in a place of *seudah*. In any event, the one who made *kiddush* may rely on the drinking of the *revi'it* to render it in a place of *seudah*.

Today's learning has been dedicated for the continued Hatzlacha and Bracha of Mr. and Mrs. Moshe Nourmand and family.

Chapter 12

Laws Pertaining to One Who Erred in Tefilat Shabbat and its Tashlumin

1 Every person should be careful not to err in *tefilatShabbat* since it is not a good sign and will cause an unnecessary *beracha*. Therefore, it is good to always pray reading from a *siddur* and have total concentration to pray properly.

applies to *tefilat arvit*, *shacharit* and *minchah*. However, he erred during *tefilat mussaf*, even if he is in the middle of a *beracha*, he should stop and start from *"Tikanta Shabbat."*

2 One who erred and started to pray *tefilatchol* on *Shabbat*, if he's in the middle of one of the *berachot* in the *amidah* (be it *"Ata Chonen"* or any other *beracha*) he should finish that *beracha* and start the *Shabbat amidah*. This

3 A *shaliach tzibur* who made a mistake and started *tefilatchol* in the repetition should not finish the *beracha* that he is in the middle of, but rather he must immediately switch to that of *Shabbat*. The *din* of finishing the *beracha* applies only by *tefilatlachash* and not the repetition.

Today's learning has been dedicated for the continued Hatzlacha and Bracha of Mr. and Mrs. Reuven Gholian and family.

4 One who erred after the *beracha* of *"Ha'E-l HaKadosh"* and said *"Ata,"* with the intention to continue in *Chonen*, since he thought it was *yom chol,* he should finish the *beracha* of *Ata Chonen* and then go back to *tefilat Shabbat*. However, if he knew that it was *Shabbat* and only said the word *"Ata"* out of habit, he should not finish the *beracha* of *Ata Chonen* [even during *shacharit*] but rather go straight to saying *"Yismach Moshe."*

○···○

5 One who mistakenly prayed an entire *tefilat chol* on *Shabbat* (without realizing) is not *yotzeh yedeh chovah* and should start again from the beginning. However, if he did not yet say the second *"Yihiyu Leratzon Imri Phi,"* he should go back only to the part of *Shabbat*.

○···○

6 One who finished his *tefilah* and is unsure whether he prayed that of *chol* or *Shabbat* does not pray again. The reason for this is because he has genuine reason to believe that he absolutely prayed *tefilat Shabbat*.

Today's learning has been dedicated for the continued Hatzlacha and Bracha of Rabbi and Mrs. Menashe Sadik and family.

7 One who mistakenly switched one *tefilah* for the other on Shabbat is *yotzeh yedeh chovah* and does not repeat. The reason for this is that the main *beracha*, which is the fourth one, is said in every *tefilah* of *Shabbat* ("*Elokenu V'elokeh Avotenu Retze Na Bemenuchatenu... Baruch Ata Hashem Mekadesh HaShabbat*"). However, this *din* is specifically in a case where he finished the *beracha*. If instead he remembered while still in the middle of the *beracha*, he must stop and start the correct *tefilah*. Some are of the opinion that if one mixed *tefilatmussaf* with another *tefilah* or vice versa, he is not *yotzeh* and must therefore pray the correct *tefilah,* while others refute this view and hold there is no distinction between *mussaf* and the other *tefilot,* and thus he need not fix the prayer. Since this matter is the subject of dispute, it's best to listen to the *shaliach tzibur* during the repetition of the *amidah* and have the intention to be *yotzeh yedeh chovah*.

•·····························•

8 One who mistakenly started reading "*Ata Bachartanu,*" which is the *tefilah* for *Yom Tov,* should stop and start the *tefilah* of *Shabbat* starting from after the first three *berachot,* not from the beginning. Similarly, one who started the *tefilah* of *Shabbat* on *Yom Tov,* and remembered that it was *Yom Tov* while in the middle of *birkhat Shabbat* should stop and start the *tefilah* of *Yom Tov* from after the first three *berachot.*

OOO

Today's learning has been dedicated by the Author, for the continued Hatzlacha and Bracha of my dear brother-in-law, Yisrael Ezra ben Mashiach Asher.

9 If it was *Shabbat-chol hamoed*, and instead of praying the *tefilah* for *Shabbat* one mistakenly said *"Ata Bachartanu,"* (the *tefilah* for *Yom Tov*) and recited the *Shabbat* insertions (the same as when *Yom Tov* falls out on *Shabbat*), he is *yotzeh yedeh chovah* because he mentioned *Shabbat*. Similarly, if he mistakenly prayed *tefilatShabbat* instead of *Yom Tov* and recited *Ya'aleh Veyavo* as if it were *Shabbat-chol Hamoed* he is *yotzeh yedeh chovah* because he mentioned *Yom Tov*.

10 If it was *Shabbat-chol hamoed* and one mistakenly recited the *mussaf shel Shabbat* instead of *mussaf shel chag*, he is not *yotzeh yedeh chovah* and must recite the correct *mussaf*. However, if he said *Ya'aleh Veyavo*, there is a dispute if he was *yotzeh* and he should therefore have the intention to be *yotzeh* with the repetition of the *shaliach tzibur*. Similarly, there is a dispute in the case of one who said the *tefilah* for *chag* but only mentioned *Shabbat* in the conclusion of the *beracha*, *"Mekadesh HaShabbat Ve'Yisrael VeHazmanim."* Therefore, one should intend to be *yotzeh* through the repetition of the *shaliach tzibur*.

Tefilat Tashlumin

11 One who erred or was *be'ones* and did not pray *minchah* on *erev Shabbat* should pray *arvit* of *Shabbat* eve twice (two *tefilot* with *"Ata Kidashtah"*). The first one serves for *arvit* and the second as *tashlumin* for *minchah*. Even though the second *tefilah* comes for a *tashlumin* of *chol*, since it is now *Shabbat* one must pray the *tefilah* of *Shabbat*.

Today's learning has been dedicated by the Author, for the continued Hatzlacha and Bracha of my dear brother-in-law, Yitzchak "Benny" Hadjyan.

12 One who erred or was *be'ones* and did not pray *tefilat arvit* on *Shabbat* eve, should pray *shacharit* twice and in both say, "*Yismach Moshe.*" If he made a mistake and said "*Ata Kidashta*" in one of them he is *yotzeh yedeh chovah*. Similarly, if he did not pray *tefilatshacharit* he should pray *minchah* twice with "*Ata Echad.*" If he made a mistake and said "*Yismach Moshe,*" in one of them he is *yotzeh yedeh chovah*.

13 One who erred or was *be'ones* and did not pray *tefilat shacharit* on *Shabbat* should pray *minchah* twice because *minchah* is always called the *tefilah* adjacent to *shacharit* (even on *Shabbat* when there is *tefilat mussaf* in between). The reason for this is that the *tefilot shacharit* and *minchah* both come to replace the *korban tamid,* but *mussaf* is different *korban*. Therefore, one should pray *minchah* twice.

Today's learning has been dedicated for the continued Hatzlacha and Bracha of Mr. and Mrs. Dovid Sinaei and family.

∾ও∾
• Day 111 •
∾ও∾

∾ও∾
• כג' כסלו •
∾ও∾

14 One who erred or was be'ones and did not pray tefilatminchah on Shabbat, should pray arvit of chol twice on motza'e Shabbat. One recites ""Ata Chonantanu"" in the first (which is said for tefilatarvit) and not in the second (which is tashlumin for the missed minchah). If one recited the havdalah in both or in neither, he was yotzeh yedeh chovah and should rely on the havdalah that is recited over the cup. If he was not mavdil in the first one but was mavdil in the second, only the second tefilah works for him. Since he intended not to be mavdil in the first one, this means the first one was for tashlumin which does not work; he is not yotzeh the tashlumin and therfore he should recite the tefilah a third time for the tashlumin of minchah. However, if he truthfully intended for the first one to cover arvit and the second for tashlumin but mistakenly recited havdalah in the second instead of the first, he is yotzeh yedeh chovah.

○ .... ○

15 One who erred or was b'ones and did not pray arvit on motza'e Shabbat, should pray shacharit twice the next day without reciting "Ata Chonantanu," in either tefilah. If he had not yet been mavdil over the cup he should be recite "Ata Chonantanu", "in the tashlumin for the missed arvit the next day, which is the second one.

Today's learning has been dedicated for the continued Hatzlacha and Bracha of Mr. and Mrs. Shimon Shamouelian and family.

Chapter 13 — Seudat Shacharit of Shabbat and the Prohibition of Fasting

1 One's table should be set in a pleasant manner with a nice tablecloth (just like by the night meal). One recites *"...Boreh Peri Hagefen"* on wine and this is called *"kiddusha rabbah"* (*kiddush gadol*). It is called this because *birkat hagefen* is said at all *kiddushim*. Some say that it is called this in the context of *sagi nahor* (like they call a blind person *sagi nahor*- who is *ba'al ohr rav*) and since the *kiddush* is small (and not big like the night *kiddush*) we therefore call it *kiddusha* rabbah.

2 The main part of *kiddush* is really the *beracha* of *Boreh Peri Hagefen*. However, we have the practice to say *"Mizmor Le'David Hashem Ro'ee Lo Echsar..."* and the *pasukim* of *"Im Tashiv Me'Shabbat..."* and *"Ve'shamru B'nei Yisrael,"* before the *beracha*. The Kabbalistic sources bring down that we add certain passages before this, most of which are printed in *siddurim*.

3 The accepted universal practice is to recite the *pasuk* of *"Al Ken Berach Hashem Et Yom HaShabbat Vayekadeshehu,"* before *birkat hagefen*. One should not question this custom due to the fact that it splits the *pasuk* into two, since there is an *atnach* in the *pasuk*, which places a pause in the middle of the *pasuk*.

Today's learning has been dedicated by Yosef Chaim Noorani, for the continued Hatzlacha and Bracha of the Noorani Family.

THIS CHAG'S LEARNING HAS BEEN DEDICATED
by Ha'Rav Aharon Dov Friedman and family, Leilui
Nishmat his holy mother, Chana Lea bat Yitzchak
Dovid, may her Neshama have an Aliyah.

4   After *birkat hayayin,* one should not insert any other additions, such as *"Baruch Mekadesh HaShabbat,"* or *"Baruch Shenatan Shabbatot Lemenuchah,"* or the like because this constitutes an interruption between the *beracha* and the drinking the wine.

5   If one does not have any wine for the daytime *kiddush,* one may recite *kiddush* on beer which is considered *chamar medinah.* If he is unable to make *kiddush* on beer due to the fact that it must be done with a cup that holds a *revi'it* and he has to drink a *maleh lugmav,* or because he doesn't have beer readily available, he may recite *kiddush* on coffee, tea, or a citrus juice or the like and recite a *"shehakol"* on it. This can only be done in a pressing situation and only by the day meal.

6   We have the custom to sit during the reciting of the daytime *kiddush,* and even those who stand by the nighttime *kiddush* sit during the daytime *kiddush.*

7   After the *kiddush,* one washes his hands and makes a *beracha* on *lechem mishneh* just like the night *seudah,* after which the meal is eaten. This *kiddush* must also be concurrent with a *seudah.*

8 The *kavod* of the day meal is higher than that of the night meal. Accordingly, one should eat dishes that are dear to him or increase in a dish he didn't eat at the *seudat lel Shabbat*. It is a *mitzvah* to eat hot foods on *Shabbat* because this gives *kavod* and *oneg Shabbat*. One should also have much meat, wine and choice-fruit for *seudat Shabbat* according to his abilities.

9 It is a *mitzvah* to eat even the smallest amount of fish at all three of the *seudot Shabbat*.

10 If *seudat brit milah* fell out on *Shabbat*, one should first sing songs of *Shabbat* for its *kavod* and only afterwards sing songs for the *milah*. The reason for this is because *Shabbat* happens more often. When faced with two items, and one occurs more often than the other, we give precedence to the one which happens more often. This is the principle of *"Tadir V'sh'eino Tadir, Tadir Kodem."* Another reason is that *Shabbat* is called *"kodesh"* and is constant and *mekudeshet*.

11 If a *brit milah* falls out on *Shabbat* day it is performed after *tefilat shacharit*. The person given the *kavod* to the *berachot* of *brit milah* can be *yotzeh yedeh chovah* of *kiddush* for everyone with the cup with which he made the *berachot brit milah*. One should not prevent this with the logic that *mitzvot* are not supposed to be bundled together.

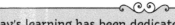

Today's learning has been dedicated by Ariel Afrah, Leilui Nishmat Michael Dovid ben Moshe and for the Hatzlacha of Ariel ben Homa and Yarden Miriam bat Elham.

12 Some have the custom to leave cooked eggs on their stove-top before *Shabbat* to be eaten during the day *seudah*. The reason for this is to commemorate the *avelut* of *Moshe Rabbenu* who passed away on *Shabbat*. Those who are *mehadrin* eat them also at *seudah shelishit*.

13 One should eat many types of fruit and smell different types of fragrances in order to make one hundred *berachot* on *Shabbat*. If one is accustomed to napping during *Shabbat* afternoon he should maintain this practice as it is *oneg* for him, provided that he doesn't sleep to the extent of *bitul Torah*.

14 After *seudat Shacharit* we set time to read from *Nevi'im* and to be *doresh* in *aggadah*. Laborers and *ba'alei batim* who are not regularly engaged in *Torah* study throughout the week should engage more in *Torah* on *Shabbat* and the *talmidei chachamim* should add to their *oneg* of eating and drinking a little extra.

Today's learning has been dedicated by Lior Barkodar, "In Honor of my beautiful wife, Rebecca, who makes every Shabbat truly Amazing."

15 If *Rosh Chodesh* falls out on *Shabbat*, one should eat an extra dish more than his regular *Shabbat* menu. It is written in the *Talmud Yerushalmi* that if Rosh Chodesh falls out on *Shabbat*, one must have a *seudat Rosh Chodesh* on Sunday. Even though we do not have this practice, blessing will come upon all those that are careful about this.

—————————————————

16 If one did not have a cup for *kiddush* of the morning and ate, but obtained wine later, it is a *mitzvah* to beautify the *Shabbat* and recite *kiddush* before *seudah Sselishit*.

The Prohibition of Fasting on Shabbat

17 It is prohibited to fast until the sixth hour *(chatzot)* on *Shabbat*, even if one was learning or praying until then. Therefore, it is not good for the *shaliach tzibur* to prolong his singing to the point that the prayers do not end until after the sixth hour. One who drinks tea or coffee in the morning before he goes to pray is considered not fasting, even if he doesn't eat his *seudah* until after midday.

Today's learning has been dedicated by Alen and Arielle Reyhan, for the continued Hatzlacha and Bracha of the Reyhan family.

18 One who finds it harmful to eat and instead gains *oneg* from not eating, should not eat. It is almost forbidden for him to eat if it causes him agony on *Shabbat*. This only applies if even a *kebetzah* or *kezayit* pains him. However, one who is able to eat that amount must have a *seudat Shabbat*.

mundane speech, as this will help with his atonement. However, if one is completely overwhelmed and depressed from the dream, he may fast on *Shabbat*. He should sit in the the entire day engaged in *Torah* study according to his ability, and he should fast after *Shabbat* on a different day to atone for the sin of annulling *oneg Shabbat*, and he will be cured.

19 One who has bad dream on *lel Shabbat* should not fast on *Shabbat*, even if it was one of three bad dreams listed in the *Shulchan Aruch (Siman 288)*. Rather, one should sanctify the *Shabbat* by reading *sefer Tehillim* and engaging in *Torah* study according to his ability. He should also abstain from

20 If it is *oneg* for one to make his *seudah* earlier (for example, if the night meal was fully digested) he can make it earlier. If making the meal later is *oneg* for him, e.g. he has not fully digested the night meal yet, he can make it later.

Today's learning has been dedicated for the continued Hatzlacha and Bracha of Mr. and Mrs. Yehoshua Khakshoy and family.

21 We do not cry out or blow *shofar* over any sorrow on *Shabbat* except for the strife of alimony in which case we cry out but do not blow. Similarly for a city which is surrounded by *anasim* or by a river, a boat that was lost at sea, and even for an individual who fled from *anasim*, bandits or *ruche rajah*, we cry out and beg to Hashem in *tefilat Shabbat*. We only blow the horn in order to rally the people to help save their brothers.

22 On the *Shabbat* during one's seven days of *avelut, rachmana litzlan*, he is permitted to learn the *halachot* of *avelut* or anything else which is permitted on *Tisha B'av* or during *avelut*. However, one who is not an *avel* but would like to learn the *halachot* of *avelut* should not do so if it causes him sorrow. However, if it does not cause him any sorrow, he is permitted to learn it.

Today's learning has been dedicated for the continued Hatzlacha and Bracha of Rabbi and Mrs. Avraham Tabrikian and family.

THIS MONTH'S LEARNING HAS BEEN DEDICATED
for the continued Hatzlacha and Bracha of
Daniel ben Aziz.

• Day 119 •

• א' טבת •

Chapter 14   Minchah of Shabbat

1 *Le'chatechilah*, one should pray *minchah* before eating *seudah shelishit*. However, if he is *b'ones* and ate it before *minchah*, he is still *yotzeh yedeh chovah*. According to the *Ari z"l*, one is not *yotzeh yedeh chovah*, even *bediavad*, if he eats *seudah shelishit* before *minchah*.

2 When one prays *minchah gedola* on *Shabbat*, it is forbidden to begin early and read the *Torah* before the time for *minchah*. Likewise, one should not say *"Va'ani tefilati"* nor *"Uva Letzion"* before the correct time for *minchah*. The reason for this is because our Rabbi's established everything for us meticulously and with exalted intentions which one cannot veer from at all.

3 Before *tefilat minchah* on *Shabbat* the custom is to recite *"Lamnatzeach Al Hagitit."* and the *parasha* of *tamid* along with *"Pitum Haketoret"* (just like during *chol*), and then say *"Ashrei," "Uva Letzion,"* and the *Kedushah Desidrah*.

4 We take out the *sefer Torah*, call up three people for *aliyot* and read ten *pesukim* from the upcoming *parasha*. One should endeavor to receive the third *aliyah* because it contributes to the *Tikun Hayesod*.

∾⊙∾
• Day 120 •
∾⊙∾

∾⊙∾
• ב' טבת •
∾⊙∾

5 We have the practice to recite *"Mizmor Shir Leyom HaShabbat"* after the reading of the *Torah*, followed by *kadish* and the *amidah*. One must be very careful in praying *tefilat minchah* on *Shabbat* because it contains great ascents in the heavens.

6 While it is more correct to say in *"V'yanuchu Bo,"* in *tefilat minchah*, those with the custom to say *"V'yanuchu Bam,"* have what to rely on. However, they must say, *"Shabbatot Kodshechah Vayanuchu Bam,"* and not the misnomer *"Shabbat Kodshechah Vayanuchu Bam."*

7 The *Inyan* of *Kedushah* in the *shaliach tzibur's* repetition of *tefilat minchah* on *Shabbat* has a great *sod* to it. Therefore, one must be very careful in it's *kavannah*.

8 After the repetition we say *"Tzidkatechah."* This corresponds to the three *tzadikim* who died on *Shabbat* - *Yosef Hatzadik, Moshe Rabenu* and *David Hamelech*. Therefore, one should say it while standing because it is in place of *Tzadok Hadin*. There are those who explain the reason for saying *"Tzidkatechah"* is for the *reshaim* who go back to *Gehinom* after *Shabbat*.

Today's learning has been dedicated the Khalili, Lavian, Ashorzadeh, Rahmanfar, Eshaghian and Shreiber families, Leilui Nishmat Moshe ben Chaim. Yehi Ratson that the merit of this holy Sefer stand for us and our children, so that the Torah should not cease from us, and may our home be filled with all the Blessings of the Torah.

∽◦∾
• Day 121 •
∽◦∾

∽◦∾
• ג' טבת •
∽◦∾

9 *Tzidkatechah"* is not recited if on that day *tachanun* would not have been said were it a weekday.

◦···◦

10 In the house of a *chatan* or an *avi haben*, we do not say *"Tzidkatechah."* Similarly, in the house of an *avel* we do not say *"Tzidkatechah"* even though we do not practice *avelut* in public on *Shabbat*. This is because abstaining from saying *"Tzidkatechah"* is not exclusively a show of *avelut* since we don't say it in the house of a *chatan* or *avi haben* either. In Yerushalayim the practice is not to say it in a house of an *avel*.

11 The practice used to be not to hold a *midrash* between *minchah* and *arvit*. The reason for this was because when a *chacham* passes away, all *batei midrashim* stop learning. Since *Moshe Rabenu* died at that time, and no one is greater to us than *Moshe Rabenu* (the father of the *Teudah*), we therefore had the practice not to establish *midrash*. In any event, nowadays one should not hold back from learning since it's definitely better to listen to *mussar* rather than converse in *devarim betelim* in a *bet midrash*.

∽◦◦◦∾
Today's learning has been dedicated for the continued Hatzlacha and Bracha of Sarah bat Rema.

Chapter 15 — Seudah Shelishit

1 One should be very particular to eat a *seudah shelishit*. Even if he is full he may fulfill it by eating just a bit more than a *kebteza*. However, if it is hard for him to eat even a *kebteza* he may eat a *kezayit* (and wash his hands without a *beracha*). If he is unable to eat anything, he should not subject himself to pain in order to fulfill *seudah shelishit*. The wise person is mindful not to eat too much by the day meal to leave room for *seudah shelishit*.

2 The time for *seudah shelishit* is simultaneous with *minchah*, which is from six and a half hours into *Shabbat* day and onwards. One does not fulfill the *mitzvah* if he eats before this time. *Le'chatechilah*, one should pray *minchah* before he eats *seudah shelishit*. However, if he is *b'ones* and ate *seudah shelishit* before praying *minchah*, he is *yotzeh yedeh chovah*. The *Ari z"l* is of the opinion that one who eats *seudah shelishit* before *minchah* is not *yotzeh yedeh chovah*, even *bediavad*.

3 We do not make *kiddush* over wine at *seudah shelishit*, yet it is good to embellish the *seudah* by reciting "*Hagefen,*" and drinking wine. However, if one has only one cup of wine left, he should save it to be used for *birkat hamazon* which is a *din* from the *Gemara,* whereas drinking wine during *seudah shelishit* is only a *midat chasidut*.

OOO

Today's learning has been dedicated by Allen Zarian, Leilui Nishmat Yonatan ben Reuven, may his Neshama have an Aliyah.

4 Even during *seudah shelishit* one must wash on two whole loaves of bread. However, if he only has one loaf, *bediavad* he may wash on that one loaf alone. If he does not have even one whole loaf, he should not skip the *seudah* but rather he should eat the piece that he has.

⸰⸳⸳⸳⸳⸳⸳⸳⸳⸳⸳⸳⸳⸳⸳⸳⸳⸳⸳⸳⸳⸳⸳⸳⸳⸳⸳⸳⸳⸳⸳⸳⸳⸳⸰

5 *Seudah shelishit* is much more important than *seudah revi'it*. Therefore, if he has one whole loaf and a piece of bread as well, he should wash on the full loaf for *seudah shelishit* and leave the other piece of bread for *seudah revi'it*. There are some who err about this and do the opposite.

6 *Seudah shelishit* must be eaten with bread. However, if one is too full he may fulfill *seudah shelishit* with one of the five grains or with something that is *melafet* the bread such as meat, fish or fruits. One who is *mezalzel* the *seudah* by eating it without bread for no proper reason will face judgement for it. Therefore, one should be very careful in this matter.

⸰⸳⸳⸳⸳⸳⸳⸳⸳⸳⸳⸳⸳⸳⸳⸳⸳⸳⸳⸳⸳⸳⸳⸳⸳⸳⸳⸳⸳⸳⸳⸳⸳⸳⸰

7 Women are *chayav* in *seudah shelishit*. Many women do not know this and therefore one should inform and encourage them to fulfill this *mitzvah*. Women must also make *hamotzi* over two loaves of bread.

Today's learning has been dedicated for the continued Hatzlacha and Bracha of Ahuva bat Sarah.

8 It is a *mitzvah* to eat fish at *seudah shelishit* and all that can should make the *seudah* on it. There is a custom to eat eggs at *seudah shelishit* in commemoration of *Moshe Rabenu* who was *niftar* on *Shabbat* evening during the time of *minchah*.

Shabbat day need not do so during *seudah shelishit* as there is no requirement *al pi Kabbalah*.

9 Those who have the practice *(al pi Kabbalah)* to go around the table on *lel Shabbat* and on

10 *Le'chatechilah,* one must eat *seudah shelishit* before *sheki'at hachamah*. If, for whatever reason, one delayed until after *shekiayh*, he may start *seudah shelishit* within thirteen minutes after *shekiayh*, and so is our practice.

Birkat Hamazon

11 If one forgot to recite *"Retzeh Vehachalitzenu,"* during *birkat hamazon* for *seudah shelishit*, he does not have to start again. If he remembered right after saying, *"Baruch Ata Hashem boneh Yerushalayim,"* he should then say, *"Baruch Ata Hashem Elokenu Melech* Ha'olam Asher Natan Shabbatot Lim'nuchah L'amo Yisrael Be'ahava L'ot Ulebrit, Baruch Ata Hashem Mekadesh HaShabbat."

O O O

Today's learning has been dedicated for the continued Hatzlacha and Bracha of Dr. Schorr and family.

12 If one finished *seudah shelishit* after *Shabbat* ended, he still recites "*Retzeh Vehachalitzenu*," in *birkat hamazon* because it follows when the meal started. However, one should skip the word "*Hazeh*." If one prayed *arvit* before reciting *birkat hamazon,* he should not insert "*Retzeh Vehachalitzenu*," in his *birkat hamazon.*

13 If one finished *seudah shelishit* after *Shabbat* ended, and *Motzeh Shabbat* was also *Rosh Chodesh*, he should recite only "*Retzeh Vehachalitzenu*" in *birkat hamazon* and not *Ya'aleh Veyavo.* [He definitely cannot recite both because doing so would be contradictory as *Rosh Chodesh* only started after *Shabbat* ended.] The reason for this is because *seudah shelishit* was only eaten for the purpose of *kavod Shabbat.*

14 The *birkat hamazon* recited after *seudah shelishit* is considered part of the hundred-count of the *berachot* for *Shabbat Kodesh*, even when recited after night has fallen. The fact that one started the meal during the day for *Shabbat* renders it's *birkat hamazon* a part of *Shabbat.*

Today's learning has been dedicated for the continued Hatzlacha and Bracha of Rabbi and Mrs. Oratz and family.

15 One who finished *seudah shelishit* after *Shabbat* ended should not recite *birkat hamazon* over a cup of wine if he does not usually do so. However, if he has the practice to always recite *birkat hamazon* over a cup of wine at *seudah shelishit* (even though he does not do so at the first two *seudot* on *Shabbat*) then he should make a *beracha* on the cup of wine. He may also drink the wine (even if he has not yet recited *havdalah*) in order to fulfill the *mitzvah* of making *birkat hamazon* over a cup. However, he does not mention *Shabbat* in the *birkat me'en shalosh*.

16 One who does not usually make *birkat hamazon* over a cup should not do so if *Shabbat* has already ended. In any event, if he still desires to do so, we don't bother him about it because he has what to rely on.

17 If the *seudah shelishit* made for a *chatan* during his seven days of *mishteh* continued past nightfall, it is permissible to drink from the cup of *sheva berachot* (and the cup of *birkat hamazon*). The *mevarech*, the *chatan* and the *kallah* may all drink. If one wants to be *machmir* he should have just a small taste of the wine. This applies to the *chatan* and *kallah* as well.

Today's learning has been dedicated by Shmuel and Leora Dayan, in honor of their wedding anniversary.

Rinsing Dishes After the Seudah

18 After eating *seudah shelishit*, it is prohibited to rinse utensils such as plates, knives and forks. Even if one wants to use them again, e.g. to eat with after *seudah shelishit*, it is best to be *machmir* not to rinse them since there are those that say it is only permitted to wash for the three *seudot* and not more. In any event, if he does not have any other utensils and they are needed after *seudah shelishit*, one may be lenient in washing them.

○··○

19 After eating *seudah shelishit*, it is permitted to rinse utensils used for drinking, such as cups, because one may drink throughout the entire day and there are no set times for drinking. In any event, if it is clear to him that he will not drink anymore it is prohibited to wash them.

○··○

20 It is permitted to clear *seudah* utensils from the table on *Shabbat*, even after *seudah shelishit*, so that the room will look clean and neat or to prevent insects from coming. However, it is forbidden to clean the table during the last minutes of *Shabbat* if he no longer needs to use that room. Even if it is still the middle of the day, he should close off that room until after *Shabbat*.

Today's learning has been dedicated by Eliyahu Levaddin, Leilui Nishmat Yechezkel ben Acha Saleh, may his Neshama have an Aliyah.

21 One that ate *seudah shelishit* may clean the table if it is needed to place *siddurim* on top of it or if the table is situated in a spot that is not respectful to those present. However, if they do not need the table and it's not in a bad place (e.g. it is sitting in a corner) one should not clean the table.

○...○

22 Even if *Yom Tov* falls out on *motza'e Shabbat*, one must make *seudah shelishit* on Shabbat with bread like every other *Shabbat*.

○...○

23 It is forbidden to taste any food or drink before reciting *havdalah*. However, *mitzad hadin,* one is permitted to drink water. *Al pi HaAri z"l*, one should not drink even water before *havdalah*, especially during *bein hashemashot*. In any event, one who is very thirsty and it's difficult for him to pray *arvit* may certainly drink water because it is permitted *mitzad hadin*.

Today's learning has been dedicated for the continued Hatzlacha and Bracha of Mr. and Mrs. Shmuel Mahgerefteh and family.

| Chapter 16 | Tefilat Arvit on Motza'e Shabbat |

1 It is proper and correct to delay praying *tefilat arvit* on *motza'e Shabbat* to add more of *chol* to *kodesh*. In any event, even those who are *machmir* and do not perform melachah after *Shabbat* until an hour and a quarter past *sheki'at hachamah* in accordance with *Rabenu Tam* are allowed to pray *tefilat arvit* with the *tzibur* before this time. They do not need to be *machmir* to pray *arvit* after an hour and a quarter passes from *sheki'at hachamah*.

2 There are those with the custom to recite the *Mizmor* of *"Elokim Yechonenu..."* and other *Mizmorim* printed in siddurim before *arvit*. This *minhag* is good and commendable to depart from *Shabbat* with song and praise and to also prevent one from doing *devarim betelim*. It is well established that one who delays the closure of *Shabbat* sees success.

3 We have the practice to recite *"Vehu Rachum..."* and *"Barechu"* in a slower, more drawn out fashion to add from *chol* to *kedushah* [of *Shabbat*]. Another reason for this is to delay the return of *neshamot* to *Gehinom* after *Shabbat*. The *din* does not come back on them in full force until all of *Klal Yisroel* has finished *Shabbat*. Therefore, anyone who extends *Shabbat* is doing a good thing and his deeds will stand in his favor.

○○○

Today's learning has been dedicated by Ben and Irene Kiaei, Leilui Nishmat Reuben ben Baruch and Parvin bat David, may their Neshamot have an Aliyah.

"Ata Chonantanu"

4 We insert *"Ata Chonantanu"* in the *"Chonen Hada'at"* beracha. If one forgot to do so (and already concluded the entire *"Ata Chonen"* beracha) he should complete his prayer and not go back to say it, nor should he insert it in the *"Shomeah Tefilah"* beracha. This is because he must still recite *havdalah* over a cup of wine. However, one must be careful not to do any *melachah* until after reciting *havdalah* on a cup of wine or saying, *"Baruch Hamavdil Ben Kodesh Lechol."*

5 In a case in which one forgot to insert *"Ata Chonantanu,"* and knows that
a) he does not have wine for *havdalah* that night;
b) he will not be able to get wine the next day;
c) he has no one to hear *havdalah* from; if he remembered before the *tefilah* of *"Shome'ah tefilah,"* then he should insert *"Ata Chonantanu"* in *"Shomeah tefilah."* If he has already passed *"Shome'ah tefilah,"* he should return to *"Ata Chonen."* If he already finished the *amidah* he must start again from the beginning because he will not be able to make *havdalah* otherwise.

6 If one forgot to insert *"Ata Chonantanu,"* and ate before reciting *havdalah*, he must repeat the *amidah* of *arvit* and insert *"Ata Chonantanu."* This is because the *Chachamim* penalize him for forgetting *havdalah* both of the *tefilah* and over the cup. However, when repeating the *amidah,* it is best to make a condition that it should be a *tefilat nedavah* on the possibility that it is unnecessary.

Today's learning has been dedicated by Eliyahu Levaddin, Leilui Nishmat Miriam bat Elazar, may her Neshama have an Aliyah.

7 In a place where most of the *kehilah* consists of *amei ha'aretz* who cannot recite "*Ata Chonantanu*" by heart (due to lack of lighting to read from the *siddur*) it is a *mitzvah* for the *shaliach tzibur* to say it out loud so that everyone will say it with him or have *kavanah* with his recitation. However, if most of the *tzibur* can recite it themselves, the *shaliach tzibur* should not say it out loud lest he confuse others. Rather, he should say just say the first two words of "*Ata Chonantanu*" out loud in order to remind everyone insert it.

8 When saying the words "*Meda Vehaskel*" in "*Ata Chonantanu,*" one must be careful to pronounce it as a '*sin*' and not mistakenly sound like "*Shichool Banim,*" Heaven forbid.

"Vihi Noam"

9 After the *amidah* of *arvit* one rceites "*Vihi Noam...*" because it is the *mizmor* of *beracha* which *Moshe* blessed *Yisrael* with when they finished building the *mishkan*. We have the practice to repeat the *pasuk* of "*Orech Yamim Asbiehu v'arehu bishu'ati.*" The *inyan* of "*Vihi Noam*" is wondrous and great because it serves to extend the *kedushah* of *tosefet Shabbat* to the rest of the upcoming week until the next *Shabbat*. Therefore, one must recite the entire *mizmor* while standing. However, if one is unable to stand for all of it, he should at least say the *pasuk* of "*Vihi Noam*" while standing and then sit down for the rest.

Today's learning has been dedicated for the continued Hatzlacha and Bracha of Mr. and Mrs. Michael Baruch Sagizadeh and family.

10 We recite *"Vihi Noam"* every *motza'e Shabbat*, even when *Yom Tov* or *chol hamoed* fall out during the upcoming the week, because *al pi hasod* *"Vihi Noam"* must always be recited. Therefore, even if the *kahal* is not saying it one should recite it personally.

11 We have the practice to recite *"Vihi Noam"* and the subsequent *seder kedushah* in a pleasant and slower tone in order to delay *B'nei Yisrael* from the finishing of their seder, which in turn defers the *resha'im* from returning to *Gehinom*. On *motza'e Shabbat*, the one in charge of the *ruchot* shouts at them to go back to *Gehinom* because *Bnei Yisrael* finished their *seder*.

12 There are places with the practice not to recite the *pasuk* of "Vihi Noam" in a *bet avel* and instead start from *"Yoshev Beseter Elyon."* Some places don't even say *"Yoshev Beseter,"* rather only the last *pasuk,* *"Orech Yamim Asbiehu..."* According to *Kabbalah* however, one should say both *"Yoshev Beseter"* and the *pasuk* of *"Vihi Noam,"* in a *bet avel*.

13 The *kedushah* of *"Uva Letzion"* recited on *motza'e Shabbat* should be said very carefully. When saying *"V'ata Kadosh,"* one should not be *makpid* to say it specifically standing or sitting because it may be said in either fashion. There are places outside of *Eretz Yisrael* that have the practice to recite it while standing.

OOO

Today's learning has been dedicated for the continued Hatzlacha and Bracha of Mr. and Mrs. Shloimy Golfeiz and family.

14 It is forbidden for one who smokes regularly during the week to prepare the box of cigarettes before *Shabbat* ends to enable himself to smoke immediately after *Shabbat*. In addition to the *issur* of *muktzeh*, he causes himself harm because it is written in the *Zohar* that the dead curse those who are quick to light candles on *motza'e Shabbat* before the *kedushah* and *havdalah* over a cup at home. (This is all besides the fact that smoking causes much damage to one's physical health.)

The Time of Rabenu Tam

15 It is a holy obligation for a *chared l'dvar Hashem* to abstain from *melachah* and not light the *havdalah* candle until past the time equal to four *milin* (seventy-two minutes) in *shaot zemaniyot*. This is in accordance with the opinion of *Rabenu Tam*, whom *Maran Shulchan Aruch* wrote the *halacha* follows. It is a *mitzvah* to publicize this to the learned people and those holding in *Torah*. Even though the standard *minhag* is to be lenient like the understanding of the *Gaonim* who hold thirteen and a half minutes after *shekiayh* is called night, in any event, is proper for a *chared l'dvar Hashem* to be *machmir* like the opinion of *Rabenu Tam* and *Maran Shulchan Aruch*.

16 It is forbidden for a *talmid* who already prayed *arvit* on *motza'e Shabbat* to record his *Rebbi* give a *derashah* or a *slichat mussar* at *seudah shelishit* while the *Rebbi* is still in *Shabbat*. However, the *talmid* may ask permission from his *Rebbi* and if he acquiesces he may he record him after the *Rebbi* recites "Baruch Hamavdil bein Kodesh Lichol."

Today's learning has been dedicated for the continued Hatzlacha and Bracha of Mr. and Mrs. Yedidya Natan and family.

Chapter 17 — The Laws and Order of Havdalah

1 It is a *mitzvat aseh* from the *Torah* to sanctify the *Shabbat* with words, as the *pasuk* says, *"Zachor Et Yom HaShabbat Lekadsho."* This means remembering it with *shevach* and *kiddush*. One must remember *Shabbat* when it commences and again when it concludes. This is accomplished by *kiddush hayom* and *havdalah* respectively. Some disagree and hold that *havdalah* is *miderabanan*. If one recited *havdalah* in *tefilah*, all agree that the *havdalah* over a cup of wine is *miderabanan*.

2 It is forbidden to taste any food or drink before *havdalah*. However, water may be consumed *mitzad hadin. Al pi HaAri z"l*, one should not even drink water before *havdalah*, especially during *ben hashemashot*. The prohibition of eating or drinking before *havdalah* applies equally to women. If one made *havdalah* over a cup, it is permitted to eat and drink, even though he hasn't made *havdalah* in the *tefilah* yet.

Today's learning has been dedicated for the continued Hatzlacha and Bracha of Mr. and Mrs. Gavreal Radford and family.

3 It is prohibited to perform any *melachah* before reciting *havdalah*. If one recited *havdalah* in the *tefilah*, he may perform *melachah* even before making *havdalah* over a cup. If one must do *melachah* before his *havdalah* in the *tefilah*, he must say "*Baruch Hamavdil Ben Kodesh Lachol*" without the *Shem Hamalchut* beforehand. Similarly, women who don't say *havdalah* in the *tefilah* (since most women don't have the practice to pray on *motza'e Shabbat*) should be taught to say, "*Baruch Hamavdil Ben Kodesh Lachol*," before performing *melachah*. Even so, women are obligated to hear *havdalah* over a cup from men afterwards in accordance with the *takanat chachamim*.

4 The order for *havdalah* is as follows: wine, *besamim*, candle and then *havdalah* (it's pneumonic being "*Yavneh.*") One must be careful not to use a *pagum* cup (one which someone else had previously used.) One may solve this issue by adding more wine or water to the cup. However, in a pressing situation where he has no other cup of wine to use for *havdalah*, he may use a *pagum* cup.

5 One must be careful in all aspects of the cup of *havdalah* just the same as the cup of *kiddush*. Although, it is best not to add water to the cup of *havdalah*, if one has less than a *revi'it* of wine and must add water to complete the *revi'it*, he should do so.

Today's learning has been dedicated for the continued Hatzlacha and Bracha of Mr. and Mrs. Yosef Dovid Rowshanshad and family.

Items of Havdalah

6 One does not recite *havdalah* over bread. However, one may recite *havdalah* over beer or any other drink so long as it is *chamar medinah* and not water.

•·······································•

7 If one is unable to drink wine or simply has no wine or beer for *havdalah*, he is not permitted to recite *havdalah* over milk, tea, coffee, citrus juices or the like. The reason for this is because these drinks are not considered *chamar medinah*. In such a case, one should rely on the *havdalah* in the *tefilah* of *arvit* or hear *havdalah* from the *shaliach tzibur* or someone else. One who makes *havdalah* on tea, coffee, or the other drinks above is possibly violating the *issur* of making a *beracha levatalah* and it is forbidden for others to answer *"Amen."*

8 If one is unable to drink wine or does not have wine or beer for *havdalah*, he may recite it over a white beer since it is intoxicating as long as he, or someone else listening to the *havdalah*, drinks a *revi'it* amount. If only a *maleh lugmav* is consumed, it is a *safek* to say *beracha acharonah* (see *Shulchan Aruch 190:3*). This applies only to white beer. In general, whether Ashkenazi or Sefaradi, one should not make *havdalah* over dark beer.

•·······································•

9 Both the *mavdil* and those listening must sit for *havdalah* on *motza'e Shabbat* and *Yom Tov*.

O O O

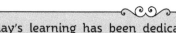

Today's learning has been dedicated for the continued Hatzlacha and Bracha of Mr. and Mrs. Meir Hakimi and family.

10 One who wants to be *yotzeh yedeh chovah* from the *shaliach tzibur* should direct his attention to the cup during the *beracha* and not move from his place until the end of *birkat havdalah*. One should not be like those who miss words because they are looking to leave or to find their sons or friends to leave with them, thereby removing their *da'at* from the *beracha* which they cannot hear entirely.

11 We have the custom to recite "Hinei E-l Yeshuati...," "Kos Yeshuot Esah...," and "Layehudim Hayetah Orah..." before the *havdalah* for *siman tov.* There are those who add more *pesukim*, like the Sefaradim who start from the *pasuk* in *Yeshaya 41:27* which begins with "Rishon Letzion Hinei Hinam..." (and don't say the *pasuk* of "Hinei E-l Yeshuati").

Birkat Besamim

12 One holds the *kiddush* cup in his right hand and the *hadas* in the left when he recites the *beracha* on the wine. He then takes the *hadas* into his right hand and the wine in his left (not to put the cup down on the table) to recite the *beracha* on the *hadas* before setting it down. He then recites a "Boreh Me'oreh Ha'esh" on the candle and then returns the cup back into his right hand. There are individuals who, when making the *beracha* for *besamim*, place the cup on the table and then make the *beracha*. One must advise these individuals that they are not acting in accordance of the *halachah* and let them know that they should hold the cup in the left hand and not set it down during the *berachot* for *besamim* and *ner*.

Today's learning has been dedicated for the continued Hatzlacha and Bracha of Mr. and Mrs. Yitzchak Saeidian and family.

∿ფ∾
• Day 138 •
∿ფ∾

∿ფ∾
• כ' טבת •
∿ფ∾

13 When reciting the beracha for hadas or besamim, he should hold them the direction in which they grow.

○·····················○

14 If one does not have besamim on motza'e Shabbat, he need not go find some since they are used only to rejuvenate our nefesh which grows heavy with the withdrawal of Shabbat. This is caused by the chalishat hada'at which comes from losing one's neshamah yeterah of Shabbat. The besamim strengthen the nefesh since all good smells strengthen the nefesh.

15 One who is chozer beteshuvah during Shabbat is allowed to recite a beracha on besamim on motza'e Shabbat (and it is not considered a hefsek between birkat hagefen and drinking the wine). Despite that at the time of kabbalat Shabbat he was mechalel Shabbat and did not gain the neshamah yeterah, he does gain it at the moment he does teshuvah and is considered a Yisrael Kasher who can make a beracha. There are those that say that even if he was chozer beteshuvah on motza'e Shabbat he is allowed to make the beracha.

Today's learning has been dedicated for the continued Hatzlacha and Bracha of Mr. and Mrs. Yehoshua Zaghi and family.

One who is fasting on *Shabbat* can recite a *beracha* on *besamim* after *Shabbat*. This is unlike *Yom Kippur* where we don't make *birkat besamim*. Since he ate on *leil Shabbat* the *neshamah yeterah* entered him. Another distinction is that the five afflictions are in effect on *Yom Kippur* and there is no pleasure for the *neshamah yeterah*. However, on *Shabbat*, one is just accepting upon himself only the affliction of not eating or drinking. As well, on *Yom Kippur* the whole world is in affliction while on *Shabbat* the whole world is in *oneg* and one therefore makes a *beracha* like the *minhag* of the world.

○···○

 It is the universal *minhag* for an *avel* to recite a *beracha* on *besamim* on *motza'e Shabbat*. This is also the *minhag* of *Yerushalayim* and the proper *minhag* to follow.

○···○

One who cannot smell only recites the *beracha* to be *motzi yedeh chovah* the *ketanim* who have reached the age of *chinuch*. However, since the *beracha* is not *chovah* rather only a *minhag chachamim*, he cannot be *motzi* the *gedolim* in the room who do not know how to make a *beracha* (because they don't need to seek out its achievement). The *din* is like any other *birkat hanehenin* in which one does not make the *beracha* for others if he is not benefitting.

~&~
Today's learning has been dedicated for the continued Hatzlacha and Bracha of Mr. and Mrs. Yitzchak Mazor and family.

19 We have the custom to recite the *beracha* on a *hadas* as best possible. We use the *hadas* from the *lulav* because we want to continue performing *mitzvos* with it. The *ba'alei Kabbalah* say that there is a *sod* to make a *beracha* on *hadas*. Regarding the *hadas* of the *lulav*, we make the *beracha* over it only during the rest of the year. However, we do not do so on *Sukkot* because it has been assigned for its own *mitzvah*. One should only make the *beracha* over it if it still has a scent.

20 There are *chassidim* and *ansheh ma'aseh*, that say, *"Ishei Reiach Nichoach L'Hashem,"* after smelling the *hadas*. However, this is not done during *havdalah* because it would constitute a *hefsek* between the *beracha* and drinking of the wine.

21 There are those who, when being *motzi havdalah* from another, make their own *beracha* on the *besaamim* and *ner* when the *mavdil* makes the *beracha* of *hamavdil*. This is not in accordance with the *halacha* because they must listen and pay attention to the *beracha* of *havdalah* in order to be *motzi yedeh chovah*. In addition to this, it is a bigger *mitzvah* for everyone to be *yotzeh yedeh chovah* in the *mavdil's beracha* in line with *"b'rov am hadras melech."* If one is far from the light and unable to use it, he may then keep in mind not to be *yotzei* with the *mavdil* and instead make the *beracha* himself afterwards. In any event, those who are accustomed to say the *beracha* to themselves must be careful not to do so in the middle of *birkat hamavdil*. Rather, the *mavdil* should wait until everyone finished making their own *berachot* and only then continue the *beracha* of *hamavdil* to be *yotzeh* everyone.

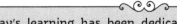
Today's learning has been dedicated for the continued Hatzlacha and Bracha of Mr. and Mrs. Aviel Mokhtar and family.

Birkat Haner

22 On *motza'e Shabbat*, one makes the *beracha* of *"Boreh Meoreh Ha'esh,"* over a candle. The reason for this is because *motza'e Shabbat* was when fire was first created. The *Gemara* (*Pesachim* 44a) relates that on *motza'e Shabbat*, HaKadosh Baruch Hu planted knowledge in *Adam Harishon* and he rubbed two rocks together to spark light. However, if one does not have a candle, he need not search for one because we only do this for the remembrance of the first fire. According to the *Zohar* though, it is good and proper to look for a candle.

23 It is *mitzvah min hamuvchar* to make the *beracha* on an *avukah*, that is a candle with two or more wicks because it generates brighter light. It is also more *mehudar* to use a wax candle.

24 The *beracha* for the candle is made only when one will benefit from it. Meaning, one should be close enough to the candle that it will help him tell the difference between two coins. Even so, it is a *mitzvah min hamuvchar* to come closer to benefit greatly from it. If one made the *beracha* far away from the candle he is *yotzeh yedeh chovah,* but only *bediavad*. If possible, it is better that to hear the *beracha* from another and have intention to be *yotzeh* through them.

○○○

Today's learning has been dedicated for the continued Hatzlacha and Bracha of Mr. and Mrs. Matityahu Yashar and family.

25 We have the custom to look at our palms and fingernails to see the shine of the light differentiate between them, similar to the difference between two coins. Furthermore, the nails are a *siman beracha* because they are *parot v'rabot* to the world. We also look at our palms because there is a *siman* between the lines to make a *beracha* on. One should bend the tops of the fingers on his right hand into his palm so that he can see his nails and palm simultaneously. One's thumb should be tucked and hidden under the four fingers in front of the candle and in front of the person himself.

○·····································○

26 One who wears glasses need not take them off while reciting the *beracha* of *"Boreh Meorei Ha'esh"* in order to see the flame directly because the candle is uncovered.

○·····································○

27 One should not make the *beracha* over an electric candle because the glass bulb is a barrier to the flame. Another reason is that it is not a fire which is lit, rather it is a metal which is heated up that causes illumination.

○·····································○

28 One who is blind does not make a this *beracha* because it does not help him to differentiate between two coins.

○·····································○

Today's learning has been dedicated for the continued Hatzlacha and Bracha of Mr. and Mrs. Moshe Parizad and family.

Obligation of Women

29 Women are obligated in *havdalah* to the same degree they are obligated in *kiddush*. Therefore, husbands must be *motzi* them if they are not experts in *havdalah*. It is proper for husbands to have in mind not to be *yotzeh* with the *shaliach tzibur* and instead make *havdalah* with their wives.

∘∙∙∙∙∙∙∙∙∙∙∙∙∙∙∙∙∙∙∙∙∙∙∙∙∙∙∙∙∙∙∙∘

30 One who recites *havdalah* in the *bet hakenesset* and goes back home to be *motzi* his wife and children should pause after *"Hagefen"* to allow the *bnei habayit* to make their own *beracha* on the *besamim* and *ner* if they are able to make those *berachot*. (The one making *havdalah* should not answer *"Amen"* afterwards because that would constitute an interruption between his *beracha* and drinking the wine). After they do so, he then recites the *beracha* of *"Hamavdil Ben Kodesh L'chol"* and drinks the cup. (If the *bnei bayit* don't know how to make the *berachot*, he should recite the *berachot* for the *besamim* and *ner* himself). This all applies where he is the *shaliach tzibur* or has a specific reason to be *yotzeh* with the *havdalah* in the *bet hakenesset*. However, if there is no need to do so it is better that he has in mind not to be *yotzeh* with the *havdalah* in the *bet hakenesset* (he can accomplish this by saying, *"Baruch Hu U'varuch Shemo"* to the *beracha*), and recite the *havdalah* at home for everyone according to the sequence of the *chachamim* without any reservation.

Today's learning has been dedicated for the continued Hatzlacha and Bracha of Mr. and Mrs. Yoyo Arieh and family.

Drinking the Wine

31 One finishes *havdalah* after the *birkhat haner* with *"Hamavdil Ben Kodesh L'chol,"* and then drinks a *revi'it* (86 grams) of wine. If the *mavdil* can't drink, he should give it to someone who listened to the *beracha* and kept in mind to be *yotzeh yedeh chovah* by drinking from the wine. In any event, one who erred and did not drink a *maleh lugmav* (most of a *revi'it*) is not required to repeat *havdalah*.

32 Those listening to the *ba'al habayit* or the *shaliach tzibur* should be *makpid* not to speak before the *mavdil* drinks the wine. Therefore, those who wish others a *"Shavuah Tov"* before the *mavdil* drinks the wine are making a mistake. One should explain to them, in the right fashion, that they should wait until after the *mavdil* drinks the wine.

33 The *mavdil* should have the practice to drink the entire cup of wine and not leave some for the *bnei habayit*. This is to ensure that he can make a *beracha acharonah* because if he only drinks a *maleh lugmav* he would be in a *safek beracha acharonah* position.

Today's learning has been dedicated for the continued Hatzlacha and Bracha of Mr. and Mrs. Yitzchak Ariel and family.

34 Women have the practice not to drink from the *havdalah* cup since the *etz hada'at* which *Chava* persuaded *Adam* to drink from was the *gefen*. In any event, women who make *havdalah* on their own must certainly drink wine equally as men do since it is not forbidden *min hadin,* rather it's merely a *minhag* not to. Because many people are not *choshesh* for this *minhag* it does not push off the *halachah*. If it is hard for her to drink, she may drink some and give to others to drink.

35 After the *havdalah* we extinguish the candle with wine and clean our eyes with the wine because of *chibuv mitzvah*. It is written in *Pirkei D'Rebbi Eliezer* that after one drinks from the *havdalah* cup it is a *mitzvah* to pour some water into the cup and drink the water because of *chivuv mitzvah*, and he should wash his eyes with whatever water is left in the cup.

36 One is not *yotzeh yedeh chovah* by listening to *havdalah* over the phone. There are those who wrote to give permission to women in the hospital, in a pressing situation, who will only be able to hear *havdalah* via the phone.

37 One with the custom not to do *melachah* or light until 72 minutes of *shaot zemaniyot* past *shekiayh* (in accordance with the opinion of *Rabenu Tam*) on *motza'e Shabbat* is still permitted to hear *havdalah* from another person before then and is *yotzeh yedeh chovah* even *le'chatechilah*.

○○○

Today's learning has been dedicated for the continued Hatzlacha and Bracha of Mr. and Mrs. Binyamin Zedner and family.

∽ৎ৯~
• Day 146 •
∽ৎ৯~

∽ৎ৯~
• כח' טבת •
∽ৎ৯~

38 One in the middle of *shemoneh esrei* of *arvit* on *motza'e Shabbat* who hears the *shaliach tzibur* reciting *havdalah* should not pause to have intention to be *yotzeh yedeh chovah*. Rather, he should continue his prayer as regular and make *havdalah* for himself afterwards.

o···o

39 One who forgot and did not recite *havdalah* on *motza'e Shabbat* may make *havdalah* until the end of Sunday. He recites only the *berachot* of *"Gefen"* and *"Hamavdil"* but not those of the *ner* and *"Besamim."* This applies only if he has not yet tasted anything since *Shabbat* ended. If, however, he did, he may only recite *havdalah* on *motza'e Shabbat,* not Sunday.

o···o

 40 One may order a taxi on *motza'e Shabbat*

even if the taxi driver is not *shomer Shabbat* and you know that he did not make *havdalah* or say, *"Baruch Hamavdil Ben Kodesh L'chol."* It is better to take a bus since the bus does not operate only for him alone, rather it will be in service regardless.

o···o

41 It is *muttar me'ikar hadin* to travel on a bus which started service before *Shabbat* ended. This is specifically in a pressing situation where there is an urgent need to travel immediately. If not, it is proper to wait for a bus which only started service after *Shabbat* ended.

O O O

Today's learning has been dedicated for the continued Hatzlacha and Bracha of Mr. and Mrs. Yosef Mehdizadeh and family.

Piyutim and Zemirot

42 We have the custom to say *piyutim* and *zemirot* to accompany the *Shabbat* just like we accompany a king when he arrives and departs. There are those with the custom for each person in the house to say, *"Eliyahu Hanavi Zachur Latov,"* 130 times. There are those who add on the *"Petichat Eliyahu Zachur Latov,"* like the *Ben Ish Hai* would do in his home.

43 It is written in the *tosefta* that, on *motza'e Shabbat, Eliyahu Hanavi* would sit under the *etz chaim* and write the *zechutim* of the *Shomrei Shabbat*. It also states there that *Eliyahu Hanavi* accepts the punishment of *tzadikim* on himself so that they will not go to *Gehinom* due to a sin they committed, as there isn't a *tzadik* who does good and doesn't sin. Because of this, we mention *Eliyahu Hanavi* on *motza'e Shabbat* not only for the *geulah*, but also to thank him for being the *Safra Rabbah* for *Bnei Yisrael* to write the *zechuyot* of the *shomrei Shabbat*.

44 How good it is for one who has the heart to understand and be enlightened, to read *perush Rashi* and the *Re'em,* or any other *mefaresh*, on the *parashat hashavua* as a *siman tov* for him for the whole week. This will affect him to be blessed in *Torah*.

○○○

Today's learning has been dedicated for the continued Hatzlacha and Bracha of Mr. and Mrs. Dovid Yasharpour and family.

THIS MONTH'S LEARNING HAS BEEN DEDICATED
by Nouriel Niamehr, for the continued Hatzlacha
and Bracha of the Niamehr family.

Chapter 18   Seudah Revi'it

1 One should always set his table on *motza'e Shabbat* in order to escort the *Shabbat* out, even if he is eating only a *kezayit*. Even if one is full and his *nefesh* is on edge with food and drink, he should still push himself. Doing so will save himself from eating or drinking the *mey hamarim* for *refuah*.

◦··◦

2 *Seudah revi'it* is of very lofty stature because just as one needs to respect the *Shabbat* at its inception, so too must one show it respect at its departure, just as we would treat a king when he leaves town. The *kadmonim* said there is a bone in man's body called *Nesakuy*, and this bone lasts forever in the grave, even after all other bones have disintegrated, until the time of *techiyat hametim*. This bone is satiated exclusively from *melaveh malkah*.

◦··◦

3 The *le'chatechilah mitzvah* is to make *seudat revi'it* on bread. If one is *b'ones* and unable to fulfill the *seudah* with bread, he should eat *mezonot* instead. If he is unable to do it with *mezonot* either, he should fulfill it by eating fruits.

◦··◦

4 Women are also obligated in *seudah revi'it*. Eating any food every *motza'e Shabbat* for the sake of *mitzvat melaveh malkah* is a *segulah* for women not to have a hard time during childbirth. In this merit, they will have an easy childbirth *Be'ezrat Hashem Yitbarach*.

ᔦᔥᔧ
• Day 149 •
ᔦᔥᔧ

ᔦᔥᔧ
• ב' שבט •
ᔦᔥᔧ

5 It is written in the *Zohar HaKadosh* that one who does not make a *seudah revi'it* is considered as if he did not make *seudah shelishit*. Therefore, he should be careful not to skip *seudah revi'it*.

◦•••◦

6 It is not fitting to engage in any *melachah* that is not connected to *ochel nefesh* or to *Torah* learning until after *seudah revi'it*. It is proper to continue wearing *bigdei Shabbat* through the *seudah revi'it*.

◦•••◦

7 It is *mitzvah min hamuvchar* to eat *seudah revi'it* during the first four hours after *Shabbat*. It is best to try and make it as soon as possible following *Shabbat*. One should at least eat the *seudah* before *chatzot halayla*. In any event, if one is *b'ones* and unable to make it during either of these timeframes, he can fulfill the *mitzvah* until *amud hashachar*. In the *birkat hamazon* for the *seudah revi'it* one should say, *"Migdol."*

◦•••◦

8 One should endeavor to eat hot bread and a hot drink during the *seudah revi'it*, which helps with the *refuah* of the body.

Today's learning has been dedicated for the continued Hatzlacha and Bracha of Mr. and Mrs. Aviel Abaei and family.

9 If *Rosh Chodesh* falls out on *Shabbat*, it is correct to add onto his regular fare of *seudah revi'it* so that he may fulfill the obligation of *seudat Rosh Chodesh* as well.

○·····································○

10 It is forbidden to say *viduy* on *motza'e Shabbat* before *chatzot halayala* since there is still *kedushat Shabbat*.

○·····································○

11 The *Maharil* would habitually fold his *Shabbat talit* every *motza'e Shabbat* so that he could engage in a *mitzvah* immediately after *Shabbat*.

○·····································○

12 On *motza'e Shabbat*, the *neshamah yeterah* goes up above and *HaKadosh Baruch Hu* asks it, "which foods were placed in front of you and what *chidushei Torah* did you hear?" and they return it to *yeshivah shel malah*. Therefore, it is befitting and correct for every person to be engaged in *Torah* study on *motza'e Shabbat* for which he will merit "Yom Shekulo Shabbat" and a day "Shekulo Aruch."

Today's learning has been dedicated for the continued Hatzlacha and Bracha of Mr. and Mrs. Josh Gabbay and family.

Chapter 19	Forbidden Speech and Mundane Articles

1 There are things prohibited on *Shabbat* even if they are not tantamount to *melachah* or bring one to do a *melachah*. The source for this prohibition is the *pasuk* of *"Vechibadeto Me'asot Derachechah Memitzoh Cheftzechah Vedaber Davar."* Our Rabbis expounded this *pasuk* to mean one's conversation on *Shabbat* should not be like that of *chol*. Therefore, it is forbidden to say, "Tomorrow I will do such-and-such *melachah*," or "Tomorrow I will make such-and-such business deal," on *Shabbat*. One should even reduce speech of *devarim betelim* which don't mention *melachah* nor contain any *divrei genai* or *kalot rosh*. This is because if the speech contains any mention of *melachah*, *divrei genai* or *kalot rosh*, it is forbidden.

----

2 One who greets his friend on *Shabbat* should not address him the same way as he does on *chol* with a plain "good morning." Rather, he should greet him with a *"Shabbat Shalom,"* to fulfill the mitzvah of *"Zachor Et Yom HaShabbat Lekadsho."*

----

3 It is forbidden to hire workers or to direct a non-Jew to hire workers for you. It is also prohibited to discuss what to sell or buy the next day, or any business plans, with one's partner. This applies not only to one's business partner, but to anyone, including one to himself.

Today's learning has been dedicated for the continued Hatzlacha and Bracha of Mr. and Mrs. Eliyahu Shotz and family.

4 It is forbidden to tell one's friend what price he purchased an item for if he knows the friend is interested in buying it as well. However, if his friend has no need for this information then it is considered regular conversation and thus *muttar mitzad hadin*. Therefore, it is *muttar* for one to tell his friend how much money he made on a wedding or on a building project, etc.

Mundane Articles

5 It is prohibited to read documents of debt and ledgers as well as any other business documents on *Shabbat*. It is even forbidden to look at them without reading them.

....

6 It is prohibited for one to read notes or letters if he already knows what they contain. It is also forbidden to look at them without reading them. However, if he received it on *Shabbat* and never read it yet, he is permitted to read it silently because it may contain an immediate or physical necessity. If the letter is sealed, one may tell a non-Jew that he is unable to read the letter because it is not opened, which the non-Jew will deduce to open it for him. However, he may not explicitly tell the non-Jew to open it for him.

Today's learning has been dedicated for the continued Hatzlacha and Bracha of Mr. and Mrs. Shimon Haridim and family.

7 It is forbidden to read stories and articles of mundane matters, romance, or wars on *Shabbat*. They are prohibited on weekdays as well due to *moshav letzim*. Regarding romance, there is an additional *issur* of stimulating one's *yetzer harah* and whomever publishes them, certainly those who print them, are *machti harabim*. Book sellers that carry these types of books are included in that category. These books are *muktzeh* and cannot be moved on *Shabbat*.

---

8 It is forbidden to learn anything but *Torah* on *Shabbat*. This *issur* applies even to books of knowledge.

---

9 Even though there are those who say it is *muttar min hadin* to read the news in a periodical (this refers to a *charedi* periodical, as others may not be read even during the week) it is still appropriate for *yarei shamayim* to abstain from doing so because it causes *bitul Torah* and one should reserve *Shabbat* for *Torah* learning. As well, often reading the newspaper causes grief when there are articles of tragedy, and it is prohibited to be in *tza'ar* on *Shabbat*. The above-mentioned *halachah* was regarding reading news. However, commercial or business advertisements are forbidden to be read or even looked at according to everyone.

---

10 It is forbidden to read captions of pictures or drawings on *Shabbat* because of a *gezeira* lest it lead one to read mundane things. However, pictures of *Rabbanim* given to children on *Shabbat* after they read *tehillim* is acceptable. One need not be *machmir* to print the name of the *Rav* on the back of the picture.

Today's learning has been dedicated for the continued Hatzlacha and Bracha of Mr. and Mrs. Baroch Laleh and family.

~ᴐᴐꙷ
• Day 154 •
ᴐᴐꙷ

~ᴐᴐꙷ
• ז' שבט •
ᴐᴐꙷ

11 It is forbidden to read the caption of a wall or curtain containing different animals or stories of people (e.g. the battle between *David* and *Goliath*) on *Shabbat* because it might lead one to read other things. However, it is permitted to look at different pictures and drawings pertaining to the weekly *parasha* distributed to children at school, because this is the method of teaching them and to instill passion for the *parashat hashavuah*.

12 It is permitted for the *gabbai* to hand out bills on *Shabbat* to those who previously pledged a donation to the *bet hakenesset*. This is specifically when he only does so from one *Shabbat* to the next. (In a place where there is no *eiruv*, he should remind them not to bring their bills home.)

13 It is forbidden for one to read the *ba'aleh haḡahah* (the pages used to proofread a *sefer* before it is printed) to know where the errors which need to be fixed lie. However, if one is using them to learn from, it is *muttar*.

14 It is forbidden to set up an election for the *"va'ad bet hakenesset"* on *Shabbat*, even if their intentions are for a *mitzvah* and to strengthen the *bedek habayit*. Rather, they should set up the election on *motza'e Shabbat* or any other day of the week.

Today's learning has been dedicated for the continued Hatzlacha and Bracha of Mr. and Mrs. Ben Ghalili and family.

15 One who accepted upon himself not to have idle conversations on *Shabbat* should not speak any *devarim betelim* at all, even if it has to do with the *Shabbat* food. For example, when he is sitting with his family eating the *seudat Shabbat* and they are discussing whether the food was tasty or fully-cooked, it is forbidden for him to chat with them. Even though it is a *midat chasidut*, because he accepted upon himself not to do so he is bound by a *neder*.

○..○

16 Even though, *mei'Ikar hadin*, there is no *issur* for one to contemplate his business, because of *oneg Shabbat* it is a *mitzvah* for him to push it out of his mind completely and act as if his job is completed. The reason for this is because he must direct his concentration toward his creator to stimulate love and awe with a great sense of happiness. This certainly applies where he is worried about suffering a loss caused from not working on *Shabbat*, because one must be in a state of true "*Menuchat shalom Hasheket vavetach*" on *Shabbat*.

Today's learning has been dedicated by the Author, for the continued Hatzlacha and Bracha of my dear brother-in-law, Raziel ben Mashiach Asher.

17 There is what to rely on regarding the custom of presenting a gift to the *bar mitzvah* boy on *Shabbat* on behalf of the *bet hakenesset*. In any event, it is better for the *gabbai* of the to give the gift before *Shabbat* through another person, in such a way that the person raises the gift and say, "I am being *zoche* in this gift for so-and-so." (This will accomplish that the object changed hands before *Shabbat*.) Similarly, one should do this any time he wishes to give his friend a gift on *Shabbat* because it will render it *muttar* on *Shabbat* so long as there is no problem with *muktzeh*. If for whatever reason he did not do so, he should have in mind that the recipient of the gift should not be *zoche* to it until after *Shabbat*. In a place with no *eruv* it is prohibited to transport the gift from place to place.

○·······································○

18 It is *muttar me'ikar hadin* in a time of need (e.g. where you only see the person from week to week) to give out wedding, *bar mitzvah,* or similar invitations on *Shabbat* since it is considered *l'dvar mitzvah*, especially when there are *pesukim* printed on the cards. (In a place where there is no *eruv*, one should remind them not to bring the invitations home). In any event, it is better to be *machmir* and give them out during the week.

Today's learning has been dedicated for the continued Hatzlacha and Bracha of Mr. and Mrs. Avraham Dovid Ha'kohen Odzer and family.

1 Our *chachamim* prohibited *Shabbat* wages, meaning accepting wages in exchange for work done on *Shabbat*. This applies even if there is no *issur* involved while doing the work because of a *gezeira* from *mekach umemkar*. Therefore, a guard with standing wage-per-workday agreement is prohibited from getting paid for working on *Shabbat*, even when receiving the payment along with the rest of the week's pay. It is certainly forbidden to accept money for the guard duty he performed on *Shabbat*. However, if the agreement was a weekly or monthly salary, it is permitted for him to accept the wages for the *shemira* that he performed. This is because the wage he receives for the *Shabbat* guard duty is included in the total salary of his contract.

In any event, it is forbidden for the *shomer* to tell his employer to him to give him his *Shabbat* and he should instead say, "pay me my weekly/monthly salary which incorporates *Shabbat*."

⸰··⸰

2 A *chazzan* who prays only on *Shabbat* or *Yamim Noraim* and one who blows the *shofar* on *Rosh Hashanah* is permitted to receive payment for those specific jobs as it is not considered a "*Shabbat* wage." This is because the *chachamim* did not extend the *issur* to *dvar mitzvah*. The same *din* applies to a *mashgiach* for *kashrut* as well as a speaker for *Shabbat* and *Yamim Tovim*. *Beracha* will come to those who are *machmir* and incorporate their salary by performing something during the week.

Today's learning has been dedicated for the continued Hatzlacha and Bracha of Mr. and Mrs. Eli Kohansion and family.

3 A doctor called to someone's house on *Shabbat* is permitted to accept money after *Shabbat* for his service and there is no issue of receiving "*Shabbat* wages."

4 It is permitted to pay before or after *Shabbat* for using a *mikveh* during *Shabbat*. This is because what one pays for includes the heating and cleaning crew that take care of the *mikveh* during the week and after *Shabbat* so that it may be used on *Shabbat*. It is therefore considered an incorporated wage.

5 A guest may pay for his stay at a hotel, even if he eats and sleeps there solely on *Shabbat*. On account of the owner's constant responsibility to keep the hotel clean, the payment is considered incorporated and there is no issue of paying a "*Shabbat* wage."

Today's learning has been dedicated for the continued Hatzlacha and Bracha of Mr. and Mrs. Shlomo Khalili and family.

6 It is permitted to pay for tickets to a zoo or the like before *Shabbat*. This is because the general upkeep is included in the price of admission. (This is merely regarding the aspect of *Shabbat* wages. However, it is clear that one should abstain from going to the zoo on *Shabbat* and instead sanctify the day with *shiurei Torah* and *derashot*.)

7 It is permitted for one to switch his rotation of working in a kitchen or a hospital or the like to a rotation on another day or even another *Shabbat*. There is no issue of *Shabbat* wages.

8 One need not worry about issues of *sechar Shabbat* over the daily interest which banks credit customers (with a *heter iska*). This is because the interest is viewed according to business day, which ends when the bank closes in the afternoon. The weekday is included in the amount.

Today's learning has been dedicated for the continued Hatzlacha and Bracha of Mr. and Mrs. Pedram Reuven Farzadfar and family.

Chapter 21 — Amirah L'non-Jew on Erev Shabbat and Shabbat

1 It is forbidden to tell a non-Jew to do *melacha* for us on *Shabbat*. This is despite the fact they are not obligated to keep the *Shabbat*, and this applies even if one were to tell him before *Shabbat* and even if one only needs that *melacha* done after *Shabbat*. This *issur* was instituted by the *Rabanan* to prevent *Shabbat* observance from becoming marginalized to the point that Jews would do *melachah* themselves.

2 If one makes an arrangement with a *non-Jew* to do *melacha* for him for an agreed-upon price, and the *non-Jew* has discretion when to do the work, he is able to do it on *Shabbat*. The reason for this is because the price was pre-set and the non-Jew decided on his own to do it on *Shabbat* in order to finish it quicker, even though the Jew was not particular about it being done then. Since the Jew was fine with it being done after *Shabbat*, it is *muttar*.

Today's learning has been dedicated by Yehuda Gabaie, Leilui Nishmat Sarah Dolati bat Yechezkel, may her Neshama have an Aliyah.

3 The *hetter* mentioned above is only when the word is done *b'tzina*, or private. That is, that the *melacha* is not identifiable as being for a Jew. However, if people can tell that it is specifically a *melacha* for a *Yisrael*, it is forbidden. The reason for this is that people cannot tell that there was a pre-set price for the work and will then think that the Jew hired a *non-Jew* to work for him on *Shabbat*. Therefore, it is forbidden because of *ma'arit ayin*. (The definition of *tzina* is that the populace does not recognize the job being done as specifically for a *Yisrael*. However, the *non-Jew* is allowed to work in public still, being that the criteria were met). This *hetter* also applies only when the non-Jew does the *melacha* from his own initiative on *Shabbat*, but it is forbidden to tell him to do the *melacha* on *Shabbat*. In addition, the *non-Jew* must do it in his own work place and not the house of a *Yisrael* because this also looks as if the Jew hired him to do work on *Shabbat*.

• •

4 It is permitted to give a job to a non-Jew during the week, for example sewing clothing or shoes, because the wage is fixed and set and he isn't telling the non-Jew to do the *melacha* on *Shabbat*. There also is no issue of *ma'arit ayin* in doing this because no one can tell that the work is for a Jew since the non-Jew is doing it in his work place.

Today's learning has been dedicated by Mr. and Mrs. Meir Hakimi, Leilui Nishmat Refael ben Meir, may his Neshama have an Aliyah.

THIS CHAG'S LEARNING HAS BEEN DEDICATED
by Raziel Ebriani, for Hatzlacha and fruitfulness
for all of Klal Yisrael, in both Ruchniyut and
Gashmiyut.

5 It is permitted to give one's car to an auto shop owned by a non-Jew on *erev Shabbat*, where all the workers are non-Jews, on condition that you are able to pick up the car on Sunday and the price was fixed beforehand. This is only when there is enough time to fix the car either before *Shabbat* or after *Shabbat* before he picks it up. With these prerequisites, the non-Jew may work on the car on *Shabbat*, but one may not tell him to. However, to give his car to the mechanic when the non-Jew will only have enough time to complete the work by working on *Shabbat*, *le'chatechilah* should not be done because it is as if he is out-right telling the non-Jew to work for him on *Shabbat*. In any event, in a time of need one can be lenient, even if the worker will finish the job on *Shabbat*. However, Ashkenazim are *machmir* on this.

6 One may not hire builders or harvesters (or the like) to do a job on *Shabbat* because people passing by cannot tell that their wage was pre-set. Also, things which are *mechubar* are considered public knowledge to be belonging to a *Yisrael*.

○○○

○○○

Amira to a Non-Jew on Shabbat

7 It is forbidden for a *Yehudi* to tell a non-Jew to do for him something which is forbidden for the *Yehudi* to do himself. This applies whether the *issur* of doing the *melacha* is a *deorayta* or a *derabanan*. In addition, it is forbidden for one to tell a non-Jew during the week to do such a *melacha* like this for him on *Shabbat*.

....

8 Just as it is forbidden for one to tell a non-Jew to do a *melacha* for him on *Shabbat*, it is also forbidden to hint to the non-Jew to do a *melacha* for one's self as well, because this also qualifies as telling him to do

the *melachah*. This *din* applies when one says it in a way that the non-Jew will take to mean as telling him to do a *melacha*. However, one may hint to him in an indirect way, such as "the light doesn't illuminate nicely," or, "I can't read from the light." There is no problem of getting *hana'a* from a *melacha* that a non-Jew did for him in this scenario because this isn't really *hana'a* as he could've read from the light without this if he really needed to. (However, if the *Yehudi* has full *hana'a*, i.e. if the non-Jew turned on a light for him, it is forbidden for the *Yehudi* to have *hana'a* from that *melacha* until *motza'e Shabbat*. One must also wait the amount of time it takes for to do that *melacha*- *kedei sheya'aseh*.)

Today's learning has been dedicated for the continued Hatzlacha and Bracha of Mr. and Mrs. Binyamin Mehdizadeh and family.

9 If one has trouble falling asleep while the light is on, it is permitted for him to say "it is hard for me to sleep while the light is on in the room," (saying it in a way that explains the need for doing the *melacha*) which will make the non-Jew realize to shut off the light. However, it is forbidden for one to say, "why didn't you shut off the light for me last *Shabbat*?" (in the command form), so that he will understand and turn the light off now.

°·············°

10 One is allowed to tell a non-Jew after *Shabbat* "why didn't you do such and such this past *Shabbat*?", even though it is implicit from his words that the non-Jew should do it for him the following *Shabbat*. This is not a problem of the *issur* of commanding one to do a *melacha* for you because we are only stringent on that aspect when hinting to him <u>on</u> *Shabbat*. In this case, he is only hinting to him in a form of commandment <u>after</u> *Shabbat*.

11 If one forgot to light a fire on *erev Shabbat*, or forgot to plug in the *plata* or *tanur*, even though he can hint to the non-Jew through *sippur devarim* and explain to him in a way that he will understand on his own and light the fire or plug in the cord to the outlet, this will not help him. This is because one may not get any benefit from food which was heated up by a non-Jew for the need of a *Yisrael* on *Shabbat*. Even if one invites the non-Jew to eat the food with him, it is still not permitted to eat because the main purpose of the non-Jew's action was for the *Yehudi's* need. However, if the non-Jew is present specifically for *Shabbat* and receives a predetermined wage before *Shabbat* for everything he does on *Shabbat*, one may be lenient (according to Sefaradim) and have *hana'a* from food heated up on *Shabbat* because the non-Jew is doing it based on his own knowledge.

Today's learning has been dedicated for the continued Hatzlacha and Bracha of Mr. and Mrs. Yechezkel Gabaie and family.

12 If one forgot to turn on a light in his home before *Shabbat*, as long as he has another light which he would be able to rely on (even uncomfortably) it is *muttar* for him to hint to a non-Jew to turn on the light. This must be done in a way of hinting through a story. For example, saying "my house is dark", and the non-Jew realizes on his own to turn on the light. Only then is it *muttar* to use the light the non-Jew lit to do things one could have accomplished without the light. However, if he has no light on in the house at all, or he would like to use the light to do something which he otherwise couldn't, he should call in a non-Jew and ask him to retrieve something from the dark room (in which the *Yehudi* would like the light turned on). The non-Jew will turn on the light for his own use so that he can find the object, and then one may use the light that was turned on because it wasn't done specifically for him.

°·····················°

13 It is *muttar* to tell a non-Jew to do something on *Shabbat* if the *issur* is only *derabanan* when it is for someone who is a bit sick, someone who is in desperate need (i.e. will otherwise suffer a substantial loss of money), or for the sake of a *mitzvah*. Because the issur is merely a *derabanan* and the *issur* of *Amira l'non-Jew* is also *derabanan*, it is a *shevut deshevut*, and in these cases the *chachamim* were not *gozer* for *issur*.

Today's learning has been dedicated for the continued Hatzlacha and Bracha of Mr. and Mrs. Elisha Loloyan and family.

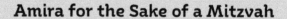

Amira for the Sake of a Mitzvah

14 It is forbidden to tell a non-Jew to do an *issur deorayta* on *Shabbat*, even for the sake of a *mitzvah*. Therefore, it is forbidden to tell a non-Jew to light a candle for you to learn or pray. However, for a *mitzvah* for the *rabim* there is what to rely on with those who are *matir* a *shevut* in a *mitzvah* circumstance. Therefore, if the light went out in a *bet hakenesset* on *leil Shabbat* or *leil Yom Kippur* in the middle of *keriyat shema* or *tefilah*, it is *muttar* to tell a non-Jew to turn on the light for the many people who are reading the *keriyat Shema* or praying from a *siddur*. In any event, if possible, it is best to do this by telling a non-Jew to tell another non-Jew to do it, because there are those who hold that this way is a *shevut deshevut*.

15 There are grounds to be lenient to allow one to transfer objects via a non-Jew on *Shabbat*, from one *reshut hayachid* to another *reshut hayachid* through a *reshut harabim*, in a *mitzvah* circumstance. The reason for this is because it is a *shevut deshevut* in a *mitzvah* circumstance. There are also grounds for leniency in cases of *hachnassat orchim* or cases of *darchei shalom* or similar scenarios.

Today's learning has been dedicated for the continued Hatzlacha and Bracha of Rabbi and Mrs. Yosef Shotz and family.

Amira in a Circumstance of Substantial Loss

16 It is *muttar* to hint to a non-Jew, even with a *lashon* of directive, to do something for one's self on *Shabbat* to prevent a substantial loss of property. This includes even if the non-Jew's actions will result in an *issur Torah*. Since one is anxious about his assets, the *chachamim* were worried that if they are not *matir* this, one may come to do the *issur* himself. Therefore, if a fire broke out on *Shabbat* in the house or in the store, it is *muttar* to tell the non-Jew "anyone who extinguishes the fire will not lose". However, it is still forbidden to tell the non-Jew outright "if you distinguish there will be no loss," even in a case of substantial financial loss.

Amira for the Sake of a Choleh

17 It is *muttar* to tell a non-Jew to do something on *Shabbat* for the need of healing a *choleh* who is confined to bed [he need not be in imminent danger], even if the action is an *issur Torah*. Therefore, it is *muttar* to tell a non-Jew to turn on a light for the *choleh* in order that he may see his needs.

Today's learning has been dedicated for the continued Hatzlacha and Bracha of Rabbi and Mrs. Shlomo Haghighi and family.

Amira Before Shabbat

18 It is *muttar* for a *Yisrael* to tell a non-Jew by way of hinting before *Shabbat*, to do for him a *melacha* on *Shabbat*, even if the hint was quite clear and instructive. For example, he may tell him "why didn't you do such-and-such for me last *Shabbat*," and the non-Jew will recognize on his own that he should do it the following *Shabbat*.

Amira During Bein Hashemashot

19 It is *muttar* during *bein hashemashot* (the time between *sheki'at hachama* and *tzet hakochavim*) to tell a non-Jew to do a *melacha* which is forbidden from the *Torah* if it is for *tzorech mitzvah* (i.e. telling him to light a candle) or in a general case where there is *tirda* and pressure for time. It is *muttar* even if one has already accepted the *kedushat Shabbat* on himself with the *tzibur* by answering "*Barechu*" or saying "*Bo'ee Kallah*." The same *hetter* applies by *bein hashemashot* of *motza'e Shabbat*, since by *motza'e Shabbat* there is also no *gezeira* of *shevut*.

Today's learning has been dedicated for the continued Hatzlacha and Bracha of Rabbi and Mrs. Yosef Kalman Neuberger and family.

1 It is forbidden to organize or prepare anything on *Shabbat* for the need of *motza'e Shabbat* or any weekday since one disrespects the *kavod* of *Shabbat* by preparing on *Shabbat* for *chol*.

2 It is forbidden to unfold a bed on *Shabbat* (to set it up for sleep) if it is not needed to be slept on during *Shabbat* but rather will only be used *motza'e Shabbat*. The reason for this is because one is preparing for after *Shabbat*. However, if the bed is in a place where people pass by, it is *muttar* to organize the bed on *Shabbat* so that the house will look neat.

3 One may not explicitly say on *Shabbat* that he is going to sleep in order that he will not be tired on *motza'e Shabbat* and be able to do his *melachot*. However, it is *muttar* to sleep on *Shabbat* even if his intention is to be awake on *motza'e Shabbat*.

Today's learning has been dedicated for the continued Hatzlacha and Bracha of Rabbi and Mrs. Rafi Gold and family.

4 It is permitted to return the leftover foods to the refrigerator after the meal. Similarly, there are grounds to *matir* transferring soup from a larger pot to a smaller pot in order to save it in the fridge. Also, it is *muttar* to put food into the freezer on *Shabbat* so that it does not spoil as there is no *issur* of preparation from *Shabbat* to *chol* in doing so.

5 Anything that has no *tircha* and which one is accustomed to doing without thinking of its benefit is *muttar* to do on *Shabbat*. This applies even when the outcome of his actions helps him for the *chol*, so long as he doesn't explicitly mention that the action is being done for *chol*. Therefore, if one takes a *talit* to a *bet hakenesset* (when there is an *eruv*) it is *muttar* for him to return home with the *talit*. Also, it is *muttar* to return a book to its place after one has finished learning from it. It is also *muttar* for someone to leave his house on *Shabbat* in the evening, even on a day which is burning hot, and take a vest with him (when there is an *eruv*) so that he can wear it later on that night while he is on the way. However, he should not say that he is taking it for the evening. Similarly, it is *muttar* for one to leave his house, even when close to *chashecha*, with the house key (when there is an Eruv) so that he can re-enter his house after *Shabbat*.

Today's learning has been dedicated by Mr. and Mrs. Meir Hakimi, Leilui Nishmat Shmuel ben Yitzchak, may his Neshama have an Aliyah.

6 It is forbidden for one who needs to travel immediately following *Shabbat* to prepare his luggage and pack it on *Shabbat* (even if the items are not *muktze*) because this is *hachana* from *Shabbat* to *chol*.

7 It is forbidden to roll a *sefer Torah* on *Shabbat* in preparation for its reading during the week. However, if one reads a few *pesukim* from it, this is considered as having learned on *Shabbat* for the sake of *Shabbat* and it won't be called *hachana*.

8 One should not take a *siddur* to *bet hakenesset* on *Shabbat* in order to pray from it on *motza'e Shabbat* (even where there is an *eruv*). Rather, he should pray from it beforehand during the day as well.

9 It is *muttar* to learn something on *Shabbat* in preparation for the next day and there is no *issur* of *hachana*.

Today's learning has been dedicated by the Author, for the continued Hatzlacha and Bracha of my dear brother, Chaim Daniel ben Elazar.

Chapter 23   Making Noise on Shabbat

1 It is forbidden to make noise with a musical instrument on *Shabbat* because of a *gezeira* lest one come to fix the musical instrument. However, to tap on a door and the like in a non-musical fashion is *muttar*. Even if one taps with a utensil it is *muttar* as long as it's not to a rhythm.

2 To knock on a door with its affixed knocker is forbidden according to Ashkenazim, even without a rhythm, because the ring is made for that purpose. However, according to Sefaradim there are grounds to be lenient.

3 It is *muttar* to whistle on *Shabbat* because one is not doing any *ma'aseh*. It is even *muttar* to whistle to a tune. However, *beracha* will come upon one who is *machmir*.

Today's learning has been dedicated by the Ebriani Family, Leilui Nishmat Saltanat Miriam bat Nehamia, may her Neshama have an Aliyah.

4 One who has keys made in such a way where they are sensitive to a specific sound, for example to a whistle or the clapping of hands, and when one forgets where he placed them he either whistles or claps his hands and the key itself starts to ring, it is *muttar* to whistle on *Shabbat* to find the keys. The reason is because he is not doing any *ma'aseh* with this and also because the whistling doesn't directly cause the key to ring, rather it releases a rubber which creates contact between two connections found in the key which cause the ring to sound. This is considered only a *grama*.

Dancing and Clapping

5 It is forbidden to dance on *Shabbat* and similarly to clap one's hands on *Shabbat*, since one may come to make a musical utensil. This *issur* also applies even for the *simcha* of a *chattan* and *kallah*. There is no allowance for this at all, especially for Sefaradim and *Edut Mizrach* who accepted the *halacha* rulings of *Maran Shulchan Aruch* who ruled dancing to be forbidden even nowadays. Therefore, the *minhag pashut* in our circles is for it to be forbidden. If one is acting leniently in this matter, it is befitting to give him *mussar* and inform him that he is going against *halacha*. Only on *Simchat Torah* is it *muttar* to dance and clap for the *kavod* of the *Torah*. To clap during a speech on *Shabbat* is *muttar* because his intentions are not directed towards a song.

Today's learning has been dedicated by Eliyahu Levaddin, Leilui Nishmat Michael Dovid ben Moshe, may his Neshama have an Aliyah.

6 It is *muttar* to clap with a *shinuy*, i.e. to clap one's palm onto the back of the other palm. Similarly, to walk in a circle with songs and praises is *muttar* on *Shabbat* because this does not fall under the principle of dancing, which our *chachamim* forbade. The dancing which they forbade was dancing in a way in which one raises one leg and places the other one down.

○·································○

7 It is forbidden to tap one's hand on a table to a specific rhythm during a song. Similarly, one should not bang his feet on the floor to make the song more pleasant. However, it is *muttar* to bang on a table with one's hand or with a utensil to silence the crowd. Similarly, it is permitted to knock on a door, either with a hand or with a utensil, so that they open the door for you. However, one should not knock on the door in a specific rhythm like that of the singers.

○·································○

8 A *shaliach tzibur* who is in awe of *Hashem* and fears His word, should *le'chatechilah* not use an instrument made like a small fork to gather his voice in the *tefilah* and *zimrah*. However, those who are lenient on their own, without asking a *chacham*, should not protested against because they have what to rely on.

○~C_⌢_Ͻ~○
Today's learning has been dedicated for the continued Hatzlacha and Bracha of Rabbi Binyamin Rowshanshad and family.

9 A door which, when opened, rings (non-electric) bells in order to let the owner know that someone is entering, is *muttar* to open on *Shabbat*, even though doing so creates a nice sound similar to a song. This is because one does not intend nor need to make the sound, rather he merely wants to open the door to enter inside, in which case there is no *gezeira* of *hashma'at kol*. However, blessing will come upon one who is *machmir* and takes off the bells before *Shabbat*.

10 Even though the bells found on a *sefer Torah* or on its plate were designed to make noise, one should not protest those who are accustomed to place them on the *sefer Torah* on *Shabbat* because it is for *tzorech mitzvah* and not intended for music. Rather, the intention is for people to hear the sounds in order to be informed that the *sefer Torah* was taken out. This was not the type of musical sound which the *chachamim* made forbidden and the *minhag pashut* is to permit this globally.

Today's learning has been dedicated for the continued Hatzlacha and Bracha of Rabbi and Mrs. Tahor and family.

Chapter 24 — Hand Watches, Alarm Clocks and Shabbat Clocks

1 If a watch stopped ticking, one should not wind it on *Shabbat*. However, if the watch is still ticking as normal, it is permitted to wind it in order to allow the continuation of the watch's ticking on *Shabbat*. Similarly, one may set a working watch that is behind or ahead of the correct time to the accurate time because the watch is still working and it has on it a *torat kli*.

°·····································°

2 One may wear an automatic watch that winds and sets itself based on the movement of one's own hand. Since one is permitted to directly wind up a watch that is currently working, how much more so one can wear an automatic watch that winds itself based on the movement of the person's hand. There are many reasons why it's permitted and one should not be *machmir*.

°·····································°

3 It is *muttar* to wear a battery-powered wrist watch. However, one should be careful not to click the button on the watch at night to illuminate the watch in order to see the time. Doing so transgresses *havara*, kindling, and is forbidden from the *Torah*.

°⁓·⁓°
Today's learning has been dedicated for the continued Hatzlacha and Bracha of Mr. and Mrs. Moshe Bandari and family.

4   An electronic watch which requires one to click the button in order to see the numbers is definitely forbidden to be used on *Shabbat* because it involves the *issur* of *havara* and *kibui*, or extinguishing, on *Shabbat*.

5   It is forbidden to press a button on an electronic watch to see the date on *Shabbat*.

6   It is forbidden to change the time on a battery-powered watch. Similarly, if it has an alarm clock, it is forbidden to set it or to stop it from ringing on *Shabbat* since doing so involves connecting and cutting off electrical currents.

Alarm Clocks

7   It is *muttar* to press the button on a non-electric alarm clock on *leil Shabbat* that will cause the alarm to ring at the set time *Shabbat* morning. Similarly, it is permitted to press the button so that it does not ring at the previously set time.

8   It is *muttar* to wind the hands of a non-electric alarm clock to the desired time. Similarly, if one had the intention for the alarm to ring at a certain time, but on *Shabbat* he wants to change it to ring either earlier or later, he may wind it to the time he would like it to ring.

Today's learning has been dedicated for the continued Hatzlacha and Bracha of Rabbi and Mrs. Moshe Kimchi and family.

THIS MONTH'S LEARNING HAS BEEN DEDICATED
by Elazar Samimi, for the continued Hatzlacha and Bracha of the Samimi Family.

9 It is *muttar* to click the button on a non-electric alarm clock to shut off the ringing. Similarly, it is *muttar* to cover it with cushions so that one does not hear the ringing.

10 A clock that doesn't work, whether it is sitting there because it is damaged or whether just because he doesn't need it during the day, is *muktza* and is forbidden to move.

11 If one's watch stops on *Shabbat* while he is wearing it, he may keep wearing it until he reaches a safe place to take it off in order that it shouldn't get stolen.

12 If one has an alarm clock built in a way that when the room is dark he cannot see the numbers or hands, and there's a small button on the side of the clock that senses the light and causes the numbers and hands to light up based on the amount of light in the room, it is *muttar* to open the windows in the room on *Shabbat* since there is no concern of *ketiva* or anything else.

○ ○ ○

○ ○ ○

Shabbat Clocks

13 A *Shabbat* clock which is made to shut off an outlet at a given time, is *muttar* to fix in a way that it will turn off at a later time on *Shabbat*. However, one should not change it to turn off at an earlier time unless it is for a *chole*h. Similarly, if one had the intentions for the light to go on at a certain time, one may do something that will cause the lights to stay on longer. However, to make the light turn on at an earlier time should not be done, unless it is for the sake of a *mitzvah* such as learning or the like.

14 Everything stated in the previous *halacha* (13) applies specifically to a clock that continues to operate fully when one changes the time for it to shut off or the lighting. For example, a clock where one moves the back plate to set the time, or a clock where the hands are released by clicking it to move to a certain time, and when one replaces the hands they fall into place without clicking. However, a clock which one must stop its operation to change it, for example where one must open the screws of the clock to move the hands and then screw it closed, is only *muttar* to change in a case of great necessity. The reason for this is because opening the screws causes the clock to stop working and it will only restart when one screws it back together. However, if one placed another pin beforehand for a later time, and only then removed the first pin, it is *muttar* even when there is no big need.

○○○

Today's learning has been dedicated by Daniel Saidian, Leilui Nishmat Yoseph ben Shmuel Ezat, may his Neshama have an Aliyah.

Chapter 25 — Washing and Cosmetics on Shabbat

1 It is forbidden to wash one's whole body or most of one's body with hot water on *Shabbat*. There is no difference whether one washes his whole body at once or washes his body limb by limb, one after another. However, it is *muttar* to wash one's face, hands and feet and other limbs so long as he does not wash most of his body.

○..○

2 If one washes his whole body every day and will be in much *tza'ar* if he doesn't wash himself, or if he is sick, it is *muttar* for him to wash his whole body on *Shabbat* even with hot water that was heated up before *Shabbat*. In any case, he should be careful not to wring or squeeze his hair.

○..○

3 It is *muttar* to dip in a *mikveh* to dispel *tumah* on *Shabbat*. However, one should be careful to make sure the water is not hot, but rather cold. Even though one should not protest those who are lenient and dip into lukewarm water for *taharah* reasons because they have what to rely on, still it's preferable not to dip in the lukewarm water. One must also be careful not to squeeze his hair.

Today's learning has been dedicated by Mr. and Mrs. Yosef Mehdizadeh, Leilui Nishmat Meir ben Yisrael, may his Neshama have an Aliyah.

4 A woman who's *tevilah* fell out on *leil Shabbat* and the water in the *mikveh* is warm, should preferably dip during *bein hashemashot*, which is thirteen and a half minutes after *shekiayh*. If it is not possible to dip during *bein hashemashot*, she may dip even after that time in the warm water and should not push off her dipping because of the water being warm. After the dipping, she should not wring her hair with her hands. Similarly, she should not wipe her body and hair with a thin towel but rather with a big and thick towel. She should dry herself gently and slowly until the water from her hair is absorbed by the towel.

5 It is *muttar* to wash one's whole body with cold water. One should be careful not to wash with a cloth or sponge so that he doesn't come to transgress *sechitah*. Ashkenazim have the *minhag* not to bathe even with cold water.

....

6 It is *muttar* to wipe one's body and hair with a large towel that is meant for wiping. However, one should not wipe with power, but rather gently and slowly until the water from the hair is absorbed by the towel. Similarly, when one takes a drink he should be careful not to dry his mustache with his hands, but rather he should use a napkin.

Today's learning has been dedicated for the continued Hatzlacha and Bracha of Rabbi and Mrs. Sam Iser and family.

7 It is forbidden to swim on *Shabbat*. As well, one should not bathe in the sea even without swimming.

○····················○

8 It is *muttar* to bathe one's whole body in the *chamei teveria* on *Shabbat*. However, this is only when not for medicinal purposes, as it is forbidden to do so for healing purposes. The same *din* applies to other springs as well that it's forbidden to use them for medicinal or healing purposes on *Shabbat*.

○····················○

9 It is *muttar* to use the hot water from the *dud shemesh* (sun-heated boiler) to wash one's face, hands, and feet or to wash utensil and the like. However, *beracha* will come upon one who is *machmir* on this.

○····················○

10 It is forbidden to open the hot water tap on *Shabbat* if the water was heated up by electricity (i.e. it was heated up by central heating or by a boiler) when the water is still *yad soledet bo*. The reason for this is because turning on the hot water causes cold water to enter the water container and get cooked by the hot water already there.

Today's learning has been dedicated for the continued Hatzlacha and Bracha of Rabbi and Mrs. Moshe Rooshanshad and family.

11 There are grounds to be lenient for *bnei Edut Hamizrach* to wash their hands with soap on *Shabbat*. However, *beracha* will come upon one who is *machmir* on this. For *acheinu* Ashkenazim, it is proper for them to be *machmir* unless there is a big need, for example a *choleh* who needs to wash his hands with soap after a checkup for hygienic reasons. In any event, it's preferable to use flowing water.

....

12 It is forbidden to put rose water or other liquid *besamim* into water which is meant for washing or *netilat yadayim* because of *molid re'ach*. However, if one mixed them in before *Shabbat*, it is *muttar* to wash with them on *Shabbat*.

....

13 It is *muttar meikar hadin* to use toothpaste to brush one's teeth with a toothbrush. This is specifically for one who brushes his teeth daily and has no *chashash* of drawing blood while brushing. However, without this one should be *machmir*. This whole *hetter* is only when one has *tzaar* from being prevented from brushing his teeth with a toothbrush. In addition, one should be careful not to rinse his toothbrush under water after he has finished brushing. It's best to be *machmir* and set aside a special toothbrush for *Shabbat*-only usage. All in all, it's best to use running water instead of toothpaste.

....

14 It is *muttar* to move a towel after one wiped with it and soaked it because we are not worried that one will come and squeeze out water absorbed in it.

....

Today's learning has been dedicated for the continued Hatzlacha and Bracha of Nofar Meshy bat Nourit.

15 It is forbidden to hang a wet towel specifically in order to dry it. However, it's *muttar* to hang it in its regular place even if it will dry there. However, it's forbidden to leave it on top of a heater or radiator.

°···°

16 It is *muttar* to use paper towels even though they may rip during usage. Similarly, it is *muttar* to use paper tissues.

Manicures and Cosmetics

17 It is forbidden for a woman to apply blush (red color) to her face on *Shabbat* because of the *issur* of *soveah*. Similarly, because of this reason it is also forbidden for a woman to apply mascara to her eyes. As well, it is forbidden to apply lipstick to redden her lips even if they were colored before *Shabbat*. It is also forbidden to use transparent lipstick.

°···°

18 It is *muttar meikar hadin* for a woman to apply powder (for makeup) to her face on *Shabbat*. Even if the powder is colored, there are grounds to be lenient because it's not permanent as long as the powder is not mixed with any ointment or cream. However, if her face had been smeared with ointment during the day, it is forbidden for her to apply powder even if it doesn't mix with the ointment because the powder will stick nicely to her face from the ointment.

Today's learning has been dedicated by Yosef Chaim Noorani, for the Hatzlacha and Bracha of the Noorani Family.

19 It is forbidden for a woman to smear ointment on her face or hands to refine her skin.

---

20 It is forbidden to apply nail polish to one's fingernails whether the polish is colored or transparent.

---

21 It is *muttar* to apply rose water or other fragrances on one's face or hands on *Shabbat*. Similarly, one may be lenient for his hair or beard. However, it is forbidden to apply a fragrance to one's clothing or *mitpachat*.

22 It is *muttar* to use an air-purifying spray. Similarly, it is *muttar* to use an aerosol can to spray good smelling aura on one's hands or face.

---

23 It is *muttar* to clean the dirt from the ends of one's nails. However, one should not pull off a part of the nail as a result of cleaning the nail.

---

24 Glasses whose lenses change color from the sun (photo-gray or progressive) and change back to normal when returning indoors are *muttar* to be worn on *Shabbat* and one need not worry about issues of *soveah*.

Today's learning has been dedicated by the Azizi Family, Leilui Nishmat Sarahy bat Nissan, may her Neshama have an Aliyah.

Chapter 26 — Washing Utensils and Cleaning the House and Table

1 It is *muttar* to wash eating utensils such as plates, knives or forks that became dirty for further *Shabbat* use like, for example, if he still has another *seudah* left to eat and he needs those utensils. However, one should not wash them after *seudah shelishit*. Drinking utensils such as cups may be cleaned all day long since they are fit to be used for drinking throughout the day, even when not in the middle of a *seudah*. However, if he knows that he will not use it for the rest of *Shabbat*, it is forbidden to wash it.

o···o

2 If after eating *seudah shelishit* he decided to eat another meal, it is proper to be *machmir* not to wash the utensils because there are opinions who hold that one may only wash utensils for three meals and not more. In any event, if one does not have any other utensils and he needs them for after *seudah shelishit*, there are grounds to be lenient to wash them.

o···o

3 The *hetter* to clean an eating utensil for further *Shabbat* use applies even to clean them on *leil Shabbat* for *yom Shabbat* or *seudah shelishit*. However, if one has an additional set of utensils, it is proper to be stringent and not wash the dirty dishes, rather use the clean ones, so that he does not do extra *tircha* on *Shabbat*. However, if one has very expensive dishes that he only uses on special occasions, it is considered as if he has no additional dishes and he may wash the dirty dishes.

Today's learning has been dedicated by the Youshei Family, for the continued Hatzlacha and Bracha of Shimon Youshei and family.

4 It is *muttar* to rinse with water those utensils which are dirty if one is worried about ants, flies or other insects, or also a silver utensil that may become damaged if one does not remove the food scraps from it even if one does not have the intention to use them anymore over the course of that *Shabbat*.

5 It is *muttar* to place dirty dishes into water on *Shabbat* if one is worried that the food residue will stick to the walls of the utensil, thereby making it hard to clean on *motza'e Shabbat*. This is because placing them in the water is merely preventing a change to the existing situation. However, if the residue has already stuck and dried to the walls of the utensil, it is forbidden to leave the utensil in water because doing so serves to make the cleaning easier after *Shabbat*.

6 It is forbidden to use steel wool or a sponge. Similarly, anything that is made of sponge material to clean kitchen utensils is forbidden to use on *Shabbat*. In addition, a natural or artificial *Lifa* (a fiber used to clean utensils) is also forbidden. However, it is *muttar* to use a *Lifa* made from synthetic material which does not absorb anything if the bristles of the *Lifa* are separated from each other and don't condense.

7 It is *muttar* to clean a baby bottle with a brush made of synthetic bristles that are not packed close to each other.

Today's learning has been dedicated by Mr. and Mrs. Yosef Mehdizadeh, Leilui Nishmat Nouranieh bat Dovid, may her Neshama have an Aliyah.

8 It is *muttar* to separate knives, spoons, and forks which became mixed together to their proper places so that one may use them for the following meal. They are not considered a mixture of *pesolet* and *ochel* because one wants them all equally.

○..○

9 It is forbidden to unclog a sink full of water with a plunger on *Shabbat*. However, if it isn't fully clogged (water is draining slowly) and plunging it will allow it to drain normally, it is *muttar* to do so with a household plunger which doesn't require a professional. Similarly, it is *muttar* to pour hot water into a clogged sink so that the fats blocking the drain will melt, thereby allowing the water to drain in a normal fashion.

○..○

10 A garbage can which contains refuse unfit for animal consumption is forbidden to move at all on *Shabbat*. However, if the garbage becomes full and there is no other place for one to throw out one's trash, it is *muttar* to move it and empty it into the dumpster. As well, if there is an unbearable stench in the garbage then even when the garbage is not yet full it is *muttar* to empty it into the dumpster and bring the can back into his home. However, if the garbage can is made of clay, then it is forbidden to bring it back into the house if one lets go of the can unless he puts water inside.

○━━━━━━━━━━━━━━━━━━━○

Today's learning has been dedicated by Mr. and Mrs. Meir Hakimi, Leilui Nishmat Tooran bat Rachamim, may her neshama have an Aliyah.

Cleaning the Floor and the Carpeting

∾�∾
• Day 189 •
∾�∾

∾�∾
• יב' אדר •
∾�∾

11 It is forbidden on *Shabbat* to sweep an unsurfaced floor with a broom because he might come to fill holes. However, if the floor is surfaced, it is *muttar* to sweep the floor. According to Ashkenazim, it was even forbidden to sweep a paved floor if the other houses were not surfaced. A *gezeira* was therefore also made for paved floors because of the unsurfaced floors. However, nowadays where all floors are surfaced, it is permitted even for Ashkenazim to sweep the floors with a soft broom.

12 One should not clean carpets with a broom or instrument that is made for cleaning carpets, even if the instrument does not work with electricity. In any event, it is *muttar* to sweep the carpets with a soft broom and collect the refuse that is on it.

13 It is forbidden to wash floors, even if they are surfaced, whether one is using a cloth or the back of a squeegee. If a lot of water spills in a particular surfaced area, it is *muttar* to draw the water with a squeegee. However, one may not absorb the water with a cloth even if it's specifically used to clean the floors, lest one come to soak the cloth with water. If a small amount of water spilled, it is *muttar* to absorb the water with a cloth made specifically to clean floors. However, one should be careful not to soak the cloth.

Today's learning has been dedicated by Yehuda Gabaie, Leilui Nishmat Meir ben Akhai, may his Neshama have an Aliyah.

14 It is *muttar* to sprinkle (not wash) water on the floor of the house, since his intention is not to fill up holes but rather to prevent the dust from rising up. This *hetter* also applies to unsurfaced floors.

○..○

15 One cannot not remove cobwebs because of the *issur* of *muktzeh*. There is even an opinion that the *issur* of uprooting something which is connected applies here as well because the cobweb is connected to the house. Certainly, one cannot kill the spider itself. However, if the cobweb is not connected to the house but rather connected to utensils or furniture, it is *muttar* to remove the web through *tiltul min hatzad*, by using a broom handle and the like.

○..○

16 It is *muttar* to make one's bed on *Shabbat* if it sits in a place where people walk by. The reason for this is *kavod Shabbat* that his house will look neat. It is *muttar* to unfold a bed in order to lie on it on *Shabbat*. However, if one wants to unfold it in order to lie on it on *motza'e Shabbat*, it is forbidden to do so as this constitutes preparing for after *Shabbat* during *Shabbat*.

○..○

17 It is *muttar* to wipe a windowpane which is steamed over on *Shabbat* with a squeegee or a rag that is made specifically to clean steam or wipe utensils and the such.

Today's learning has been dedicated by the Khalili, Lavian, Ashorzadeh, Rahmanfar, Eshaghian and Shreiber families, Leilui Nishmat Rachamim ben Yonah. Yehi Ratson that the merit of this holy Sefer stand for us and our children, so that the Torah should not cease from us, and may our home be filled with all the Blessings of the Torah.

Cleaning the Table

18 It is *muttar* to remove utensils of a meal from the table on *Shabbat*, even after *seudah shelishit*, so that the room will look clean and neat or so that insects don't gather on it. However, it is forbidden to remove the utensils from the table in the final moments of *Shabbat* if he no longer needs to use that room that day. Similarly, even if it is in middle of the day and he decides to close the room and leave it until *motza'e Shabbat*, it is forbidden to clear that room.

○...○

19 If beer or any other beverage spills on one's tablecloth and he would like to remove it with a spoon or knife to clean the tablecloth, he should be careful not to press too hard lest he come to do *sechitah*.

Therefore, one should only remove the floating liquid that is above the tablecloth. If it is a colored drink, one must be careful not to color other space on the tablecloth when removing the liquid. If he spills water he must be extra careful about removing it because squeezing water is a *toldah* of *melaben*.

○...○

20 Liquids (water, wine, etc.) which spill only a little bit on a table are *muttar* to be wiped with a cloth made for this purpose, so long as one is careful not to squeeze any liquid from the cloth. However, if a large amount spilled it is forbidden to wipe it up because one might come to squeeze liquid from the cloth. However, it is *muttar* to remove the water with a squeegee.

Today's learning has been dedicated for the continued Hatzlacha and Bracha of Rabbi and Mrs. Mordechai Shoob and family.

∽৩ও
• Day 192 •
৩ও∽

∽৩ও
• טו' אדר •
৩ও∽

THIS CHAG'S LEARNING HAS BEEN DEDICATED
by Rodney and Hilda Javidnia, to see much Nachat from their children.

21 It is *muttar* to put a bit of water on a clean cloth made specifically to clean tables, and clean the table in a light fashion. However, if the cloth has food stuck to it, it is forbidden to add any water to it.

∘⋯⋯⋯⋯⋯⋯⋯⋯⋯⋯⋯⋯⋯⋯∘

22 It is *muttar* to moisten a piece of paper with water to clean a table and the like. There are no issues of *melaben* or *sechitah* with this.

∘⋯⋯⋯⋯⋯⋯⋯⋯⋯⋯⋯⋯⋯⋯∘

23 It is forbidden to polish a silver or copper utensil on *Shabbat*. Not only is a regular cloth dipped in a cleaning solvent forbidden, but also one may not wipe it even with the cloth specifically made for shining (even without any solvent) because polishing is forbidden. However, it is *muttar* wipe a glass utensil well, even to the extent that it shines.

○○○

∘⋯⋯⋯⋯⋯⋯⋯⋯⋯⋯⋯⋯⋯⋯⋯⋯⋯⋯⋯⋯∘

○○○

Chapter 27	Cleaning Clothing and Folding on Shabbat

1 One who shakes off dew from a new black garment is *chayav* because this shaking is as good as washing it. This applies if he is particular to wear it only with shaking it out. Additionally, this *din* is specifically where the garment is both new and black and that he will only wear the garment if it was shaken off. However, if any of these conditions are not met, it is *muttar*. There are those that say since we don't really know the *halachic* definition of a "new garment" one should be careful in any situation, whether it looks new or not.

2 It is forbidden to shake out a new garment, which one is *makpid* on, if it was soaked in water or rained on, regardless of its color. However, one is allowed to shake out an old garment. Still, one must be careful not to do it so strongly lest he come to transgress *sechitah*.

3 It is permitted *me'ikar hadin* to shake the dust off of a garment even if it has all three conditions (new, black, and he is *makpid* to wear it without shaking). If one is *machmir* in this matter, *beracha* will come upon him. Our Ashkenazi brethren are stringent in this matter. In any event, it is *muttar* according to everyone to gently wipe the dust off with his hand or a dry rag.

⊙⊙⊙

Today's learning has been dedicated by Yehuda Gabaie, Leilui Nishmat Refael Mordechai ben Meir Moshe, may his Neshama have an Aliyah.

4 It is *muttar* to rub off mud which fell on his clothing, even if the mud is dry and crumbles and grinds up into thin dust. This is *muttar* only when one does not rub the clothing from outside, which looks like *melaben*, but rather from the inside (where he holds the garment from the inside and rubs the mud until it falls off).

5 An iron which is placed outside of the entrance to one's house to wipe his shoes off on is forbidden to be used on *Shabbat* if he wipes with strength. However, to wipe gently is *muttar*, especially if the mud is moist. It is also *muttar* to wipe one's shoes off onto a wall or the steps of a ladder.

6 A leather shoe or any other leather utensil, or clothing made from synthetic fibers such as nylon, are *muttar* to rinse in water to clean them. This is only when one does not wash them, meaning that one does not rub their sides on one another. However, if the shoes are made from rubber it is *muttar* to rub them because rubber does not absorb at all and there is no *chashash* of *kiboos*. [This is the same as by a wooden utensil where there is no *chashash* of washing.]

Today's learning has been dedicated by Yishai Natan, Leilui Nishmat Kafi bat David, may her Neshama have an Aliyah.

7 It is forbidden to shine one's shoes with a brush or a cloth even without polish. However, to remove dust with one's hand or with a cloth is *muttar* only when one does so gently in a way that he does not shine them.

8 It is *muttar* to remove feathers from one's clothing on *Shabbat*, even if the garment is new and one is *makpid* not to wear it with the feathers on it. Additionally, it is *muttar* to remove them with a brush. However, *beracha* will come to one who is *machmir* to use only his hands instead of a brush.

9 It is *muttar* to change and put a case on a pillow or a quilt, even if it is not for *tzorech mitzvah* but rather for personal want, for example, if he forgot to do it before *Shabbat* or he saw a cleaner one on *Shabbat* that he would like to change it to.

Today's learning has been dedicated by the Ebriani Family, Leilui Nishmat Rebi Shimon ben Avraham, may his Neshama have an Aliyah.

Folding Clothing

10 One may not fold a garment or tablecloth or the like in the same manner it was previously folded. Rather, one must follow the following five conditions when folding it on *Shabbat*:

1) One will use that garment later on *Shabbat*.
2) The garment is new and has not been laundered yet.
3) The garment is white, not colored.
4) He has no other garment to wear or use on *Shabbat*.
5) He must fold it by himself without another person's help.

In any case, it is always *muttar* to fold it in a different way than it was previously folded.

○·····················○

11 It is *muttar* to fold one's *talit* on *Shabbat* differently than the prior folding, even if he will not use it for the rest of *Shabbat*. However, one should not protest against those who fold their *talit* the same way as beforehand because they have what to rely on.

○·····················○

12 It is *muttar* to fix a dent in a hat which became bent out of shape. Similarly, it is *muttar* to fix the collar of a jacket and the cuff of one's pants.

Today's learning has been dedicated by Shimon Ommatyar, for the continued Hatzlacha and Bracha of the Ommatyar family.

Chapter 28 Hanging Laundry on Shabbat

1 It is forbidden to hang wet laundry on a rope on *Shabbat* in order to dry because we are worried others will suspect him of laundering on *Shabbat*. It is even forbidden to spread them out in *chadrei chadarim* (totally private rooms) because everything which the *chachamim* made forbidden due to *ma'arit ayin* is forbidden even in *chadrei chadarim*.

2 If one went ahead and hanged clothing on *Shabbat be'Isur*, we don't make him take it down from the rope.

3 A garment which is wet from water or sweat, even if only a little bit, is forbidden to be hung or spread out in a way that is clearly for the sake of drying it. However, it is *muttar* to hang it over a chair in a way that is not discernibly for the sake of drying it. This applies only where one does not hang it close to a source of fire which is *yad soledet bo*.

Today's learning has been dedicated by the Samimi Family, Leilui Nishmat my dear grandfather, Atta ben Elazar, may his Neshama have an Aliyah.

4 It is *muttar* to hang or spread out a wet raincoat on *Shabbat* in order to dry it (provided that it is not hanged next to a source of fire which is *yad soledet bo*). This is because everyone knows that it became wet from the rain and will not suspect him of laundering it on *Shabbat*.

○‥‥‥‥‥‥‥‥‥‥‥‥‥‥‥○

5 It is *muttar* to hang dirty diapers so that they may dry, even if they are only dirty from urine, provided that he would like to use them again that day. This is so long as one does not spread them out next to an oven which is *yad soledet bo*.

○‥‥‥‥‥‥‥‥‥‥‥‥‥‥‥○

6 It is *muttar* to spread out hand towels that became dirty as a result of many people wiping with them as long as some of the dirtiness is noticeable. The *din* by a *mitpachat* is the same - it is *muttar* to spread it out if some of the dirtiness is noticeable.

○━━━━━━━━━━⟨ ⟩━━━━━━━━━━○
Today's learning has been dedicated for the continued Hatzlacha and Bracha of Chaya Mushka bat Ariella.

Taking Down the Laundry from the Rope

7 Laundry, as well as cloth diapers or any other children's clothing, which were laundered before *Shabbat* are *muttar* to be taken off the drying line and used on *Shabbat* after they have dried. This is even when they were still wet during *bein hashemashot* to the extent of *topheach al menat lehatphiac*. (In other words, if you touch the item to your hand, you can then make another object wet by touching the other object to your hand.) They do not have the status of *muktzeh*.

8 Laundry clips have the *din* of *kli shemelachto le'issur*, and it is *muttar* to move them for *tzorech goofam* (to use them in a non-*issur* fashion) as well as *tzorech mekomam* (i.e. to take down the laundry hanging from them on *Shabbat*).

9 When rain falls on *Shabbat*, there is a *hetter* to take down the laundered clothing from the line so that the clothes will not get soaked from the rain, even if one will not use them on *Shabbat*.

Today's learning has been dedicated for the continued Hatzlacha and Bracha of Ramon Yehuda ben Sabriye Moaloud.

| Chapter 29 | Tying and Untying Clothing on *Shabbat* |

1 One is *chayav* for tying a *kesher shel kayama* knot that is also used in *ma'aseh uman* (craftsman) fashion (i.e. a knot meant for a camel or a knot meant for a boat). However, tying a *kesher shel kayama* knot that is not of *ma'aseh uman* fashion (i.e. he ties a rope to a bucket or ties a restraint over the mouth of an animal), is only forbidden *miderabanan* because it is a regular person's knot. Similarly, tying a *ma'aseh uman* knot that is not a *kesher shel kayama* is only forbidden *miderabanan*.

2 A knot which is neither a *kesher shel kayama* nor a *ma'aseh uman* is *muttar le'chatechilah* to be tied on *Shabbat*. All knots which are *muttar* to tie are also *muttar* to untie.

3 Some say that any knot which is not meant to be undone on that day itself is considered a *kesher shel kayama* and forbidden to tie on *Shabbat*. Some disagree and reason that any knot which would not stay tied for seven days is not considered a *kesher shel kayama* and is therefore *muttar* to tie on *Shabbat*. The *halacha* is to be lenient in accordance with the latter opinion. Therefore, it is *muttar* to tie any knot which will not last for seven days because we do not consider it a *kesher shel kayama*.

Today's learning has been dedicated for the continued Hatzlacha and Bracha of David Listhaus and family.

4 Some say that one must be careful not to tie a double knot on *Shabbat*, even if he is not doing so for it to last. The reason for this is because we are not experts to know what is considered a *ma'aseh uman* and therefore take precaution that maybe a double knot constitutes *ma'aseh uman*. Some object this and permit double-knotting if one does not have the intention that it should last. The *minhag* is to be lenient and permit this, however blessing will come upon one who is stringent about this. In addition, in a case of necessity one should not be stringent. It is proper to be careful not to come to double knot a single knot which was tied before *Shabbat* in order to strengthen it.

5 Any knot that one sometimes decides to end up keeping indefinitely is considered a *kesher shel kayama* and is forbidden to tie on *Shabbat* even if he didn't intend to do this when he tied it. However, a knot that one does not leave indefinitely, rather only for a specific time frame, may be tied on *Shabbat* if it was clearly his intention to undo it on *motza'e Shabbat*.

○..○

6 Any knot which is forbidden to tie on *Shabbat* is also forbidden to tighten if it became loose (e.g. a double knot in which the top knot became undone). Therefore, one must be careful not to tighten the loose knots on his *tzizit*.

Today's learning has been dedicated by Chaim Daniel and Tiferet Rochel Samimi, in honor of their Wedding Anniversary.

7 It is *muttar* to tie a necktie, even with intent to leave it indefinitely. Yet it is good to be *machmir* and avoid knotting the tie in a fashion that will last for seven days. However, to loop the tie without a knot or to tie one knot without a loop is *muttar*, even with the intention to leave it indefinitely.

8 If one tied his shoelaces on *erev Shabbat* with a loop and knot, and without intent double-knotted it, he is allowed to unknot it on *leil Shabbat*. If he is unable to untie it, it is *muttar* to cut the shoe laces and switch them. One should not do this in front of an *am ha'aretz*, lest he come to be more lenient on himself.

9 It is *muttar* for a woman to tie her *mitpachat* (head scarf) on *Shabbat* with the same double knot as she does during the week. However, *beracha* will come upon one who is stringent and only ties it with a loop and knot.

10 It is *muttar* to tie a decorative bow on *Shabbat*. It is not considered a *kesher* because it is pulled together lightly. As well, one may untie such a bow on *Shabbat*.

Today's learning has been dedicated for the continued Hatzlacha and Bracha of Tzivie Rosen and family.

෨෪ஂ
• Day 203 •
৩৩৸

෨෪ஂ
• כו' אדר •
৩৩৸

11 Some have the *minhag* to give bags of candy to the *tzibur* and children when there is a *simchat mitzvah* in the *bet hakenesset*. If these bags were double-knotted, there is room to be lenient and permit the use of these bags on *Shabbat*. In any event, one should not *lechatechilhah* tie the bags like this, but rather one should tighten them with rubber bands.

○························○

12 One may not tie a knot on *Shabbat* (even a single knot) with the margins of a nylon bag in similar fashion to the knots made on the edges of *tzizit* strings, even if the knot is made with the bag itself and not with a string. As well, one may not untie such a bag. If there is a necessity to open the bag to take out food from inside it, one must tear the bag open, thereby ruining it, to take out the food. In any event, one may make a loose knot and if by accident it was pulled tight, it is *muttar* to open it.

○························○

13 One who is honored with *gelilat sefer Torah* (i.e. our Ashkenazi brethren who tie a belt around the *Torah*) during *minchah* on *Shabbat*, is *muttar* to tie the *sefer Torah* belt with a loop and knot. (This is despite the fact that it will not be undone until Monday morning). However, if he sees that the belt is long and he is able to tie the *sefer Torah* with just one strong knot and tuck in the rest, then it is best to do so. This is only if he is positive that the knot will not become weak, and, heaven forbid, cause damage or *bizayon* to the *sefer Torah*.

○ ○ ○

Today's learning has been dedicated for the continued Hatzlacha and Bracha, Torah, Mitzvot, Ma'asim Tovim and good health for the donor and all of the generations.

14 New clothing which are tied together, like socks or gloves, should be detached from one another before *Shabbat*. However, if one forgot to do so, he is allowed to sever the string in a *derech kilkul* fashion. (However, it should not be done in front of an *am ha'aretz.*)

15 It is *muttar* to remove the pins that were placed in the garment by the factory to hold its folds.

16 It is *muttar lechtechilah* to pull a shoelace through an old shoe on *Shabbat*. However, it is forbidden to pull shoelaces through a new shoe that never had shoelaces in them.

17 Clothing made of synthetic material are *muttar* to be put on to wear and to take off even though it seems to cause sparks to fly out. One does not have to worry about the *issur* of *havarah...*

Today's learning has been dedicated Leilui Nishmat Daniel ben Karim Yechezkel, may his Neshama have an Aliyah.

Chapter 30	Sewing and Tearing on Shabbat

1 One who sews two stitches, i.e. he enters the needle with the string and pulls it through twice, on *Shabbat* is *chayav*. This is when one ties the head of the string from one place to another so that the stich will last and not open up. One is *chayav* if he sews more than two stitches even if he did not tie it because the stitches will last.

2 It is forbidden to pull a string in order to tighten a loose stitch. Some say that it is also forbidden pull a string attached a to loose button.

3 The cord threaded into the brim of a rain coat hood is *muttar* to pull or loosen on *Shabbat*. Even though pulling it causes the hood to shrink and tightens around one's head and loosening it undoes this, it is still *muttar* because there is no *tefirah* or sewing that will last since he will end up taking it off anyways. There is also no issue of comparison to sewing since there is a special hole in the brim of the hood for the cord.

Today's learning has been dedicated for the continued Hatzlacha and Bracha of Mordechai and Taly Aryeh and children Gavriel and Ovadia.

4 It is forbidden to remove a button from an article of clothing, even if the string that attaches it is loose. Similarly, it is forbidden to remove the threads left over after a button is lost.

5 It is *muttar* to insert a safety pin into clothing for any necessary reason. For example, to hold together an article of clothing in a place where a button fell, or to hold together a tear in the clothing. *Meikar hadin*, it is even *muttar* to insert it into the clothing three times. However, *beracha* will come upon one who is *machmir* and only inserts it into the clothing twice.

6 It is forbidden to put new feathers into a cushion or quilt. However, feathers which fell out from the cushion or quilt may be placed back in but must be careful not to sew. One must also be careful not to stuff clothing into a casing in order for it to become like a pillow for one to sleep on.

Today's learning has been dedicated for all of us to have the merit to bring Mashiach and the Geulah speedily in our days, Amen!

THIS MONTH'S LEARNING HAS BEEN DEDICATED BY
Mr. and Mrs. Chezky and Yaffi Klein, Leilui Nishmat Binyamin
Tzvi ben Avraham Refael and Esther Fayga bat Menachem
Mendel, may their Neshamot have an Aliyah.

Tearing Paper

7 We do not tear paper because it is tantamount to *metaken kli*. If one is *makpid* to cut it to a specific size, he is also *chayav* over the *melacha* of tearing.

8 It is forbidden to tear toilet paper for the purpose of wiping. However, in a scenario of great necessity with no other recourse, for example where one to forgot to tear it before *Shabbat* or ran out of them, it is permissible to tear some in an abnormal fashion. An example of this is tearing it with one's foot or elbow. One should make sure not to tear the pieces into specific sizes. (Tearing with one's off-hand is not enough of change because the off-hand is only considered a *shinuy* or change regarding the *melacha* of writing). One must attempt to tear the toilet paper anywhere but the perforations in order to avoid the *issur* of tearing.

9 Gluing papers or leathers constitutes a *toldah* of sewing for which one would be *chayav*. Similarly, one who tears apart papers or pieces of leather that are glued without the sole intention to destroy them is *chayav* for a *toldah* of tearing. Therefore, one should be careful to separate the pages of a new book before *Shabbat* if he knows he will need the book on *Shabbat*. If the pages of the book are stuck together by wax or the like, it is *muttar* to open them because the wax wasn't placed to stay there permanently and therefore is not similar to sewing nor is opening the book similar to tearing. It is forbidden on *Shabbat* to cut the extra pages of a new book which were not trimmed to size by the machine.

10 It is *muttar* to use disposable diapers on *Shabbat*, but one must be careful to separate the elastic slowly from what it sticks to so that the diaper does not rip when one separates it. Even if one tore the diaper while separating it, this falls into the category of *davar she'eno mitkaven* and is *muttar*. There are grounds to permit one to open a package of diapers on *Shabbat*, but it is preferable for one to do so before *Shabbat*. One should be stringent from using diapers on *Shabbat* which one must tear open to use, and will otherwise stay closed forever.

11 It is *muttar* to clean a baby with a damp wipe, however it is forbidden to tear it from the roll of wipes. Rather, one must separate them before *Shabbat* and place them in a bag or a closed box to prevent them from drying out. When wiping the baby, one should do so lightly in a way that will not squeeze out liquid.

12 It is *muttar* to tear open paper or nylon bags that have food inside provided that he does not reuse the bag for something else.

Today's learning has been dedicated by the Author, in honor of my dear Rebbi, HaRav Eliyahu Ha'Kohen Hakakian, for the Rav's continued Hatzlacha and Bracha in being Mezakeh the Rabbim.

1 It is forbidden to pluck or cut one's hair or nails on *Shabbat*, whether for himself or for someone else, whether by hand or with a utensil, and even when done through a *shinuy*. It is forbidden from the *Torah* to take out one single hair, and one is *chayav* a *chatat* for removing two or more. One is always *chayav* a *chatat* for plucking a white hair from among black hairs, even during the week, because of the *issur* of "Lo Yilbash Gever Simlat Isha".

2 It is forbidden to cut off a callus, whether by hand or with a utensil and even for someone else. Similarly, it is forbidden to remove a piece of skin hanging off one's hand or another part of the body.

3 If one has a nail which is mostly detached and is causing him much pain, he may remove it by hand or through a *shinuy*. However, it is forbidden to cut the nail with a nail clipper or a knife and the like.

4 The strip of skin surrounding the nail is also forbidden to be removed on *Shabbat*, even by hand or through a *shinuy*. It is still forbidden even if most of the skin is off the finger and it hurts.

Today's learning has been dedicated by Rabbi and Mrs. Meilech Nussbaum, in honor of their dear children, Shmulie and Dovid.

∾✿∿
• Day 210 •
∾✿∿

∾✿∿
• ד' ניסן •
∾✿∿

Hairstyling

5 It is prohibited to brush on one's hair with a comb on *Shabbat*, even if it has soft bristles, because it will inevitably remove hair. However, it is permissible to fix some of one's hair with a utensil (i.e. a brush) made with soft bristles.

Nevertheless, it is forbidden with a normal brush. We are accustomed to set aside a special brush just for *Shabbat* so that it will not look as though it is *uvda d'chol*. One may also fix his hair with his hands.

○···○

6 It is *muttar* for one to comb a toupee (with a brush made specifically for combing a wig) that is made of synthetic hair since the hair is woven tight enough to the scalp of the wig that when it is brushed, no hair will be pulled out. We are stringent when it comes to brushing a wig made of natural hair, since it seems that the hairs do get pulled out. If the wig is not fit to be worn without it being brushed first, it is forbidden to brush it since it is like being *metaken kli.*

○···○

7 It is forbidden for a woman to use hair spray on *Shabbat* in order to hold her hairdo. This is because making the hair stick together with the spray is equivalent to *binyan.*

○────────∾✿∿────────○
Today's learning has been dedicated by the Author, in honor of a dear community Rav, HaRav Reuben Arieh, for the Rav's continued Hatzlacha and Bracha in being Mezakeh the Rabbim.

8 It is forbidden for a woman to braid her hair on *Shabbat*. As well, it is forbidden for one to undo a preexisting braid. These things are equivalent to *boneh* and *soter*. It is forbidden to braid a wig on *Shabbat* because of weaving and it is forbidden to unravel it because of *botze'a*.

9 It is *muttar* to gather one's hair and fix it into the desired position with one's hand or to tie it with a ribbon or bow.

10 One should not curl one's hair or use curling cylinders. Similarly, one should not curl a child's hair because there is no difference between man or woman regarding this prohibition.

11 It is befitting that one shouldn't twirl and unravel his *peyot* on *Shabbat* because this is equivalent to *boneh* and *soter*. There is also a *chashash* that he may pull out some of the hairs. If the *peyot* are wet, for instance if one came out of the *mikveh*, there is an issue of *sechitah*.

Today's learning has been dedicated by Dara and Chana Abaei, for the continued Hatzlacha and Bracha of the Abaei family, as well as all of Klal Yisrael.

12 One should be careful not to scratch one's beard too much because hair might fall out. Similarly, women who have a lot of hair should not scratch their heads too much with their nails because this will inevitably pull out hair. Nevertheless, one can gently scratch hair on his head and need not worry that hair will be pulled out. It is even *muttar* to remove food stuck in one's beard, as long as one is careful not to pull out any hairs.

13 It is proper to be careful to wipe the dried mucus from one's nose gently, so that he does not pull out any hairs. Even though *meikar hadin* there is no *issur*, *beracha* will come upon one who is careful about this matter.

○..○

14 If one has cooked chicken with small feathers still attached to the skin that were not plucked before it was cooked, it is *muttar* to remove them when he eats them.

Today's learning has been dedicated by the Author, for continued Hatzlacha and Bracha of a dear friend and mentor who aided me in completing this Sefer, Dara Abaei.

15 It is *muttar* to walk on top of grass, whether dry or wet, on *Shabbat* even though one pulls out the grass as a result of his footsteps. This is because his intentions are not to uproot the grass and he has no need to uproot it. If the grass is tall, one should walk slowly instead of quickly, and surely should not run there, because otherwise he will definitely rip out the grass.

16 If, after one walks over the grass, he finds some stuck to his feet or shoes, it is forbidden to remove them with his hands because they are *muktza*.

17 It is *muttar* to sit or lie down on grass. Similarly, it is *muttar* to lay out a blanket or mat on top of the grass and sit on top of it. It is also *muttar* to shake the attached grass back and forth, so long as he is careful not to uproot it.

Today's learning has been dedicated by the Author, for the continued Hatzlacha and Bracha of R' Yechiel Schreck and family.

∾ఌఄఄ
• Day 214 •
ౚఄఄ

∾ఌఄఄ
• ח' ניסן •
ౚఄఄ

| Chapter 32 | Writing and Erasing on Shabbat |

1 One who writes two letters is *chayav*. One who erases in order to write two letters in the place that was erased is also *chayav*. Even writing less than two letters is forbidden, but the *chiyuv* of *chatat* is only for two letters.

○···○

2 When ink spills on top of letters or wax drips on the letters, one must be careful not to clean the smudge. If one does clean the smudge, he is basically erasing in order to write again and is *chayav* because by doing so the letters become evident.

○···○

3 If wax is found on top of the letters in the *sefer Torah* on *Shabbat*, if the letter can be seen through the wax, there are reasons to *kasher* the *sefer Torah* and to continue the reading. However, if the letter is totally covered, one should take out another *sefer Torah* to finish the reading from.

Today's learning has been dedicated by the Author, for the continued Hatzlacha and Bracha of R' Zecharia Reisch and family.

4 On *Shabbat*, it is *muttar* to open and close a book that has letters or drawings on the edges of the pages. However, it is proper to be stringent in this matter and use a different book if possible. It is certainly better *lechatchilah* not to write any letters or words on the edges of the papers.

5 If a page of a book was torn, but not in the place of the letters (or even if it was torn in the place of the letters, but he doesn't have any other book like this one) there is reason to be lenient to connect the torn sections together in order to continue reading.

However, it is forbidden to tape them together.

6 It is *muttar* to cut a cake, biscuit or chocolate in order to eat, even though it is decorated with characters, provided that the decoration was baked into the actual food item. This applies both when the characters are flush in the item and even when they are sticking out, and certainly if they are written in script and not *ktav ashuri*. However, if the characters were made with food coloring or icing, it is proper to be *machmir* and only break it by biting into the item. In any event, even the one who is lenient in this aspect has what to rely on.

Today's learning has been dedicated for the continued Hatzlacha and Bracha of my dear sister, Elianna bat Rivka Chaya.

7 It is *muttar* on *Shabbat* to use a film-strip thermometer, in which different symbols appear, if the sick person has a temperature, and disappears when removed from the mouth. There is no issue of writing or erasing (although it is preferable to use a regular thermometer because of *marit ayin*.) However, it is definitively forbidden to use a digital thermometer as is using anything else electronic on *Shabbat*.

8 It is not forbidden to wear shoes which have soles with ingrained symbols or letters, even though when one walks with them on dirt, clay, or snow the letters become engraved into the ground. This is not considered writing and one may wear them on *Shabbat*.

9 One may be lenient in using a piece of paper in which foreign (non-Hebrew) lettering of mundane topics was written to wipe off something else. One need not worry about the *issur* of erasing.

Today's learning has been dedicated by Avraham Enock, Leilui Nishmat Dovid Mendel ben Efraim, may his Neshama have an Aliyah.

Different Writings

10 One should be careful not to write on a table with liquid on his fingertips. (i.e. to dip his finger in liquid and write on the tabletop.) Similarly, it is forbidden to write any letters or illustrations on a glass window which has fog on it.

11 It is *muttar* to draw letters in the air to show a friend something. Similarly, it is *muttar* to move his fingers on a dry table to illustrate a symbol, because his illustration is not noticeable at all.

12 Typing on a keyboard on *Shabbat* is a violation of the *issur deorayta* of writing, since typeset is considered full-fledged writing. Similarly, stamping a seal is full violation of this *issur* from the *Torah*.

13 On *Shabbat*, one who writes on one piece of paper and lying beneath is another paper which the writing goes onto as well, some opinions hold he is also *chayav min haTorah* for the second copy because he is also writing on it. However, some are of the opinion that he is only *chayav meDerabanan* because it is only a *gramma*.

Today's learning has been dedicated by the Author, for the continued Hatzlacha and Bracha of my dear wife, Chagit Sara bat Elana, without whom, I would not be where I am today.

∾९ঌ৵
• Day 218 •
ৎৡ৵

∾९ঌ৵
• יב' ניסן •
ৎৡ৵

14 Fingerprinting, in which one sticks his fingers in ink and imprints it on a piece of paper, is forbidden because of writing.

15 It is *muttar* to scratch a slash (but not a symbol) with one's nail onto a piece of *klaf*. In any event, since there are some who say it is forbidden it is best to refrain from doing so. Moreover, to scratch with one's nail onto a piece of paper is forbidden according to all opinions, due to the fact that paper is soft and the marking would last.

16 It is *muttar* to fold a page in a book in order to keep the place, even though by doing this one creates a lasting fold that will be recognized. In any event, it is better to refrain from doing even during the week, because by doing this one slightly ruins the *sefer*, which is not *kavod* to the *sefer*. It is better for one to use a bookmark rather than fold the edges of the *sefer*.

Today's learning has been dedicated by the Author, in honor of a dear Rav, HaRav Michoel Ha'Kohen Shaliasaboo, for the Rav's continued Hatzlacha and Bracha in being Mezakeh the Rabbim.

Chapter 33 — Building, Destroying and Makeh Bepatesh

1 One who hammers one piece of wood onto another, whether with a nail or by hitting them together until they conjoin, has violated a *tolda* of *boneh*.

2 If one of the legs of a bench detached it is forbidden to put it back in place. It is even forbidden to put the leg back in flimsy fashion, lest one reattach it with a nail in order to strengthen it. It is also forbidden to rest the broken end of the bench on another bench and sit on it, lest one come and fix the leg.

However, if one sat on it one time before Shabbos, it is ok.

3 It is forbidden to fix a window shutter that broke or came off its track. It is forbidden to move, and even open or close the cover of the box that houses the shutter.

4 If a child pulls out a drawer of a cabinet which is attached to the ground, it is *muttar* to return the drawer to it's place on *Shabbat* as there is no *chashash* of an *issur* of *boneh*.

Today's learning has been dedicated for the continuous Hatzlacha of Machon Tiferes Lakewood.

5 It is forbidden to remove a door or window from its frame. If they fell out, they are forbidden to replace on *Shabbat* and even forbidden to move.

───────────────

6 It is *muttar* to remove and return a peg to its socket that connects the two parts of the window to keep them closed, in order to open and close the window. There is no *chashash* of violating *ohel* or *soter*, since the peg was made to be used in this very way and was used before *Shabbat* already.

───────────────

7 It is forbidden to stick in a nail or thumbtack on *Shabbat* (this is not comparable to the previous section regarding a peg). Similarly, it is forbidden to stick in a hook or a rack made of rubber or plastic material and to use the sticky material found in the middle of the rack. It is also forbidden to remove them from their place. However, it is *muttar* to hang up a picture on a nail that was already in the wall before *Shabbat*.

───────────────

8 It is *muttar* to clear the ground of fragments of a shattered window in order to prevent injury. However, one should clear it with a broom or the like and not by hand because of the *issur* of *muktzeh*. If more glass is still left in the windowpane, it is forbidden to remove because of the *issur* of *soter*. If there is a *chashash* that it might scratch a person, it is *muttar* to have a Non-Jew remove the fragments. If none can be located, it is *muttar* to for a Jew to remove the fragments in an indirect fashion, such as with one's foot.

Today's learning has been dedicated by Jonathan and Leora Kohanoff Family, in honor of Rabbi Alex Landa and Family, for his amazing dedication and inspiration to Am Yisrael.

THIS CHAG'S LEARNING HAS BEEN DEDICATED BY
Dr. and Mrs. Avraham Radparvar, for the continued
Hatzlacha and Bracha of the Radparvar Family.

9 One may adjust the height of a *shtender* on *Shabbat* (vis-à-vis loosening and tightening the bolts) so long as it is normally adjusted.

10 It is *muttar* to take out the *sefer Torah* from its case on *Shabbat* to roll it from one *parshah* to another, and one may also return it to the case afterwards.

11 One may put a lens back into the glasses frame on *Shabbat* if a regular person can accomplish this (it wouldn't require a professional). One may only do this if it can be pushed back into place, but not by screwing it into place.

12 If a spring axis used to hold up a roll of toilet paper came out of its place, it is forbidden to return it back to its place on *Shabbat*.

13 It is forbidden both to apply and remove rubber pads from the legs of a chair or table (which reduce the sound made when the object is moved) on *Shabbat*.

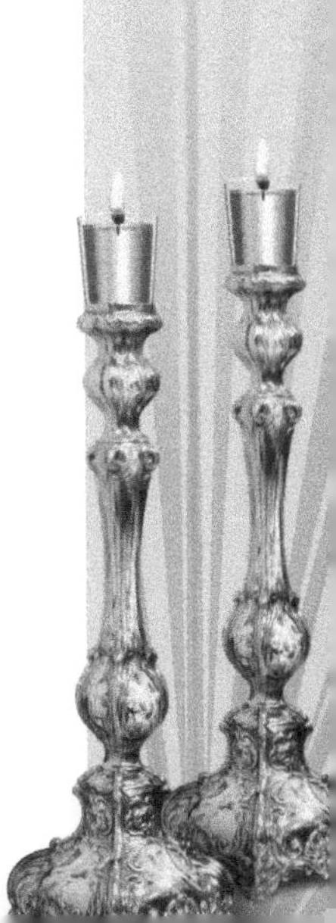

ooo

ooo

14 One may not transform a stroller into a different position if it entails screwing the pieces together. However, if it consists of just clicking the pieces together, then it is permitted.

○..○

15 It is forbidden to fix any damage done to a carriage (such as a rubber hoop which diverted from the wheel, a wheel which fell, or a spring which fell out of place) on *Shabbat*. If the damage happened on *Shabbat* itself and he can easily fix it, then it's even forbidden to move it,

because he might come to fix it on that day.

○..○

16 It is *muttar* to make seltzer on *Shabbat* so long as the machine does not use electricity to carbonate the water.

○..○

17 It is forbidden on *Shabbat* to pour powdered pudding mix or powdered potato puree into water (or vice versa) and mix it because one is creating a thick mixture. The same *din* applies to powdered Jell-O mix.

Today's learning has been dedicated by Avraham Enock, Leilui Nishmat Meir ben Yisochor, may his Neshama have an Aliyah.

Freezing Water

18 It is *muttar* to place water into an ice tray and freeze them in the freezer, especially in the summer where the days are hot and there is *oneg Shabbat* to have ice.

19 It is permitted on *Shabbat* to use nylon bags that are made specifically to make ice. However, after filling it with water, when one ties the straps that are found in the mouth of the bag, one must be careful that he not double-knot the bag; rather, he should tie a loop knot or one knot in a place where he's able to. When he wants to take out the ice, it is *muttar min- hadin* to tear the bag and when he tears the bag he not be meticulous at all.

20 It is permitted to put food into the freezer so that it does not spoil. There is no *issur* of preparing from *Shabbat* to *chol*.

21 It is *muttar* to put ice cubes into a cup of water in order to drink cold water and there is no *issur* of *nolad*. Similarly, it is *muttar* for one to take a frozen bottle of water with him and then drink the cold water after it melts (due to the heat) as there is no problem of *nolad*.

22 It is *muttar* for one who wears dentures to apply the tightening paste into the palate. There is no *issur* of *boneh* or *lush*.

Today's learning has been dedicated Leilui Nishmat Menachem Asher Ha'Kohen Zakbach, may his Neshama have an Aliyah.

23 One may make a hole into a coconut in order to get the water out and there is no *issur* of *boneh*.

24 One may not put oil on the hinges of a creaking door since there is an *issur* of *tikun manah*.

Opening Boxes and Cans

25 It is *muttar* to open sealed cans of sardines on *Shabbat* for necessity (whether for one's self or for guests) but it is preferable to open them before *Shabbat*. It is better to open the can in a way that will make the container unable to be reused as a utensil. One can also open the cover only halfway in order to accomplish this. After opening it, one should put the sardines into another utensil and throw out the can.

26 *Le'chatechilah*, one should not open canned foods on *Shabbat*. In any event, if one hadn't yet opened them before *Shabbat* and he needs them (for himself or for a guest) he may rely on the lenient opinion and open them. The reason for this is because nowadays most people don't reuse the can for other items afterwards. However, even those who are lenient prefer that he only open half (or as little as possible) of the can. By doing this, the can will not be fit to be reused since it is likely that one can cut his hand when opened in this matter. [Regular cans are more *chamur* than sardines because no one reuses sardine cans.]

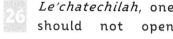

Today's learning has been dedicated by Rabbi and Mrs. Yaakov Yehuda Burstyn Leilui Nishmat HaRav Yirmiyahu Gedalya ben R' Avraham Abish, may his Neshama have an Aliyah.

27 It is *muttar* to open a soda can or a drink bag and there is no issue of the *issur* of making a utensil or destroying a utensil. There is also no *issur* of creating an opening or an *issur* of cutting. However, one must not drink from the can or bag itself and instead should pour the drink into a cup and drink from there. The reason for this is that by drinking from it straight, he has created a vessel by using it place of a cup.

cover. Although he may open it on *Shabbat*, it is good to open the bottle before *Shabbat* as a *midat chasidut*. When opening the bottle on *Shabbat*, it is preferable that one throws out the cover after he opens the bottle. [Similarly, it is *muttar* to tear the plastic that is attached around the cork of the bottle of wine.]

28 It is *muttar* to open up a bottle of grape juice that was tightly closed by a tin cap that goes around the bottle's spout, even though when one opens the bottle the cap separates from the lower ring of the

29 It is *muttar* to open up bags of on *Shabbat*. However, it is preferable to open them through a *shinuy*, in a different method than how one cuts it open during the week. In any event, it is better to open it on *erev Shabbat*.

Today's learning has been dedicated Leilui Nishmat Hanoch Slod, may his neshama have an Aliyah.

Chapter 34 — Making an Ohel and Mechitza

1 One who makes a permanent *ohel* on Shabbat is *chayav* for transgressing the *melachah* of *boneh*. Therefore, we do not *le'chatechilah* make even a temporary *ohel* nor do we even take down a temporary *ohel*, lest one come to make or take down a permanent *ohel*.

- -

2 It is forbidden to make an *ohel* on Shabbat, even if it is not meant to last. However, it is *muttar* to add onto a temporary *ohel*. Therefore, if a mat was spread out over the area of at least one *tefach*, it is *muttar* to spread out the rest of the mat on Shabbat, provided that the original *tefach* was not part of the binding. Therefore, if the mat was spread out as a roof before Shabbat, one must have at least one *tefach* already spread before Shabbat so that it would be *muttar* to spread further on Shabbat.

- -

3 On Shabbat, it is *muttar* to spread a sheet or mat over wood with the width of one *tefach* that was arranged before Shabbat, because this is viewed as adding to a temporary *ohel*. Similarly, if the width of the wood is not a *tefach*, but the wood is placed one next to the other in such a way that there is not more than three *tefachim* between each piece of wood, it is *muttar* to spread a sheet over them.

O O O

Today's learning has been dedicated Leilui Nishmat Shimon Matalon, may his Neshama have an Aliyah.

4 It is forbidden to spread a mesh net or mosquito net on top of a child's carriage, over one's bed, or over a playpen of a child, even for protection from the sun or bugs. However, if one spreads the netting at least one *tefach* (not including the cylinder) before *Shabbat*, it is *muttar* to spread the rest out on *Shabbat*. When one wants to roll it back, he should roll it back to the original *tefach* that was there when *Shabbat* started but not any less because that would constitute breaking the *ohel*.

⸰⸳⸳⸳⸳⸳⸳⸳⸳⸳⸳⸳⸳⸳⸳⸳⸳⸳⸳⸳⸳⸳⸳⸳⸳⸳⸳⸳⸳⸰

5 It is *muttar* to open the awning on a child's carriage if it is connected to the carriage from before *Shabbat*. If one connected the awning on *Shabbat*, even if he did it in a way that was *muttar*, he should not open the awning on *Shabbat*. Once one has established the *ohel* (of the awning) before

Shabbat, he may then add on the mesh or mosquito netting over the whole carriage. He should start spreading it from the awning down.

⸰⸳⸳⸳⸳⸳⸳⸳⸳⸳⸳⸳⸳⸳⸳⸳⸳⸳⸳⸳⸳⸳⸳⸳⸳⸳⸳⸳⸳⸳⸳⸳⸳⸳⸳⸰

6 There is reason to be lenient and allow opening and closing a small umbrella connected to a stroller, even though it is opened up like a regular umbrella, if it was already affixed to the stroller before *Shabbat* (just like it is *muttar* in opening up the awning on the child's carriage).
However, there are opinions that hold one should not open or close the stroller umbrella on *Shabbat*, just like one may not open or close any umbrella on *Shabbat*.

○○○

Today's learning has been dedicated by Jonathan and Leora Kohanoff Family, in honor of Rabbi Cavalier and Family, for his special way with the community and the inspiration to Klal Yisrael.

∾৩৩∾
• Day 228 •
৩৩৩

∾৩৩∾
• כב' ניסן •
৩৩৩

7 A collapsible lounge chair, which folds over in the center when one wants to carry it and spreads open from the middle when one wants to sit, is *le'chatechilah muttar* to open on *Shabbat*. Even though it has partitions on the bottom, it is not comparable to making an *ohel* in the sense that one is really not doing anything to create an *ohel* since before *Shabbat* the chair already had partitions and on *Shabbat* one is simply opening it up. For this very reason, it is *muttar* to open and close a canopy on *Shabbat*, but only if the canopy was already connected to the legs before *Shabbat*.

°·····················°

8 It is *muttar* to open folding chairs, deck chairs, folding tables, or a child's playpen on *Shabbat*, because they are made to habitually do so. It is also *muttar* to fold them. It is forbidden to attach an awning for protection from the sun. However, if the awning was already attached to the chair before *Shabbat* it is *muttar* to be opened and closed on *Shabbat*.

°·····················°

9 It is forbidden for one to open an umbrella on *Shabbat* for protection from rain. This is even when the umbrella was opened before *Shabbat*. Furthermore, in a place where there is no proper *eruv* in a *reshut harabim* it is certainly forbidden according to all opinions. Similarly, it is forbidden to carry it, even in a place where there is an *eruv*, because of *muktzah*.

°·····················°

10 There is room to be lenient on the issue opening and closing a garden umbrella which is stuck into the ground prior to *Shabbat*. However, some are of the opinion that one should not open or close it on *Shabbat*.

─────∾৩৩∾─────

Today's learning has been dedicated Leilui Nishmat Moshe Ben-Shalom, may his Neshama have an Aliyah.

11 It is forbidden on *Shabbat* to wear, even in one's house, a hat which has a brim longer than a *tefach* (eight centimeters) if it is hard enough that it does not bend. This is because doing so constitutes creating a temporary *ohel* on *Shabbat*. In any event, nowadays we are not *makpid* not to wear such a hat because the *issur* applies only when the hat has a *tefach*-long brim, and only when the brim is hard and unbendable. Nowadays, most hats don't have such brims and they are not made in order to act as an *ohel*, rather they are made for style and aesthetic appeal.

⸺⸺⸺⸺⸺⸺⸺

12 Some have a custom on *Simchat Torah* to spread a *tallit* over the children's heads that receive an *aliyah l'Torah*, and they have whom to rely on. One should not consider it forbidden due to making a temporary *ohel* because people hold it with their hands and do not spread it over pillars or the like. As well, one should not protest over putting a *tallit* over the *sefer Torah,* while it is outside, for protection from rain.

⸺⸺⸺⸺⸺⸺⸺

13 There are those that say that it is forbidden to return a drawer back to its place if it had been fully removed and there is a *tefach*-sized space in the depth of the area because this is creating an *ohel*. This also applies to tables that have drawers with a space of a *tefach*. Similarly, one should be careful to not completely remove the ice drawer of the fridge (where there is a space of a *tefach*), rather one should only remove it partially. In any event, there is reason to be lenient in all of these cases.

○○○

Today's learning has been dedicated by the Khalili, Lavian, Ashorzadeh, Rahmanfar, Eshaghian and Shreiber families Leilui Nishmat Behjat bat Brachas. Yehi Ratson that the merit of this holy Sefer stand for us and our children, so that the Torah should not cease from us, and may our home be filled with all the Blessings of the Torah.

14 It is *muttar* on *Shabbat* to cover food with a large utensil in order to guard the food from the sun or bugs or the like, even if there is a space of more than a *tefach* between the food and the bottom of the utensil. The reason for this is because it is not the regular way of creating an *ohel*, and the *chachamim* did not make a *gezeirah* on this type of temporary *ohel*.

Positioning a Mechitza

15 It is *muttar le'chatechilah* on *Shabbat* to make a temporary *mechitza*, even if one is making it to protect himself from the sun or for shade, as it is not considered an *ohel* in this manner. Similarly, if he is constructing a *mechitza* to prevent the candles from blowing out or for *tzniut* reasons (i.e. for *tefilla b'minyan)* it is *muttar*.

⚬...⚬

16 A *mechitza hamateret* is forbidden to make on *Shabbat*, even if it is a temporary *mechitza*. For example, if one's *sukkah* had only two walls and one made a temporary wall as the third wall, this is a *mechitza hamateret* because it functions to make the *sukkah* kosher. As a result, adding this third wall constitutes building and is therefore forbidden. (The same *din* applies when the *mechitzah* serves to allow carrying within its new confines, whereas without it carrying was forbidden.)

⚬⚬⚬

Today's learning has been dedicated Leilui Nishmat Yehoshua Engelard, may his Neshama have an Aliyah.

17 It is *muttar* to hang a curtain in front of a doorway on *Shabbat*, even if it is being placed there permanently. The reason for this is because the curtain flutters in the breeze and does not obstruct a passerby; it is not considered a permanent *mechitza* rather merely temporary, which is *muttar* if not made *lehatir*.

18 It is *muttar* to open a *mechitza* that is tied to a wall on *Shabbat*, even if it was not spread a *tefach* from before *Shabbat*. This is *muttar* even if opening it functions to be *matir davar*.

19 It is permitted to tell a non-Jew to make a *mechitza hamateret* that is not permanent on *Shabbat*, if the *yehudi* needs it for the sake of a *mitzvah*. For example, one may ask a non-Jew to make this *mechitza* in order for him to pray in a clean area.

Today's learning has been dedicated Leilui Nishmat Moshe Engelard, may his Neshama have an Aliyah.

Chapter 35	Laws Pertaining to Animals on Shabbat

1 In *sefer Shemot 23:12*, the *Torah* says *"Sheshet Yamim Ta'aseh Ma'asecha U'vayom Hashevi'i Tishbot, Lema'an Yanuach Shorecha Va'chamorecha Ve'yinafesh Ben Amatecha Ve'hager."* The *Torah* warns that even the animals of *bnei Yisrael* should rest; this *din* applies to all living creatures. Therefore, it is forbidden to place a package on one's animal for it to take outside. However, it is *muttar* for the animal to go out with something attached to it for its healing, such as a bandage on a wound. Similarly, any item that is needed for its security is tantamount to a clothing item and *muttar* for the animal to go outside with. However, extraneous security items are forbidden on *Shabbat*. Similarly, if this specific animal does not require this security item while the other animals do, it is still forbidden for this specific animal, as it constitutes cargo.

2 It is forbidden for an animal to go out in a place devoid of an *eruv* with cargo that may fall off, even if it is for the animal's security. The reason for this is that *Chazal* made a *gezeira* to prevent the owner from accidentally picking it up and carrying it four *amot* if the cargo were to fall to the ground.

Today's learning has been dedicated for the continued Hatzlacha and Bracha of Shlomo ben Miriam.

3 It is forbidden to let out an animal to graze that leaves with a bell around its neck to prevent it from getting lost. This is a *gezeira* made because of the *issur* of *hashma'at kol* (that people would hear the sounds made). There is also a *chashash* that others will think that one is bringing the animal up for sale.

4 It is forbidden to rent or lend one's animal to a non-Jew, because he might come to do *melachah* with it on *Shabbat* and that will violate the obligation one has to rest his animals.

5 If one has an animal that was created through *sefer Yetzirah*, the owner is not commanded to rest it because these *halachot* of animals on *Shabbat* only apply to natural-born animals.

Today's learning has been dedicated by Allen Zarian, Leilui Nishmat Eliyahu ben Rebi, may his Neshama have an Aliyah.

Issur of Directing

6 There are two *mitzvot DeOrayta* and one *mitzvah DeRabanan* by animals on *Shabbat*: The first *mitzvah DeOrayta* is that one must rest his animal so that it does not carry any load or pull a wagon on *Shabbat*, as the *pasuk* (cited above) states, *"Lema'an Yanuach Shorecha V'chamorecha."* It is forbidden for the owner to put any cargo on top of the animal and if someone else did, he is obligated to remove it. One is only commanded to remove the load from his own animal. However, if the animal belongs to a non-Jew, he is not commanded to take it off. The second *mitzvah DeOrayta is* directing an animal to do *melacha*. This means that when the animal is loaded with a burden, one cannot direct the animal, from behind, where to go. We learn this from the *pasuk "Lo Ta'aseh Kol melachah...*

U'behemtecha" which connotes an action shared by both the human and the animal together. This *issur* applies even to the animal of a non-Jew. The *mitzvah DeRabanan* is to not use one's animal at all on *Shabbat*, even to lean on it or the like.

Today's learning has been dedicated by Jonathan and Leora Kohanoff Family, in honor of the author, for undertaking this huge task and helping all the Neshamot with keeping Shabbat.

Using an Animal

7 It is forbidden to use one's animal on *Shabbat*, even if the animal does not do any *melachah* for him. Therefore, one may not ride on his animal or hang anything on it. This applies even in using the side of the animal. If one went on the animal, even if he did so on purpose, he must dismount immediately because of *tza'ar ba'alei chaim*. The reason behind the *issur* of riding an animal is because of a *gezeira* to prevent one from breaking off a stick in order to direct the animal. By doing so, one is *chayav* because of uprooting which is a *toldah* of *kotzer*.

8 It is *muttar* to unload anything from an animal that one needs as long as he does not wobble the animal in doing so. It is also *muttar* to take down anything from an animal on *Shabbat* that causes the animal any suffering even if he shakes the animal while doing so.

○·····································○

9 It is forbidden to ride in a carriage which is harnessed to an animal on *Shabbat*, even if a non-Jew is leading it. This is because even sitting in a carriage falls into the category of the *issur* to use an animal on *Shabbat*.

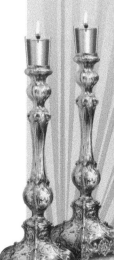

Today's learning has been dedicated Leilui Nishmat Chaim Seller, may his Neshama have an Aliyah.

10 If a non-Jew rides a Jew's animal in order to bring it to drink, one does not have to prevent this since the non-Jew carries himself and it therefore does not fall under the category of "a burden that one has to prevent his animal from carrying." However, one must prevent the non-Jew from placing his clothing (or anything else that is forbidden to carry on *Shabbat*) on top of the animal due to the *chiyuv* of resting one's animal.

⸺

11 It is *muttar* for a blind man to walk out into *reshut harabim* with his guard dog, even though he is holding on to the dog's leash. However, the head of the leash should not go under his hand more than a *tefach* because it is equivalent to one who is carrying with his hand.

⸺

12 It is forbidden to carry a live animal or bird since they fall under the category of *muktzah*. Even for the animal's benefit or for the space, it is forbidden to move the animal. Even if the animal may cause a financial loss (for example, the bird flies on top of the utensils and may break them), it is still forbidden to move them with one's hands. Rather, one should scare the animal away from the utensils, since the *issur* of moving *muktzah* still applies in a scenario where one may sustain a financial loss.

Today's learning has been dedicated Leilui Nishmat Moshe Mordechai Elhadad, may his Neshama have an Aliyah.

THIS MONTH'S LEARNING HAS BEEN DEDICATED
in Honor of a true Eishet Hayil.

• Day 237 •

• א' אייר •

13 Those who keep dogs, cats or birds as pets, and place the animal on their lap or arm on *Shabbat*, are violating the *issur* of moving *muktzah* on *Shabbat*. As well, when guests come over for *Shabbat*, they should be careful not to move them or place the animal on their lap or arm either. However, it is *muttar* to feed animals on *Shabbat*.

Feeding Animals

14 It is *muttar* on *Shabbat* to put food in front of one's goose, chicken or dove that relies on the owner to provide the food. However, it is forbidden to go out of one's way to give food to the birds that take care of their own sustenance (i.e. a dove). Similarly, one should not feed a stray kitten because it does not rely on him. However, if one sees the kitten crying and he has leftovers that he was planning to throw out anyway, he may throw them away from the kitten so that the kitten can go take them itself. By doing so, one is not going out of his way specifically for this animal.

○...○

15 It is *muttar* to feed a silkworm, since its source of sustenance comes from the owner. Similarly, it is *muttar* to feed fish in an aquarium or a domestic cat or the like that relies on the owner.

16 There are some with the *minhag* to place wheat in front of birds on *Shabbat Shira*. Even though there are those who say the *minhag* is not proper because the birds don't rely on them for food, one should not be *makpid* because it is being done for the sake of a *mitzvah.* It is said that even the birds sang *shira* at *krias Yam Suf* and it brought joy to *bnei Yisrael.*

○..○

17 There are those that say that if one sees an animal that cannot find its own food and is hungry, it is *muttar* to put food in front of it on *Shabbat* as this fulfills the *pasuk "Ve'rachamav Al Kol Ma'asav."* Similarly, it is *muttar* to put food in front of a dog, even if the dog does not belong to him. However, some opinions maintain that one may only feed his own dog. Therefore, one should throw the food away from the dog and let the dog go "get it" itself. By doing so, one is not going out of his way specifically for this animal.

Today's learning has been dedicated Leilui Nishmat Yosed Dovid Elhadad, may his Neshama have an Aliyah.

1 One who milks his animal on *Shabbat* is *chayav* because of *mefarek*. It is *muttar* to tell a non-Jew to milk one's cow on *Shabbat* in order to prevent *tza'ar ba'alei chayim*, as an excessive amount of milk causes the animal pain and puts it in physical danger. However, the milk is forbidden to drink that day. After *Shabbat*, one should buy the milk from the non-Jew for a small amount of money, so that the milk doesn't appear as if it was milked on *Shabbat* for a *yehudi*.

2 In a place where there is no non-Jew to be found, it is permitted to milk the animal onto the ground in such a way that the milk will go to waste. One should be particular to not milk the animal all at once as he does during the week. Rather, when the udder fills up with milk, one should milk the animal moderately to relieve the pain of being "full." It is *muttar* to milk the animal into a foul utensil that is filled with garbage or the like because it becomes spoiled immediately. After one is done milking the animal into such a utensil, he may spill it out.

Today's learning has been dedicated Leilui Nishmat Yaakov Elchanan Strakovski, may his Neshama have an Aliyah.

3 The *heter* of milking an animal to waste in a place where there is no non-Jew applies specifically in the case where there is no calf or kid to nurse from the animal. However, if there are calves or kids to nurse from the mother, there is no *hetter* for a *Yisrael* to milk the cow to waste and instead one must use the baby animals to relieve the milk supply. Nevertheless, even with the presence of nursing baby animals one may rely on a non-Jew to relieve the milk supply.

○..○

4 Even though there is reason to be stringent against milking even onto food, if there is no non-Jew present and someone milks it in a way that most of the milk absorbs into the food, one should not protest this.

○..○

5 One who milks into an empty utensil, or one that had a small amount of the food that the milks drowns is *mechalel Shabbat* with an *issur* of *sekilah*. There is no leniency to apply in such a case.

○..○

6 It is forbidden to milk an animal on *Shabbat* even through a *kattan* (one who is under the age of *bar mitzvah*). However, when one must milk the animal for its health (in which case the milk is anyways going to waste), it is preferable to have the *kattan* do the milking because *mitzad hadin* it is permitted.

Today's learning has been dedicated Leilui Nishmat Nachman Kirschbaum, may his Neshama have an Aliyah.

7 In a place where one milks an animal electronically, it is *muttar* to place the tube on the cow's udder. The reason for this is because the electricity shuts off via an automatic clock and the tubes milk the animal into a utensil. Therefore, placing the tubes on the udders constitutes merely a *grama* of *melacha* and is permissible.

8 It is permitted for one to unload something for an animal as long as he needs that item and he does not shake the animal while removing the item. If there is a problem of *tz'aar ba'alei chayim,* one may unload the animal, even if it causes the animal to move.

9 It is forbidden for one to sit on a chariot, that is connected to animal being driven by a non-Jew since sitting on the chariot constitutes using an animal on *Shabbat*.

10 People who have pet dogs, in which they place their dogs on their laps on *Shabbat*, are doing an *issur*. Similarly, if one has a cat or a pet bird, he may not move them on *Shabbat*. Guests who are invited for *Shabbat* should also be careful not to play with the animals on *Shabbat*.

11 One may feed his pet on *Shabbat* if he is responsible for the pet. This applies to pets at home such as cats and fish as well.

Today's learning has been dedicated by Dara and Chana Abaei, for the continued Hatzlacha and Bracha of Moshe Hayim and Batsheva Abaei.

Chapter 37 — Hunting and Taking a Life on Shabbat

1 *Tzidah* (hunting) is one of the *avot melachot*, which means that if one hunts an animal *be'mezid* in the normal fashion, he is *chayav sekilah*; if he did it *be'shogeg* he is *chayava korban chatat*. *Tzidah* was performed in the *mishkan* because they needed to trap the *chilazon* in order to color the *techelet*.

2 One is *chayav* for trapping wild birds in a cage-like trap, or birds or deer in a hut. However, if the animal is not normally trapped with that item, he is *pattur*, but it is forbidden to do so nonetheless.

3 If a bird enters a house through a window or door, it is forbidden to close the door or window even though it is not the regular way to trap the bird. In a case where one is cold (or has a similar unrelated reason to close the window) it is *muttar* to close the door or window if his intention is to solve his other issue and not to trap the bird. This is allowed only because there is no *d'oraisa issur* of *tzidah* in this case. However, it is forbidden to do this in cases of other animals and birds that do have the *issur* of *tzidah*.

4 One who scoops out a fish from the water into a cup of water is *chayav* for violating the prohibition of *tzidah*.

○○○

Today's learning has been dedicated Leilui Nishmat Rabbi Eliezer Goldberg, may his Neshama have an Aliyah.

5 It is forbidden to set up a trap in order to trap a mouse on *Shabbat*. It is also forbidden to open the trap (containing the mouse) in front of a cat so that it may eat the mouse. As well, the trap is *muktzeh* because it is an item used to accomplish an *issur*. Therefore, if one set up the trap before *Shabbat* and it trapped a mouse at night, one must be careful not to let the mouse go until after *Shabbat* ends.

○·····································○

6 One who traps snakes or any other creeping creatures that cause damage on *Shabbat* is *chayav* if he does it for *refuah* purposes. However, one may trap it in order to prevent the animal from attacking. Even in a place where the snakes do not regularly kill and are not chasing him (rather are merely lying still), while it is forbidden to kill them, it's still *muttar* to trap them. One must trap them by placing a utensil over them or by tying them.

○·····································○

7 One may trap an animal or bird that is in one's property, including an animal that is habituated in the house and is domesticated. However, one may not grab the animal with his hands because they are *muktzah*. Instead, one may chase them into a narrow area and secure them there. As well, this *din* applies when the animal does not rebel; otherwise it is forbidden to catch an animal that rebels if the yard is big enough that were it not for the animal being domesticated, it would require trapping to catch it.

○ ○ ○

Today's learning has been dedicated Leilui Nishmat Rabbi Yehuda Leib Rubin, may his Neshama have an Aliyah.

∽ల౩∾
• Day 244 •
∾ర౬౫

∽ల౩∾
• ח' אייר •
∾ర౬౫

8 A cow or horse or the like do not have the *issur* of *tzidah* since their nature is not to run away from humans. Therefore, it is *muttar* to bring them to their pen on *Shabbat*. However, if they rebel and one is unable to catch them without a trick, it is forbidden to catch them.

9 A cat has the same *din* as any other animal, in the sense that it is forbidden to catch on *Shabbat*. Therefore, if a cat entered one's house, it is forbidden for him to close the door until the cat exits. This is even though one's intension is not to trap it.

10 It is *muttar me'ikar hadin* to close a box or a utensil which has flies inside, even though they inherently will be trapped, because his intentions are not to trap them. However, blessing will come upon one who is *machmir* and blows away the flies first and only then closes the box. As well, one need not check carefully to make sure every fly is gone when he blows them away.

11 There is no *issur* of *tzidah* when it comes to people. Therefore, it is *muttar* for parents to lock their children in the house when they go out, so that the parents will know for sure that the children will not go out.

12 It is *muttar* to free any animal that is trapped since the *issur* is only in trapping an animal, not in setting it free. However, because it is *muktzah* one may not take it out with his hands.

O O O

Today's learning has been dedicated Leilui Nishmat Shmuel Klugsbald, may his Neshama have an Aliyah.

Taking a Life

13 Trapping the eight creeping creatures that are written in the Torah (in *parshat shemini*) would make one *chayav*. One who bruises them is also *chayav* even if blood did not come out of them (rather merely collected under the skin like a bruise). However, if one punches any of the other creeping creatures that are not mentioned in *parashat shemini*, he is only *chayav* if he causes it to bleed.

14 It is forbidden to kill wasps, flies or mosquitos, and doing so is equivalent to killing a camel. Therefore, one must be very careful in this matter, especially by mosquitos in the summertime. Because they are painful, many people get upset and kill them the same as during the week. Therefore, one must be particularly careful about this on *Shabbat*.

15 It is *muttar* to spray a bug repellant into a room that has mosquitos or flies which cause pain to the people sitting there on *Shabbat*. However, this is specifically when one does not spray the repellant directly onto the bugs but rather in the air. There must also be an open window so that the bugs may escape from the room. In any event, if there is another way to get the flies out, or if there is not such a big pain to sit in the room with flies, it is proper to abstain from spraying, even with the above conditions.

OOO

Today's learning has been dedicated Leilui Nishmat Eliyahu Cohen, may his Neshama have an Aliyah.

16 It is *muttar* to spread a special liquid made to give off a bad smell on himself in order to deter mosquitoes from approaching him. However, this *hetter* is only for a liquid, but not a cream, since creams are forbidden to apply on *Shabbat* because of smearing.

•···•

17 It is permitted to flush a toilet on *Shabbat*, even if there are flies or the like on the toilet seat and by flushing the water, he will cause the bugs to fall into the water and die. It is best for one to use a lighter flush, if possible.

•···•

18 It is *muttar* to pick out lice from one's head and kill them on *Shabbat*. The reason for this is because in *halacha* a louse is not considered a creature, rather it is viewed as having grown from one's sweat. However, as per the *takanat chachamim*, it is forbidden to pick lice from one's clothing and kill them, as he might also find fleas in the clothing and kill them as well.

Today's learning has been dedicated by the Radfard Family, Leilui Nishmat Moshe ben Modechai and Moshe ben Yechezkel, may their Neshamot have an Aliyah.

19 It is *muttar* to kill any animal or creature whose bite will put one's life in danger. An example of this is a poisonous snake or a rabid dog, even if the animal is far from him and is not even chasing him or anyone else. Because we are worried that it might attack and cause a danger to one's life, one may therefore kill it. Similarly, it is *muttar* to kill a wasp when it is near a baby. This is the *din* regarding any animal that might kill, but it is dependent on the time and place.

20 It is better for one to be careful not to pull out one's tooth with a string, for we are worried that this will cause bleeding. Similarly, one should be careful to scratch himself gently on *Shabbat* because there are times when the skin opens up and blood comes out without one even noticing.

21 It is *muttar* to take out a thorn that got stuck to one's body, whether by hand or with a needle, but one must be careful not to draw blood. In an event, if he was careful but was unsuccessful and blood ended up being drawn, there is no problem.

Today's learning has been dedicated Leilui Nishmat Simcha Bunim Diskind, may his Neshama have an Aliyah.

Chapter 38 — Plowing, Sowing and Harvesting

Charisha – Plowing

1 One who plows even a tiny bit is *chayav*. One who lops the roots of a tree or trims off the dry twigs or young shoots in order to beautify the ground is *chayav* for even a tiny bit as this is a *toldah* of *choresh*. Similarly, one who evened out the surface of a field (for example, he lowered a mound by flattening it or filled up a valley) is *chayav* because of the *issur* of *choresh*. This too is even for a tiny amount. The same applies to filling a hole.

2 Something that he did not intend to do is *muttar* as long as it does not constitute a *pesik reisha* (an action that undoubtedly completest a *melachah*). Therefore, one may drag a bed, chair or bench, no matter what size as long as he does not have the intention to do create a ditch (which is a *toldah* of *choresh*). By the same token, it is permitted to push a baby's carriage in a public domain, as long as there is a proper *eruv,* even on a dirt or sand path and even if he turns the carriage from side to side.

Today's learning has been dedicated Leilui Nishmat Yosef Yehuda Levi, may his Neshama have an Aliyah.

Zeri'ah – Sowing

• Day 249 •

• יג׳ אייר •

3 One who waters his seeded or planted field on *Shabbat* (or anywhere that has plant growth) has transgressed the *issur de'orayta* of the *toldah* of *zore'ah*. Therefore, if one eats in a garden, it is forbidden for him to wash his hands over the grass because by doing so he is "feeding" them and causing them to grow. Even though one does not have intention to accomplish this, it is still a *pesik reisha*.

4 It is *muttar* to pour water into the toilet after one is done using it, even though the water seeps into the sewage and feeds the trees growing nearby, thereby causing fruits to grow, because this is merely *grama be'alma*. This is a *grama* because the water doesn't directly reach the trees, but rather it goes into a pit first, overflows into another pit, and only then does it feed the roots of the trees. There are also a few other reasons to permit this.

5 It is *muttar* to urinate or to pour any other acrid liquids on top of weeds attached to the ground because these liquids do not promote growth but instead stunt and prevent it. In any event, it is better to be careful not to pour these types of liquids directly onto the weeds or the seedlings but rather close to them. Even within three *tefachim* of them one may be lenient. However, it is forbidden to defecate in a plowed field that is waiting to be sowed, lest one even out a hole by doing so.

Today's learning has been dedicated by the Barkhordar Family, for the well-being and success of their children and grand-children.

6 It is even forbidden to water a pot on *Shabbat*, even if the pot is not attached to the ground (and not getting sustenance from the ground).

---

7 It is forbidden to throw plant seeds or seeds of a fruit onto wet ground. It is forbidden scatter them on dry ground if the ground is waiting to be fed with water or rain.

---

8 One may water vegetables that are detached on *Shabbat* in order to prevent them from spoiling. This is because they are presently fit for consumption.

---

9 Branches of *besamim* or *hadasim* are permitted to be placed into a vase containing water on *Shabbat*, even *le'chatechilah*. One may even put water into the vase and then place the *besamim* or *hadasim* inside. Since they are presently fit to be smelled and *muttar* to move, there is no *issur* in filling a utensil with water to place the branches in to preserve them. All the more so it is certainly permitted to add water to the vase on *Shabbat*.

---

10 Flowers or roses with closed buds which are likely to open whilst placed in water may not, *le'chatechilah*, be placed into a vase of water on *Shabbat*. Even if one took a flower out of the vase in order to smell it, he should not return it to the vase. However, if the bud did blossom, it is *muttar* to place it into a vase of water. Blessing will come upon those who are stringent in this matter regarding flowers that already opened up.

Today's learning has been dedicated Leilui Nishmat Yishai Mualam, may his Neshama have an Aliyah.

Ketzira- Harvesting

11 It is forbidden to harvest grain or legumes, grapes, dates, olives or figs on *Shabbat*, as each of these actions constitute the *Torah* prohibition of *kotzer*. The definition of this prohibition is purposely uprooting something from its place of growth.

fruits is because they are *muktzeh* since the fruits were still attached before *Shabbat* and he made up in his mind that they should not be accessible for the duration of *Shabbat*, rendering them *muktzah* even if they fall down on *Shabbat*.

12 Fruits which fell from a tree on *Shabbat* are forbidden to be eaten on that day. This is because of a *gezeira* lest one come to climb the tree and pluck hanging fruit. Another reason for the *issur* of fallen

13 It is forbidden to pluck a plant even from within a pot that is not connected to the ground. By the same token, it is forbidden to water a pot which is not connected to the ground.

Today's learning has been dedicated Leilui Nishmat David Kraus, may his Neshama have an Aliyah.

Using a Tree

14 One may not climb up a tree on *Shabbat*, whether the tree is wet or dry, nor may one hang from it. We do not use any tree attached to the ground at all, because of a *gezeira* lest one come to climb the tree to pluck fruits or leaves and branches.

○·····················○

15 If one intentionally climbed a tree on *Shabbat*, it is forbidden for him to come down until *motza'e Shabbat* as a penalty. However, if he did it by accident (i.e. he forgot it was forbidden) he may come down on *Shabbat*. If one climbed the tree before *Shabbat* with the intention to stay there throughout *Shabbat*, it is *muttar* for him to come down on *Shabbat* because he went up before *Shabbat*.

16 Just like it is forbidden to use the tree itself, it is also forbidden to use the sides of the tree. This includes something that is inserted into the tree or tied to the tree. However, it is *muttar* to use the side of the side of the tree (i.e., something that leans on the item inserted into or tied around the tree) on *Shabbat*. For example, while it is forbidden to place into or remove something from a basket which is hanging from a tree branch, it is still *muttar* to place something into a basket that is hanging from a peg inserted into the tree, since the basket is considered the side of the side of the tree.

○○○

Today's learning has been dedicated Leilui Nishmat Chen Doron, may his Neshama have an Aliyah.

17 It is *muttar* to smell flowers or *hadasim* that are still attached to the ground. It is even *muttar* to hold them in one's hand in order to smell them. However, when it comes to apples, *etrogim*, or any other edible fruit, it is forbidden to smell them when still attached to the ground, even without touching them since *Chazal* made a *gezeira* lest he come and pluck it to eat.

18 It is *muttar* to walk on top of both dry and wet grass on *Shabbat*, even if the grass is sometimes uprooted due to the strength of his trampling, since he does not intend to uproot the grass and it won't necessarily be pulled out. If the grass is tall, he should not rush, and certainly not run, because the grass is bound be pulled out when he tramples on top of them. Therefore, he must walk slowly.

Today's learning has been dedicated Leilui Nishmat Yisrael Alnekave, may his Neshama have an Aliyah.

19 One may make *birkhat ilanot* on *Shabbat* just like one may smell a myrtle branch that is attached on *Shabbat*. We are not worried that one might forget and will come to detach the plant.

Le'chatechilah, it is best for one to make the *beracha* during the week. If his only opportunity to make the *beracha* is the *Shabbat* closest to the month of *Nissan,* and he is worried that if he waits he might forget and lose out on the *mitzvah,* he may then make the *beracha* on *Shabbat*.

20 It is permitted to sit or lie down on the lawn.

Similarly, it is *muttar* to spread a blanket or mat on the lawn and sit on top of it.

21 It is *muttar* to crack *besamim* branches which are detached to give to others to smell. This is specifically one when cracks the branches with his hands. However, there is reason to forbidden severing them with a knife.

Today's learning has been dedicated by Alen and Arielle Reyhan, Leilui Nishmat Yoseph Moshe ben Meir, may his Neshama have an Aliyah.

1 If one cooks deliberately on *Shabbat*, the food is forbidden for him to benefit from forever, but *muttar* to others immediately after *Shabbat*. If one cooked by mistake, it is forbidden to him and others on *Shabbat*, but becomes *muttar* to him and others immediately after *Shabbat*.

2 One who bakes bread, cook's food, or boils water or milk on *Shabbat* is *chayav* due to the *melacha* of *mevashel*. Similarly, one who roasts meat on top of coals is *chayav* due to *mevashel*. The same applies to one who dissolves wax, fat, tar or the like. Even fruits which are eaten raw are forbidden to cook on *Shabbat* on account of *mevashel*.

3 The *melacha* of cooking does not have a correlation to the *melacha* of *hav'arah* since every *melacha* is a different category of its own. Therefore, one who cooks on a fire that was set up before *Shabbat*, or one who adds cold water to boiling water in a kettle in order to increase it, is *chayav* for *mevashel*. Many people are mistaken for thinking the *issur* of cooking involves the *issur* of making a fire, and that therefore it is not a violation of *Shabbat* to cook on a fire which was standing before *Shabbat*. This is a terrible mistake and it is *mitzvah* to publicize that the *issur* of cooking is not connected to the *issur* of making a fire or *hav'arah*.

〇〇〇

Today's learning has been dedicated by Binyamin Rachmani, Leilui Nishmat Asher ben Bashi, may his Neshama have an Aliyah.

4 Just as it is forbidden to cook with fire, it is also forbidden to cook with a *tolda* of the fire. For example, it is forbidden to place an egg on the side of a pot or to break it on an article of clothing which was heated up with fire in order to cook the egg. It is even forbidden to cook with a *tolda* of the sun (for example, if the garment was heated up by the sun) because of a *gezeira* regarding the *tolda* of fire. Therefore, it is forbidden to insulate something with sand that was heated up by the sun. However, it is *muttar* to leave something out in a place where it will get directly heated up by the sun (for example, leaving an egg or water out in the sun to heat it up). In this case, we do not make a *gezeira* because the fire and the sun themselves are not interchangeable.

Heating Up a Cooked Food

5 If one heated up food which was previously fully cooked but became cold, if the food again reached the point of *yad soledet bo*, he is *chayav* for the *issur* of *bishul*. This is specifically if there was juice in the food.

Today's learning has been dedicated Leilui Nishmat Parvin Khaya bat Itzchak, may her Neshama have an Aliyah.

6 Cold, dry food which was fully cooked before *Shabbat* and then placed in the fridge, is *muttar* to heat it up on *Shabbat* on top of an electric *plata*, even to the degree of *yad soledet bo*. Similarly, it is *muttar* to heat up the food on a tripod placed on top of the stove top. This is specifically where most of the food is dry, even if there is some sauce; however, if most of the dish is sauce, it is forbidden to heat up on *Shabbat*. In this case, there is a *din* of recooking an item which was already cooked that applies to liquid food. Blessings will come upon those individuals who are *machmir* and only heat up food that is fully dry.

7 The *heter* mentioned above of heating up fully cooked, cold food on a *plata* also applies to meat that contains congealed fat. Even though the fat melts as a result of the heat, it is still *muttar* to heat up on *Shabbat* and is not prohibited by *nolad*. On the other hand, Ashkenazim are *machmir* when it comes to this.

○··○

8 It is *muttar* to place frozen bread on a *Shabbat* electric *plata*, as well as onto a tripod which sits atop the stovetop, in order to heat it up. If there are ice chips or flakes on top of the bread, one must remove them by shaking the loaf and wiping off the ice before reheating the bread.

Today's learning has been dedicated Leilui Nishmat Chaim Rak, may his Neshama have an Aliyah.

Tea and Coffee

9 It is *muttar* to recook (reheat) something through liquid means on *Shabbat*. Therefore, it is *muttar* to place bread into a hot soup that is *yad soledet bo*, even if it is a *kli rishon*. It is also *muttar* (for Sefaradim, whose tradition is like *Maran Shulchan Aruch*) to pour boiling water from a kettle resting on a fire into a cup that has coffee inside. The reason for this is because the coffee has already been roasted before *Shabbat* and there is no *issur* of cooking after it has already been roasted. However, blessing will come upon one is stringent in this matter and instead places the coffee into the cup only after he filled it with the hot water in order to make the cup a *kli sheni*. Similarly, (even for *acheinu* Ashkenazim) it is *muttar* to pour boiling water from a hot water urn atop a fire into a cup that has instant coffee inside, since the instant coffee was cooked from beforehand. Even Ashkenazim agree that in this case there is no *bishul* after *bishul*. However, it is better to *machmir*, if possible, to only add the instant coffee to the water afterwards.

○·······························○

10 It is forbidden to pour hot water over tea leaves on *Shabbat* to make an extract (essence), because doing so causes the outer shell of the leaves to be cooked. Rather, one should make the essence *erev Shabbat*.

○○○

Today's learning has been dedicated Leilui Nishmat Elkana Shiloh, may his Neshama have an Aliyah.

11 If one finished the tea essence on *Shabbat*, it is *muttar* to pour hot water from the kettle sitting on the *plata* onto the tea leaves which had already been cooked before *Shabbat* in order to make more essence. However, if they were not cooked before *Shabbat*, rather one had merely poured hot water from a *kli rishon* on top of them before *Shabbat*, there is a *machloket* if one is permitted to pour hot water on top of the tea leaves on *Shabbat*.

Therefore, *le'chatechilah*, it is best for one to boil the tea leaves before *Shabbat* to avoid any issue of *safek*.

12 When one wants to make tea on *Shabbat*, one should not first pour the tea essence into the cup and then add boiled water from a *kli rishon*. Rather, one should first pour the hot water into the cup and then add the tea essence on top of the hot water. However, if the tea essence is also *yad soledet bo*, it is *muttar* to add the tea essence first.

13 If one did not cook the tea leaves at all before *Shabbat*, one may be lenient to make tea through a *kli shelishi*. Similarly, if one did not prepare tea essence on *erev Shabbat*, the *din* is that one may use a tea bag in a *kli shelishi*. The *kli shelishi* is made by taking water from the kettle, pouring it into a cup, and then pouring that water into a different cup, which is called the *kli shelishi*.

14 It is *muttar* to place mint or nana leaves into a hot cup of tea even if it is *yad soledet bo*, and so is our custom.

Today's learning has been dedicated Leilui Nishmat Yonatan Hevroni, may his Neshama have an Aliyah.

15 It is proper to be *machmir* not to squeeze a lemon into a hot cup of tea which is *yad soledet bo*, because lemon is considered a sharp food that cooks even in a *kli sheni*. If the drink is so hot that one would hold himself back from it, it is *yad soledet bo*. If one would drink it as is and not have to let it cool down any more, it is not considered *yad soledet bo*.

○···○

16 It is forbidden for one to add spices to a soup or a dish while the pot is still on the fire and at a temperature of *yad soledet bo*. Even if the pot is taken off the fire but at a temperature of *yad soledet bo,* it is still forbidden since a *kli rishon* still cooks even after it was removed from the fire. However, one may add salt to the pot as long as the pot is not on the fire.

○···○

17 If one poured the soup into a bowl, one may add spices to the bowl even if the soup is *yad soledet bo* since one does not need to be stringent when it comes to a *kli sheni.*

○···○

18 It is *muttar* to pour hot water, even from the spout of a *kli rishon* sitting on the fire, into cold water which is in a cup, even though this will cause the cold water to become heated to the point of *yad soledet bo*. However, there is reason to be *machmir* not to do this if there is only a small amount of cold water in the cup, since there is a worry that the it will become cooked by the large amount of hot water.

○·························❧·························○

Today's learning has been dedicated Leilui Nishmat
Yedidya Fogel, may his Neshama have an Aliyah.

19 It is *muttar* to pour cold water into a cup of hot water, since a *kli sheni* does not cook. Therefore, it is *muttar* to pour cold milk into a hot cup of coffee even if the coffee is *yad soledet bo*. Similarly, it is *muttar* to pour hot water or tea from a thermos into a cup of cold milk even if there isn't so much milk because the thermos has the status of a *kli sheni* and the milk has been cooked and boiled already (pasteurized).

20 It is *muttar* to place a pitcher of water or any other drink next to a fire to ease the coolness, but only when one places it far enough from the fire that the drink won't heat up to the degree of *yad soledet bo*. It is forbidden though to place it close enough to the fire in a way that the drink will reach *yad soledet bo* even for a brief moment because it might cook in that area.

21 If milk was boiled on *erev Shabbat* and cooled down, it is *muttar* to place it on top of the *plata* in order the ease the coolness for a baby's needs or the like. However, one must be careful to remove the milk before it reaches the degree of *yad soledet bo*.

22 If one poured hot water from a *kli rishon* over an egg on *erev Shabbat* to make it soft-boiled, it is *muttar* to pour hot water over it to heat it up on *Shabbat* even from a *kli rishon* that is on top of the fire.

Today's learning has been dedicated Leilui Nishmat Ashraf bat Mashiach, may her Neshama have an Aliyah.

23 It is *muttar* to use an urn that has a glass tube attached to it which serves to tell the water level, despite the fact that opening the spout causes the water which is not so hot to mix into the boiling water inside of the urn.

○·······························○

24 One who wakes up in the morning and sees that his food is about to burn may take an empty pot and place it on top of the *plata* or stovetop, and place the pot containing food on top of it. However, one should be careful not to place the pot with the food inside on the floor in the meantime. According to Sefaradim, one must also make sure that the food is still boiling.

24 It is forbidden to pour boiling water into a cooked food that shriveled on *Shabbat* even after it was removed from the fire. However, it is *muttar* to pour a large amount of water at once into a *kli rishon* which was removed from the fire since the cold water will not become cooked by the hot water but would rather cool the boiling water. If one *bediavad* went ahead and poured hot water, it is *muttar* to eat the food even on that *Shabbat*. The *le'chatechilah issur* is really in a case of a *kli rishon*. Therefore, it is *muttar* to pour water onto the food sitting into a *kli sheni*. [According to *Acheinu* Ashkenazim, it is *muttar* to pour even into a *kli rishon* after it is removed from the fire.]

○~~~○

Today's learning has been dedicated by the Shaliasaboo Family, Leilui Nishmat Yehuda ben HaRav Michael, may his Neshama have an Aliyah.

26 It is *muttar mitzad hadin* to pour hot water into a cup that was rinsed with cold water and still contains droplets leftover. In any event, one should shake out these droplets from the cup before pouring hot water into it. Blessing will come upon one who is *machmir* to use another cup or to wipe the cup dry. In any event, when drying a narrow cup, one should be careful not to transgress the *issur* of *sechitah*.

Insulating on Shabbat

27 On *Shabbat*, it is forbidden to insulate a cooked food which is hot to the degree of *yad soledet bo* and still sits in the *kli* it was cooked in, even if he insulates it with something that does not increase heat. However, if it is not at the degree of *yad soledet bo* or if he moved it to another *kli* (even at *yad soledet bo*, surely if fully cold) it is *muttar* to insulate the food on *Shabbat* with something that does not increase heat, even if his intentions are to relieve the coolness by doing so.

⚬·····················⚬

28 It is *muttar* to pour water that is *yad soledet bo* from a hot water urn that is on top a fire into a thermos in order to keep the water heat. There is no such *issur* of *hatmana* (insulating) here.

Today's learning has been dedicated Leilui Nishmat Yosef Mastorov, may his Neshama have an Aliyah.

29 It is *muttar* to place a cooked food, even if it is still in the *kli* it was cooked in and *yad soledet bo*, into a device that maintains the temperature of the food, like a box in which one puts the pot into and closes its cover over it. Since there is air between the walls of the pot and the walls of the device, this is not considered *hatmana*. Even if the food was not fully cooked, it is *muttar* to put it into such a device.

30 It is *muttar* to place a bottle of cold milk or any other drink, for a baby, into another *kli* of hot water which is *yad soledet bo*. Because the hot water cools down, it is not considered *hatmana* with something that increases heat.

31 It is *muttar* to put a *kli rishon* which contains hot food into another *kli* that has cold water inside in order to cool off the food.

32 It is permitted for one to remove food from a pot with a spoon or ladle even while it is on the fire if it's fully cooked. However, it is forbidden to mix around the cooked food while it sits on the fire. If the food was not fully cooked, it is forbidden to take food from the pot while it's still boiling, even when removed from the fire, because of a *gezeira* lest one come to mix food on the fire. It is surely forbidden to mix the food in this situation.

Today's learning has been dedicated Leilui Nishmat Yedidya Hayut, may his Neshama have an Aliyah.

33 If the cover fell off a pot containing food that wasn't fully cooked sitting atop the fire, it is forbidden to put the cover back on *Shabbat*. Similarly, it is forbidden to add a cover on top of the cover, since by doing so he quickens the cooking process. However, if the food is fully cooked, it is *muttar* to replace the cover or add another, but *le'chatechilah* it is forbidden to cover even fully cooked food while still on the fire.

Insulating from Erev Shabbat

34 It is forbidden to insulate any food, even from *erev Shabbat*, with an item that will increase heat to the insulated food. It is *muttar* to insulate the food from *erev Shabbat* with something that will only maintain the food's temperature and not add to it.

○..○

35 The following are things that increase heat: the waste of olives or sesame seeds, manure, salt, sand whether wet or dry, straw, cotton, worn out clothing scraps and wet grass. The following are things that do not increase heat: pillows and quilts, blankets of wool or cotton, fruits, flax chaff and sawdust from trees.

○..○

36 It is *muttar* to use clothing to insulate a pot sitting atop a burner or electric *plata* from *erev Shabbat*. This is not forbidden due to *hatmana*, but it is good to be *machmir* to place a wide *kli* on top of the pot when the pot is on top of fire, and only then place the insulating material around it, in order that the sides of the pot will not get covered. However, by an electric *plata* there is no need to be *machmir* and it is permitted to directly insulate the pot with the materials.

Today's learning has been dedicated by the Author, for the continued Hatzlacha and Bracha of my dear mother, Rivka Chaya bat Sarah.

THIS MONTH'S LEARNING HAS BEEN DEDICATED BY
Mr. and Mrs. Issac and Miriam Hadjyan, for the continued Hatzlacha and Bracha of the Hadjyan family and their dear children Moshe, Shlomo and Leeba Batya.

37 If one has food which did not get fully cooked before *Shabbat* started, it is *muttar* to place it on a burner or an electric *plata* before *Shabbat* for the sake of the *Shabbat* meal, even though the heat is good for it (*mitztamek ve'yafeh lo*). It is correct to be *machmir* to place a metal plate beneath it to make a separation between the fire and the pot as a safeguard to remind one not to change the fire. However, by a *plata* there is no need for this safeguard. Totally raw meat, or food which was barely cooked which one placed a piece of uncooked meat into right before *Shabbat*, is *muttar* to be placed on top of an open fire before *Shabbat* begins.

38 On *erev Shabbat*, it is *muttar* to place a cooked food into an electric oven, whether the food was fully cooked or not cooked at all, as long as one takes it out on *Shabbat* after is fully cooked and fit to eat. There is no *issur hatmana* in doing this because the sides of the pot are not touching the walls of the oven, and there is also no *issur shehiyah* present. There is certainly reason to be lenient when one removes or covers the knobs of the oven. There are those who do not permit this if the oven works with a thermostat, since they are worried that when one opens the oven on *Shabbat* it causes the flame to increase. Therefore, it is correct *le'chatechilah* to be *machmir* in this case. In any event, one who is lenient about this has what to rely upon, because many allow *grama* even in a situation where there is no loss, and thus all the more so here where it is necessary to take out the food which is used for a *mitzvah*.

Returning the Pot to the Fire

39 If one takes off a pot from on top a fire, and in it is a food that is fully cooked, it is *muttar* to return it back to the fire if the fire is covered with a tin as long as there is sauce, and the food remains at the degree of *yad soledet bo*. Also, one may not put the pot onto the floor or anything that is connected to the ground, such as the marble in the kitchen. However, if one placed the pot on top of the table or a chair, one may return the pot while the pot is still *yad soledet bo*. According to the Ashkenazim, the pot must remain in his hands and he must keep in mind to return it onto the fire. It is *muttar* to return a pot onto a *plata* even if he placed it on the ground because it does not look like cooking since it's not the norm to cook on a *plata*.

40 If one finds bones in the pot that are cooked and fit for eating, one may only return the pot to the fire if the bones are fully cooked and fit for eating. The prohibition of returning the pot is specifically where he is preparing to eat the bones but if he is not preparing the pot in order to eat the bones, he may return the pot with the bones to the fire even if the bones were not fully cooked. Some say that one should not pay attention to the bones but rather to the dish; if the dish is fully cooked, one may return the pot to the fire even if the bones were not cooked yet since this *din* of *mevashel kol tzorcho* has to do with the cooked dish and not the bones.

○○○

Today's learning has been dedicated Leilui Nishmat Elazar Yitzchak Koltai, may his Neshama have an Aliyah.

41 If the flame on which the pot containing fully cooked food sits is too low, there is reason to permit one to move the pot onto a bigger flame. This is on condition that the flame is covered in some way. Similarly, if the food is on top of a *plata* it is *muttar* to move the food from a place where it is less hot to a place which is hotter, so long as the food is fully cooked.

42 If the gas turned off or if the *plata* stopped working on *Shabbat*, it is *muttar* to move the pot, while the food is fully cooked and still hot, and put it onto a different *plata* in his home or the home a neighbor. If the food contains sauce, according to Sefaradim the food must be at *yad soledet bo* in order to move it. However, if the food is dry and fully cooked, it is *muttar* to move it even when cold. In any event, since there are those who say it is forbidden to move food that has sauce or liquid inside, it is correct to be *machmir* in this matter if possible. One who is lenient in this matter has what to rely upon, even *le'chatechilah*.

Today's learning has been dedicated Leilui Nishmat Ariel Tzadik, may his Neshama have an Aliyah.

Power Outage

43 If there was a power outage on *leil Shabbat* and after time the power came back on and the *plata* started working again, it is forbidden to eat the food sitting on the *plata* which was not fully cooked before *Shabbat*. This food becomes *muttar* to eat after *Shabbat*. However, if the food was fully cooked before *Shabbat*, if the power outage was long enough that the food cooled down and became reheated once the electricity returned, one should wait for the food to cool down before eating it. If the food stayed hot (i.e. the power outage was short) there are those who hold that one is permitted to eat the food while it is still hot. In any event, even in this case there is reason to be *machmir* and not eat the food while it's still hot. The reason for this stringency is because were it not for the electricity coming back on *Shabbat* the food would have become cold, and therefore this scenario is as if one is benefitting from a *melachah* of *issur*.

∾ⲟⲟⲥ∾
Today's learning has been dedicated Leilui Nishmat Yosef
Greenbaum, may his Neshama have an Aliyah.

Chapter 40 — Laws Pertaining to Separating on Shabbat

1 *Borer* is one of the 39 *melachot* of *Shabbat* and as such, one is *chayav* a *chatat* for transgressing it accidentally and *mitah* if done deliberately. In our many sins, many people fall in this area. One transgresses the *Torah*-level *issur borer* in the following three ways:

1) If one separates the bad from the good; even if one separates it by hand with the intent to eat it immediately, he is *chayav*.

2) If one separates with a *kli* that is used for separation (e.g. a sieve) he is *chayav*, even if he separates the good from the bad and it is

his intention to eat it right away. However, if he uses a *kli* that is not usually used for separating, he is *pattur* but still is forbidden *miderabanan*.

3) If while separating, he intends to eat the food later, even if he separates the good food from the bad by hand, he is *chayav*.

The only way one can separate items on *Shabbat* is by fulfilling all three of the following conditions:

1) He takes the good food from the bad food.
2) He does so with his hands (and not a *kli*).
3) His intention is to eat the food immediately.

Today's learning has been dedicated by Dara and Chana Abaei, for the continued Hatzlacha and Bracha of Aviel and Miriyam Abaei.

2 It is proper and honorable for every man to instruct his household to place every fruit or food in its own section before *Shabbat* in order to prevent them from stumbling in the *halachot* of *borer*.

○·······································○

3 If two different types of foods are mixed together, one may take the food that he prefers to eat right away, as this gives it the status *ochel*. However, it is forbidden to remove the food that he does not want to eat right away, since it is now considered the *pesolet*. In any event, if he is choosing for others, he may take the food that they prefer and like, even if he himself does not like that particular food, because for them this food is considered the *ochel*.

4 One separating in order to feed an animal (or bird) is permitted to separate what he would consider *pesolet* from his *ochel*, if it is the food for the animal, in order to feed the animal right away. The reason for this is because the *pesolet* which the animal wants is considered to be an *ochel*, and is therefore seen as separating *ochel* from *pesolet*. It is best to do this either in private or to put the *pesolet* directly into the dish made specifically for the animal. This will prevent people from suspecting him of separating *pesolet* from *ochel*, which is forbidden even if he were to eat it immediately. One who is lenient and not worried about this has what to rely upon.

○──────────୧ଵ୨──────────○

Today's learning has been dedicated Leilui Nishmat Moshe Levi, may his Neshama have an Aliyah.

THIS CHAG'S LEARNING HAS BEEN DEDICATED BY
Michael Ebriani, for the Hatzlacha and Siyata
Dishmaya in learning for all of Klal Yisrael

5 *Borer* is considered *le'alter* ("right away") and therefore *muttar* if one is sitting at a meal and separating *ochel* from the *pesolet* for the purposes of that meal, even if the meal takes three hours or more. However, if he is not sitting down to a meal he is prohibited to separate even if his intention is to eat it *le'alter*, which means within the hour. If he separates close to his meal, it is *muttar* to separate for any purpose of that entire meal, since he is ready to eat shortly after this preparation. Therefore, it is forbidden to separate *ochel* from *pesolet* until the point in time when people leave the *bet hakenesset* from *shacharit*.

6 One may even separate with his spoon or fork, because it is considered separating by hand which is *muttar* when taking the good food from the bad for immediate consumption. We do not consider these utensils as having been made to separate food, but rather this is the way that the world at large eats food.

7 It is *muttar* for one person to separate good food from the bad with one's hands for someone else's immediate consumption. However, it is forbidden to separate more than the amount which this other person will eat right away. Therefore, if one knows that his guests will not finish their entire plate, one should not separate (even *ochel* from *pesolet*) more than the amount which they will be able to eat right away. Even if one does so in order to fill up the serving plate in honor of the guests, it is still forbidden.

∾ↄ∾

• Day 273 •

ↄ∾ↄ

∾ↄ∾

• ח' סיון •

ↄ∾ↄ

8 One who separates *ochel* from *pesolet* for the needs of that meal should not separate more than what is needed for that meal. If his intention is to have leftover for after the meal or for another meal, he is *chayav* a *chatat*. If he separated food in order to eat it right away but was unable to finish all the food, he hasn't violated an *issur* as long as he was not fooling himself.

9 Even if one separates *ochel* from *ochel*, he must separate the food that he wants first before the one he'll eat second. In any event, if it is all one type but there are bigger and smaller pieces, it is *muttar* for him to choose whichever is more convenient and easier for him, be it something he'd like to eat now or something he prefers to eat later on since there is no *din* of *borer* here.

10 If one has a bowl filled with fruits but he cannot tell from the outer appearance which ones are rotten, it is *muttar* to pick up each one individually and then put it aside if it is rotten. There is no *issur* of *borer* because this is the regular way to eat.

Today's learning has been dedicated for the continued Hatzlacha and Bracha of Leeba Batya bat Miriam.

11 It is forbidden to choose between two types of fish which are two different types of food unless he does so by hand and eats it right away. This applies even if the pieces are big and recognizable on their own. Similarly, if there was the same type of fish, but one was cooked and one was fried, he must choose the one he would like to eat immediately.

12 Pieces of meat, half of which are cooked and the other half which are fried or roasted, are considered two types of food. Certainly, all the different cuts of chicken are considered different types of food. Similarly, if there are sweet and sour apples mixed together but the sour apples are so bitter that they are inedible, the sour apples are considered *pesolet* and there is an *issur* of *borer*.

13 It is *muttar* to peel garlic or onion by hand or with a knife, on condition that he eats it immediately since this is the usual way of eating it. However, it is forbidden to peel them for a later meal. This is also the *din* for all fruits that have peels like walnuts, almonds, golden apples, grapefruit and the like.

Today's learning has been dedicated Leilui Nishmat
Moshe Levi, may his Neshama have an Aliyah.

14 There are those that say that it is *muttar* to peel fruits and vegetables that are eaten with their skin (even if only in a pressing situation) such as apples, pears, cucumbers, carrots and the like. One may even use a proper peeler in this case.

○..○

15 One should not remove the bad leaves from the good when preparing vegetables such as celery, horseradish or the like, which oftentimes have rotten leaves. Instead, one must separate the good ones from the bad and it must be for immediate consumption.

This applies when the leaves are disconnected from the stalk. However, if the leaves are still connected to the stalk with the rotten leaves on the exterior, it is *muttar* to separate them and eat the good leaves right away because removing the bad leaves off the stalk first constitutes the normal way of eating a vegetable stalk.

Today's learning has been dedicated Leilui Nishmat Ariel Achdut, may his Neshama have an Aliyah.

16 If one eats fish or pieces of meat containing bones, it is *muttar* to remove the bones first by hand and then eat it right away. This is because doing so is seen as merely eating, not an act of separating. One should not remove the bones left on the plate which are separated from the fish or the meat, rather he should leave them on the side of the plate. This is because the bones are *pesolet*, and removing them would constitute separating *pesolet* from *ochel*.

17 It is *muttar* to pull out the small feathers on a chicken that were not plucked before it was cooked, as there is no *issur* here of *borer pesolet* from *ochel*. Similarly, it is *muttar* to remove the skin from the chicken since it is a part of the chicken and there is no *issur* of *borer*.

Today's learning has been dedicated Leilui Nishmat Moshe Tzarfati, may his Neshama have an Aliyah.

18 Regarding fruits which contain one large seed (such as dates, peaches, apricots, etc.) it is *muttar* to remove the seed with one's hand and eat it immediately. Since there is only one seed, it is considered as if he is taking *ochel* from *pesolet*. However, regarding fruits which have many seeds inside them, such as certain raisins, it is forbidden to remove the seeds. Even though one is holding the fruit in his hand, it is considered taking *pesolet* from *ochel* because he will have to remove the seeds individually from inside the fruit. Instead, one should put the raisin in his mouth and take the seeds out with his mouth.

19 Watermelon seeds should not be removed prior to eating even for immediate consumption because this is separating *pesolet* from *ochel*. Instead, one should pick up a piece of watermelon and shake it strongly to cause the seeds to fall out of it. After doing this, it is then *muttar* to remove the remaining seeds (even by hand) which were stuck too deeply to fall out, for this is considered the normal way to eat this food. In an event, it is better to remove them by way of a small *shinuy* (in an irregular fashion).

Today's learning has been dedicated Leilui Nishmat Mordechai Paketeh, may his Neshama have an Aliyah.

∽৩৩৽
• Day 278 •
৽৩৩∽

∽৩৩৽
• יג' סיון •
৽৩৩∽

20 The seeds and the *pesolet* of a melon may be removed for immediate consumption, since one is not able to reach the flesh of the fruit without doing so.

○···○

21 It is *muttar* to crack peanuts on *Shabbat* to eat them right away as this is the only proper way to eat them. This also applies to pistachios as well.

22 If one squeezes a lemon over salad or other food and seeds from the lemon fall into the food as a result, it is forbidden to remove and dispose of the seeds. Doing so is considered separating the bad from the good, which is forbidden even for immediate consumption. It would only be permitted to throw them out afterwards if he sucked on the seeds beforehand.

Today's learning has been dedicated Leilui Nishmat Shlomo Zalman Leibovitz, may his Neshama have an Aliyah.

23 There is a *machloket haposekim* if a yolk and egg white are considered one thing, with which one would be able to do *borer*, or two different food entities, which would then be forbidden to separate. Therefore, it is proper to be *machmir* about this and first eat whichever part he prefers, not the opposite. It is permitted for one to separate the yolk from the egg-whites by passing it from one of the shells to the other as long as he eats it right away.

24 It is *muttar* to wash fruits or vegetables which have any dirt, dust or the like, for immediate consumption. One need not worry about violating *borer*.

25 If one is drinking a cup of water or any other drink on *Shabbat* but does not wish to drink the entire contents of his cup, it is *muttar* for him to pour some back from the cup before he drinks from it. There is no *issur* of separating *pesolet* from *ochel*.

26 If a mosquito or fly fell into a cup holding one's drink, it is *muttar* to remove it because there is no *borer* by liquids. *Borer* only applies when one must search and separate *pesolet,* whereas here the item is floating on the surface of the drink and it is recognizable on its own. However, there are those who say it is forbidden because in the end he is taking out *pesolet* from *ochel*. It is correct to be *machmir* and take out the fly along with some of the drink simultaneously. As well, one can pour the fly out of the cup with some of the liquid.

Today's learning has been dedicated Leilui Nishmat Shraga Gestetner, may his Neshama have an Aliyah.

27 It is *muttar* to remove the layer of cream resting on top of milk which was boiled from *erev Shabbat* in order to drink the milk right away, as doing this does not transgress the *issur* of separating *pesolet* from *ochel*. Similarly, it is *muttar* to remove the fat from the surface of soup in order to drink the soup right away. However, if the fat splits into a few pieces, and the soup enters in between them, one should be careful not to remove the fat unless he takes out some of the soup in the same spoonful.

○...○

28 On *Shabbat*, it is *muttar* to use a tea kettle which has a strainer in its spout to hold back the tea leaves from going into the cup.

○...○

29 It is not necessary to remove a filter from the kitchen faucet before *Shabbat*, rather one may leave it and use it on *Shabbat*. There is no worry of *borer* since the water coming out of the faucet is already clear, clean, and ready to be dinken as is, and the filter is merely for extra hygiene; one need not be stringent in this and may leave the filter of the faucet. If the filter falls off, it is *muttar* to put it back on while it's dry, but only in a temporary matter (without attaching it too well) since there is worry of violating *boneh*.

Today's learning has been dedicated Leilui Nishmat Eliezer Tzvi Joseph, may his Neshama have an Aliyah.

Separating by Different Things

30 Just as there is a *din issur* of *borer* by two different foods, so too there is a *din issur* of *borer* by utensils, clothing, or books that are mixed together. Therefore, when one wants to choose a utensil, an article of clothing or a book from the next, he should choose the item which he needs, since in comparison to the rest that is considered the "*ochel*" from the *pesolet*. This is *muttar* so long as it is taken for immediate use.

31 It is *muttar* to separate the different knives, spoons and forks which were mixed together, and to arrange them in their specific places in order to use them the next meal. Similarly, it is *muttar* for the *shamash* of the *bet hakenesset* to separate the *siddurim* and *chumashim* that are mixed together, and place each *sefer* back in its place after the *tefilah*.

32 It is *muttar* to take off outer clothing from on top of a hanger, even though one does not need them, when his intention is to take out the article of clothing found beneath them. There is no problem of *borer* so long as he wears the clothing right away.

33 It is *muttar* for the *gabbai* of the *bet hakenesset* to separate the name cards of the *olim*. There is no issue of *borer*.

34 It is permitted for one to remove a tea bag from the cup of tea and there is no problem of *borer*. Some are stringent to remove the tea bag with a spoon while taking some of the tea with it as well.

Today's learning has been dedicated Leilui Nishmat Menachem Knoblowitz, may his Neshama have an Aliyah.

Chapter 41   Squeezing on Shabbat

1 One who squeezes olives in order to make oil or squeezes grapes in order to make wine on *Shabbat*, is *chayav* for the *issur* of *mefarek*, which is a *tolda* of *dosh*. It is also forbidden *m'dvrei soferim* to squeeze berries or pomegranates. Since there are some people who squeeze them like olives and grapes, they made a *gezeira* lest one come to squeeze them like olives or grapes.

○·······························○

2 Any fruit in which people in any given place are accustomed to squeeze for juice, whether for thirst or pleasure, is forbidden to squeeze out on *Shabbat*. Even when this fruit is squeezed in a locale where it is abundant, it is forbidden to squeeze it throughout the world, like the *din* by berries and pomegranates. Therefore, it is forbidden to squeeze pears or apples because people in many places squeeze them for their juice. As well, one may not squeeze golden apples or grapefruit, since nowadays many people squeeze them for juice. Similarly, there is what to be *machmir* for when it comes to squeezing tomatoes or the like on *Shabbat*, and instead one should do it on top of food.

○꩜○

Today's learning has been dedicated Leilui Nishmat Daniel Morris, may his Neshama have an Aliyah.

3 Fruits that people generally do not squeeze for juice are *muttar* to squeeze on *Shabbat* in order to drink because this is viewed as taking one food from another food.

Therefore, it is *muttar* to squeeze watermelons. In any event, one may only do this by hand and not with a *kli* made for juicing.

○·····································○

4 It is *muttar* for one to suck the juice out of a fruit with his mouth for fruits such as strawberries, pomegranates, golden apples and grapefruit. As well, one may suck pieces of meat saturated with soup and bread saturated with wine. However, it is proper to be *machmir* when it comes to grapes because squeezing grapes on *Shabbat* is a *issur* from the *Torah*. Therefore, when sucking grapes, one should only suck out the juice when it is fully in his mouth and only then spit out the grape pip, as this is *muttar* according to all.

Today's learning has been dedicated Leilui Nishmat Yosef Cohen, may his Neshama have an Aliyah.

5 One may even squeeze a cluster of grapes over a food in order to fix the taste of the food, because this juice is considered food and it is viewed as extracting food from food, which has no *issur* of *mefarek*. The *hetter* even allows one to squeeze them when not close to the meal, and even without leaving a bit of the juice left in the fruit. All the more so, it is *muttar* to squeeze other fruits like golden apples or grapefruits into food, as long as there is a lot of food on the plate, so that the juice mixes in with the food and is mostly saturated into it. However, if there isn't so much food and therefore the juice drowns it, it is forbidden. Therefore, there is reason to protest against those who put two or three teaspoons of sugar in a cup and squeeze half a cup or more of golden apples into it.

6 One is only permitted to squeeze a fruit for its juice when doing so directly into solid foods. However, one cannot squeeze it into a cup of liquid, since the drink is not considered a food in this aspect.

Today's learning has been dedicated by Aaron Ebriani, Leilui Nishmat Elazar ben Shimon, may his Neshama have an Aliyah.

7 It is *muttar* to squeeze lemons on *Shabbat*. There is reason to be lenient about this whether one squeezes the lemon into an empty *kli*, into into a *kli* containing a drink, or even to later mix it into a food. In any event, if he makes lemonade, it is correct to adhere to the opinion of the *machmirim* and make it as follows. First he should place the sugar into the cup, then afterwards squeeze the lemon on top of the sugar (so that that the juice fully or mostly swallows up the sugar), and afterwards fill up the rest with water.

....

8 If one would like to squeeze lemon into a cup of tea, it is proper to be *machmir* and not do so into a hot cup of tea that is still at *yad soledet bo*. This is because lemon juice is considered sharp that cooks even in a *kli sheni*. Similarly, one should not squeeze the lemon into a cup that contains sugar before adding the boiling water from the *kli rishon* into the cup. The reason for this is that pouring the hot water that is *yad soledet bo* directly from the hot water urn would cook the lemon juice. Instead, one should pour the water first into an empty cup (which becomes *kli sheni*) and only then pour it into the cup containing the lemon juice and sugar.

Today's learning has been dedicated Leilui Nishmat Yosef Amram Tauber, may his Neshama have an Aliyah.

9 On *Shabbat*, it is *muttar* to squeeze fruits or vegetables which were boiled or pickled in vinegar or salt water into an empty utensil if he doesn't need the juice and is only squeezing it to make it fit for consumption. Similarly, it is *muttar* to squeeze the fat out of turnips or any other boiled vegetables if he is only doing so because he cannot eat it otherwise. However, if he needs the juice, he is only allowed to squeeze it into a *kli* that already has food in it; it is forbidden to squeeze it into an empty *kli*.

⸰⸱⸱⸱⸱⸱⸱⸱⸱⸱⸱⸱⸱⸱⸱⸱⸱⸱⸱⸱⸱⸱⸱⸱⸱⸱⸱⸱⸱⸱⸱⸰

10 It is forbidden to cut a grapefruit across its width and press the it with a spoon to extract the juice to drink. However, it is *muttar* to eat the grapefruit with a spoon if he is careful not to squeeze it and if his intention is not to specifically get the juice when eating it. Nevertheless, it is best to be stringent even by this.

⸰⸱⸱⸱⸰

11 It is *muttar* on *Shabbat* to stir sugar into a drink with a spoon or the like, and it is not considered equivalent to mashing snow or ice in a cup, which is forbidden according to the *Shulchan Aruch*. The difference is that snow turns into water, but sugar simply dissolves into the drink.

Today's learning has been dedicated Leilui Nishmat Moshe Bergman, may his Neshama have an Aliyah.

12 It is *muttar* to wipe cups or bowls with a sponge which has a handle on *Shabbat*, as long as he does not hold the sponge itself and he cleans them for the need of *Shabbat*. Even though when he presses liquid out of the sponge while cleaning, he is not holding the sponge directly and therefore is only squeezing in an irregular fashion (*shinuy*) which is not forbidden because our sponges nowadays are not made from materials that grow from the ground. However, when the sponge has no handle, it is forbidden to wipe even with our modern-day sponges since one is squeezing with his hands.

·····················

13 Some say that it is *muttar* to gently wipe a baby with baby wipes if he is not tearing them, or if he tore them before *Shabbat* and placed them in a closed bag so they don't dry up. However, there are those that say it is forbidden to clean the baby with a damp wipe. In any event, one who is lenient in a time of need has what to rely upon.

Today's learning has been dedicated Leilui Nishmat Avraham Daniel Ambon, may his Neshama have an Aliyah.

Chapter 42 — Grinding, Kneading and Salting Foods

1 One who dices vegetables into very fine pieces is *chayav* because of *tochen*. This applies even to vegetables which are eaten in their raw state. However, the *issur* is only when one dices the vegetables in order to be eaten at a later time or date. Therefore, one may cut them into small pieces for immediate consumption. It is *muttar* to cut vegetables into small pieces to put into a salad as long as is it eaten right away. In any event, *beracha* will come to one who is particular to cut them into larger pieces.

2 The measurement of "right away" is as follows. It is *muttar* for one to make a salad for the current meal even if the meal will last for a few hours. If one is not yet ready to be seated at the meal, he should not make the salad until shortly before it begins. Therefore, one should be careful not to make a salad until the men have left the from *shacharit* and are ready for the meal. If one has salad left over from that meal, it is *muttar* to eat it later as long as he is not fooling himself by knowingly preparing extra amounts.

Today's learning has been dedicated Leilui Nishmat Dov Steinmetz, may his Neshama have an Aliyah.

3 It is *muttar le'chatechilah* for one to mash bananas or cooked vegetables with the prongs of a fork for a baby's needs and the such, in order to feed it to him right away. Avocados may also be mashed with the prongs of a fork for immediate consumption.

4 It is *muttar* to spread out bread in front of chickens. This is because the grain was already ground up, and there is no issue of secondary grinding. However, it is proper to be careful to spread out the food in front of them close to the time which they eat.

5 It is permitted to cut up cooked or roasted meat into very small pieces. This applies even when it is not for the current meal, because meat does not grow from the ground. Similarly, it is *muttar* to cut cheese into very fine pieces, or to crush it with a fork, even when not for the current meal. However, it is forbidden to grate cheese with a double-edged cheese grater, even for the current meal because it's not permitted to grind something with a utensil made specifically for grinding. Therefore, it is forbidden to grate carrots or radishes with a grater on *Shabbat* even if his intentions are to eat it right away.

Today's learning has been dedicated Leilui Nishmat Elazar Gefner, may his Neshama have an Aliyah.

Kneading on Shabbat

6 It is permitted for one to make mayonnaise by mixing eggs, oil, mustard, sugar and salt, on *Shabbat*. There is no *issur* of kneading in doing this. However, one must mix it gently (not hard) and it may only be done in order to be eaten immediately at the current *seudah*. It is *muttar* for one to place the mayonnaise on top of pieces of potatoes, carrots, hard boiled eggs and pickles, and mix them together, since they don't stick together well and mixing them will not create one large blend. If pieces of egg shell fell into the mixture, one may not remove them because of the *issur* of *borer*, but rather he should take out some of the mixture together with the shells.

○·······················○

7 It is *muttar* on *Shabbat* for one to prepare a food made from chopped eggs and chopped onions, or salted fish and onions, and mix them with oil until it becomes like a doughy substance. There is no issue of *lisha*. One should not protest the custom of those holy Jews who do so. One should make this food with the intent to eat it right away at the present meal.

Today's learning has been dedicated by the Author, with a tremendous amount of Hakarat Hatov, for the continued Hatzlacha and Bracha of Yeshivat Ner Yisrael, the Rosh Yeshiva, HaRav Aharon Feldman Shlita, The Mashgiach Shlita, HaRav Berel Weisbord, the dedicated Rebbeim, Avreichei Kollel and Bachurim.

8 It is *muttar* for one to prepare *tehina* on *Shabbat* by adding water, lemon, and some salt on top of the *tehina* which was pre-kneaded in a grinding house and made into a thick mixture. This is only if one does so close to the meal at which it will be eaten, and one mixes it not vigorously, but rather gently.

9 It is forbidden on *Shabbat* for one to put powdered pudding or powdered potato puree into water, or to pour water on top of it, and mix it together with a spoon because doing so creates a thick mixture. This *halachah* also applies to powdered jello it is forbidden for one to add water to it on *Shabbat*.

Today's learning has been dedicated by the Zedner family, Leilui Nishmat Avraham ben Malka and Yitzchak, may his Neshama have an Aliyah.

Salting Foods

10 Pickling a food on *Shabbat* is forbidden because of *mevashel* and because of the *issur* of *me'aved*, or tanning. Therefore, any food which is usually pickled is forbidden to salt and set down even though he will eat it during that same meal. Rather, one should dip each piece into the salt individually and eat them immediately. [One should even be careful not to dip two or more and set them down in front of him.] Even if the food is not usually pickled, but salting it causes a change in its nature to either take away its bitterness or to sweeten it, it is forbidden to salt and then set down. Examples of this are radishes, onions, garlic or any other sharp food. One must dip each piece, one by one, and eat it right away.

o...o

11 It is forbidden to salt a few pieces of radish at the same time since it looks as if one is pickling. Therefore, one should dip them one at a time and eat them immediately before going on to the next one. This applies equally to any food in which salt causes a change in its nature to take away its bitterness as well as anything that is normally pickled.

Today's learning has been dedicated by the Author, with a tremendous amount of Hakarat Hatov, for the continued Hatzlacha and Bracha of Yeshivat Mikdash Melech, the Rosh Yeshiva, HaRav Chaim Benoliel, the dedicated Rebbeim, Avreichei Kollel and Bachurim.

12 One who makes a salad from vegetables which are usually pickled, or one who makes a salad with vegetables mixed with pieces of radish, onion or garlic, must immediately pour the oil or lemon juice over it after adding the salt. Alternatively, he can pour the oil or lemon juice on top of the salad and add the salt afterwards.

enhance the taste of the tomato. If one mixes cucumbers into the tomato salad, he does not have to add the oil or lemon juice immediately after adding the salt because it is not the norm to pickle peeled cucumbers and the salt is only there to add to the cucumber's taste. In any event, *beracha* will come upon one who is *machmir* to add oil or lemon juice immediately after salting it.

13 One who makes tomato salad may add salt on top of it in order to give it taste. He need not add any oil or lemon juice right away after he adds the salt since it is not the norm to pickle ripe red tomatoes. Also, the salt is only added to

14 Eggs are *muttar* to salt for the current meal since it is not the norm to pickle them and the salt doesn't really add too much. However, it is forbidden to salt and leave them for another meal.

Today's learning has been dedicated by the Author, for the continued Hatzlacha and Bracha of my dear mother-in-law, Elana bat Sarahy

15 It is *muttar* to scatter sugar on top of strawberries or other cut fruit, even though one intends on leaving them there for a while for the fruit to absorb the sweetness. There is no *issur* of *me'aved* or *kovesh kevashim* here. *Beracha* will come to one who is *machmir* to sprinkle the sugar on top of the fruit and eat it immediately.

○·····································○

16 If one removed one of the vegetables which were pickled in a jar of vinegar or salt water, and noticed that it hadn't pickled enough to his liking, it is proper to be *machmir* and not return it to the jar on *Shabbat*.

○·····································○

17 Salty fish is *muttar* to rinse or leave in cold water on *Shabbat* in order to take out the salt, if his intention is to eat it that *Shabbat*. This is only if one can eat the fish without soaking it. However, if it cannot be eaten without soaking, it is forbidden to soak it on *Shabbat* because doing so is considered as completing a *melachah* and is forbidden because of *makeh bepatesh*.

Today's learning has been dedicated for the continued Hatzlacha and Bracha of Mr. and Mrs. Eddie Aziz Haboosheh and family.

Electronic Lamp

1 It is forbidden from the *Torah* to turn on electricity on *Shabbat*. This includes turning on a radio, a television, a car, etc. Likewise, it is forbidden to turn off electricity on *Shabbat*.

2 It is *muttar* to learn next to the light of a lamp on *leil Shabbat*, even if the lamp has a button which enables you to increase its light. One need not be *machmir* not to learn there because of a concern about mistakenly pressing the button, as this will cause *bitul Torah*.

3 If the lamp is on and preventing people from sleeping, it is *muttar* to cover the lamp with clothing so that he can fall asleep.

Today's learning has been dedicated for the continued Hatzlacha and Brachah of Mr. and Mrs. David Saeidian and family.

THIS MONTH'S LEARNING HAS BEEN DEDICATED
as a Zechut for Klal Yisrael to never again know Tzara or Galut. May the final redemption come swiftly in our days.

4 If the lights in a room were turned on *leil Shabbat*, whether on purpose or by accident, it is *muttar* to sleep in that room since it is only like a *gerama*.

5 If one has a lamp that shuts off due to the fact that it is connected to an automatic timer (which turns the lights on and off at particular times) and he would like to remove the trip-switch to prevent it from turning the lamp back on, he may only do so if he made a clear condition before *Shabbat* to take the trip-switch off after the lights go out. He may make this condition one time and rely on it for the rest of the year, but it is best to make the condition each and every *erev Shabbat*. If one forgot to make any condition, it is *muttar* to ask a non-Jew to remove the trip-switch. If the power went out, it is best to be *machmir* and leave it alone because maybe the power will come back and he will end up turning off the electricity directly.

○○○

○○○

Refrigerators

6 It is *muttar mitzad hadin* to open the door of a refrigerator (so long as he made sure that the light will not turn on from doing so) both while the fridge motor is humming as well as when it is resting. However, it is preferable and best to open it only while it is humming especially when it has been a while (10-15 minutes) since the motor stopped humming, because by then it is almost certain that opening it will cause the motor to kick back on.

7 Because all standard refrigerators have a light which goes on from opening the door, it is imperative to remember to turn off the light or otherwise prevent this before *Shabbat*. Furthermore, because it is so easy to forget to take care of this before *Shabbat*, one should turn off or remove the light and not use it even during the rest of the week. By doing so, one removes any *halachic* problems that might arise. It is worth enduring any inconvenience of a dark fridge than *chalilah* violating *Shabbat*. Experience has shown that those who do not employ the light in their fridge are not so bothered by it.

Today's learning has been dedicated by Dani Reihani, Leilui Nishmat Anbar bat Aghajon, may her Neshama have an Aliyah.

8 If one forgot to remove the bulb before *Shabbat* but would like to open the fridge because he really needs the food inside, it is *muttar* for him to tell a non-Jew to open it. If he cannot find a non-Jew, he should wait until the fridge stops humming and have a young boy remove the fridge's plug from the outlet. There are those who hold that in a case where there is no young boy present, and the plug is regularly unplugged and re-plugged during the week, then even an older person can unplug the fridge after the motor stops running. This is specifically where one removes the plug via a *shinuy* (e.g. sticking a piece of wood or plastic between the plug and the outlet). In any event, *lehalachah* one should not be lenient to have an older person remove it. Furthermore, it is forbidden to re-plug the fridge back into the outlet on *Shabbat*.

9 If one opens the fridge and realizes that the light is on, the food inside is not forbidden to be eaten. As for closing the door, one should place a chair or a towel or the like between the door and the fridge itself in order to prevent the door from closing all the way.

Today's learning has been dedicated for the continued Hatzlacha and Bracha of Dovi Portnoy and family.

10. One who is unsure if he switched off the light from before *Shabbat* has what to be lenient with in opening the door. There are also opinions who are stringent about this.

○·······································○

11. It is *muttar* to use an electric water cooler just like a refrigerator. However, it is best for one not to use it while it isn't running, since removing cold water from the cooler allows regular water to enter and triggers the motor to kick back on. One who is lenient to use such a cooler even while the motor is not running has what to rely on, especially by coolers which one cannot really tell when the motor is running.

○·······································○

12. It is *muttar* for one to place water into an ice tray and freeze it in the freezer, especially in the summertime when it is hot and this brings *oneg Shabbat*.

○·······································○

13. It is *muttar* to place food into a freezer so that it does not spoil, and there is no *issur* of preparing from *Shabbat* to weekday.

Today's learning has been dedicated by Dara and Chana Abaei, for the continued Hatzlacha and Bracha of Mayer and Tsipora Avruch.

Air Conditioning and Fans

14 During the hot days of summer, when there is acute discomfort from the heat, there is what to rely on to permit one to tell a non-Jew (if he doesn't understand in a way of hinting) to turn on a fan (ventilator) or the air conditioning. This also applies in a situation of small *mitzvah* necessity. If the unit runs according to the weather but the weather changed on *Shabbat* and the cold air is causing harm to the people in the house, it is *muttar* to tell the non-Jew to shut it off.

o·····················o

15 If a non-Jew walks into a lunchroom filled with Jews and would like to turn on the fan, one need not protest him from doing so as long as he is also eating in that room or staying there. This is because the benefit he gave himself spreads to the others automatically. However, if he turns on the fan and starts to leave, one must protest his actions. In any event, if he already went ahead and turned on the fan anyway, those in the room do not need to vacate to another room, but rather they can stay put. However, in the future they must tell the non-Jew not to turn on the fan and rather to set it up on a timer before *Shabbat* to activate for the meals.

o·····················o

16 One may be lenient and open the door to a room which has air conditioning or heating which works through a thermostat, even though this lets air come in from outside and causes the thermostat to reactivate if it stopped.

Today's learning has been dedicated by Mordechai and Taly Aryeh, Leilui Nishmat Gavriel ben Ribi Chiya, may his Neshama have an Aliyah.

Central Heating

17 It is forbidden to open the valves of the actual radiator connected to the heating system of a home. Similarly, it is forbidden to open the valves of pipes which lead hot water from the central boiler to the heating system of a home. One may only do this through asking a non-Jew.

○·················○

18 If one shares a house with a *mechalel Shabbat* who turned on the heat for him on *Shabbat*, he does not have to leave the room or close the vents so long as the scenario is that of great necessity.

○·················○

19 Regarding central heating which works in an automatic fashion in that it turns on and off multiple times over the course of *Shabbat* (causing the water to cook then cool off and then cook again) there are grounds to permit using this system without any concerns. The reason for this is because the system automatically turns on and off throughout the whole *Shabbat* and one need not worry of problems of *sheheeya*.

○·················○

20 It is forbidden to open the knob of the heater in order to use the hot water inside for drinking or to clean dishes or the like. However, for the needs of a *choleh* there is what to be lenient.

○ ○ ○

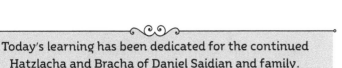

Today's learning has been dedicated for the continued Hatzlacha and Bracha of Daniel Saidian and family.

21 Regarding a heater that works off of a "*Shabbat* clock" which was set up before *Shabbat* to start or stop at certain times, it is *muttar* to change the times on the clock in order to delay the time for the heat to turn on or off. However, one may not change the time to start or turn off earlier than what was set before *Shabbat*. In any event, for the sake of a non-critical *choleh* it is even *muttar* to change the setting to turn off earlier if the heat is bothering him. Still, he must still be careful not to shut off the heat directly.

22 One should not hold his wet hands near the heater even if it is not at the degree of *yad soledet bo*. However, it is *muttar* if he wipes them off first. It is forbidden to spread wet clothing near the heater, even if it will not reach *yad soledet bo*. Similarly, one should not stand or sit near a heater while wearing wet clothes if the heater will reach *yad soledet bo* even if his intention is merely to heat up from the heater.

Today's learning has been dedicated for the continued Hatzlacha and Bracha of Meir Gabaei and family.

Electric Blankets

23 It is *muttar* to use an electric blanket which was plugged in before *Shabbat*, and one need not worry that the heat will rise or decrease on *Shabbat*. In any event, it is best for one to make a special knot before *Shabbat*, or to place a note on the knob that says "*Shabbat*" as a precaution to prevent him from accidentally changing the setting. If he forgot to plug it in before *Shabbat*, it is forbidden to connect it on *Shabbat*.

○······················○

24 Regarding an electric pillow, there is grounds to permit one to sleep with it and move it on *Shabbat*. However, it is forbidden to plug it in on *Shabbat*.

Radio, Television and Cd's

25 It is forbidden to set a radio or a TV to an automatic clock before *Shabbat* to turn on during *leil Shabbat*. One who wants to watch over his *nefesh* should distance himself from a TV completely.

○······················○

26 It is categorically forbidden to operate a transistor on *Shabbat*.

○······················○

27 It is forbidden to set up a recording device before *Shabbat* to turn on automatically and record singing, *chazzanut*, or even *derashot* on *Shabbat*. As well, one may not set up the device to play a recording on *Shabbat*.

Today's learning has been dedicated for the continued Hatzlacha and Bracha of Yosef Chaim Noorani and family.

Telephones

28 It is forbidden to use a phone on *Shabbat*. Similarly, it is forbidden to return or answer anyone that has their phone on them. However, when it comes to a non-critical *choleh* it is *muttar* to use a phone so long as a non-Jew picks up and puts down the phone.

29 One should try to unplug the phone or turn off the ringer before *Shabbat* in order that if it is caused to ring, no one will hear it.

30 If one needs to make a phone call because of *pikuach nefesh*, it is best to pick up the phone in a way different than the norm (through a *shinuy*). Picking it up with his elbow is better than two people picking up the phone in tandem.

31 One who called emergency assistance (hospital, ambulance, or doctor) in a case of *pikuach nefesh* may hang up afterwards if he will otherwise block them from taking or making a different call to deal with *pikuach nefesh*. Similarly, it is *muttar* for the one that received the call to hang up. In any event, it is best to hang up the phone through a *shinuy*.

Today's learning has been dedicated for the continued Hatzlacha and Bracha of Yisrael Meir Gabaei and family and for the Refuah Shelemah of Kol Choleh Yisrael.

·ᴄᴇᴏ·
• Day 305 •
·ᴄᴇᴏ·

·ᴄᴇᴏ·
• ז' תמוז •
·ᴄᴇᴏ·

Answering Machines

32 One should not leave an answering machine on over *Shabbat* which will result with callers leaving messages over *Shabbat*. There are many reasons for this to be forbidden and one should therefore take the necessary measures before *Shabbat*.

Fax

33 It is forbidden to use a fax machine on *Shabbat*, even if one set it up and left it open before *Shabbat*.

Electric Doors

34 It is forbidden to walk in front a door that opens automatically, because doing so triggers the electric current to turn on. Similarly, it is forbidden to open a door which turns on a light on *Shabbat*.

bell to ring when opened. It is also forbidden to leave through it since the bell will ring again as he leaves.

35 It is forbidden to enter a house through a door that triggers an electric

36 There is what to be stringent about regarding entering a house which has a security camera covering the door to show the owners who is approaching to enter their home.

Today's learning has been dedicated by the Author, for the continued Hatzlacha and Bracha of my dear daughter, Nava Tehila bat Sara.

∾✺∾
• Day 306 •
∾✺∾

∾✺∾
• יא' תמוז •
∾✺∾

Electric Bells

37 One may not use a bell on *Shabbat*, even a regular bell that does not work on electricity, and certainly not an electric one.

०·····························०

38 If one mistakenly pushed an electric doorbell on *Shabbat* and realized his mistake while his finger was still on the button, he may remove it. This is because doing so is not considered even a *kibuy derabanan* as it merely disconnects the current; in this circumstance we allow him to remove his finger because otherwise he will be quite embarrassed to keep his finger there for the rest of *Shabbat*. In any event, it would still be forbidden for him to remove his finger from the bell if doing so would turn on or off a light connected to it.

Microphones

40 It is forbidden to use a microphone on *Shabbat*, or to hear *tefilah* through a microphone, even if it was set up before *Shabbat*.

∘~∾✺∾~∘
Today's learning has been dedicated for the continued Hatzlacha and Bracha of Mr. and Mrs. Mordechai Lalehzari and family.

Hearing Aids

40 For people who have a hard time hearing and wear a hearing device, there is what to permit one to use it if he set it up before *Shabbat*. Similarly, it is *muttar* to go out with it in the public domain if it is impossible for him to go out without it so long as it is sturdy in his ear; there's no worry that it will fall out and cause him to pick it up in a public domain. It is correct to stick a piece of paper on the device before *Shabbat* to prevent him from turning off the device on *Shabbat* itself.

Elevators

41 It is forbidden for one to use a regular elevator on *Shabbat*, since the opening and closing of the elevator doors as well as the elevator itself operate through electrical circuits. On top of this, most elevators have lights on their buttons which would constitute *mavir*.

42 There is what to permit one in using an automatic elevator that goes up and down in a pre-programmed way without stopping and whose doors open and close on their own, in which no *melacha* is done to get in or out of it. Specifically, one should use this type of elevator in order to accomplish a *mitzvah*, for example to join a *minyan* or for the needs of *seudat Shabbat*, or if he is old and weak. There are those of the opinion that one may only go up in such an elevator but not come down.

Today's learning has been dedicated for the continued Hatzlacha and Bracha of Rena Levy and family.

Escalators

43 Escalators which are triggered by stepping onto them are forbidden to use on *Shabbat*, whether one is going up or coming down. However, it is *muttar* to go up or down an escalator that runs non-stop or at pre-programmed times on *Shabbat*.

Vehicles

44 If someone is traveling in a car on *Shabbat* and stops to ask bystanders for directions, it is forbidden to give him directions. This applies even if by giving the directions it will make the person's drive shorter or prevent him from stopping more times to ask people. It is still forbidden to give him directions even for the sake of *darchei shalom*.

45 It is best for one to abstain from crossing the road when a car is driving close by, since this will cause the driver to slow down and then speed up again.

Today's learning has been dedicated for the continued Hatzlacha and Bracha of Shayan Davatgar and family.

| Chapter 44 | Laws Pertaining to Muktzah on Shabbat |

1 The *Chachamim* made it forbidden to move certain objects on *Shabbat* in the same way one does during the week. The reason they made it forbidden is because just as the *Nevi'im* cautioned that one's comportment on *Shabbat* should not be same as during the week and that one's discussions on *Shabbat* should not be the same discussions as those during the week — how much more so one should differentiate which objects he takes on *Shabbat* in order to prevent *Shabbat* from appearing mundane in the people's eyes. Otherwise, people would begin moving and arranging all their objects to fill the time as they wouldn't be working on *Shabbat*. It would then appear as though there were no *Shabbat* which would undermine the whole reason for *Shabbat*, as the *Torah* says, *"Lema'an Yanuach"*.

2 The four main categories of *muktzah* are the following:

1) *Kli she'melachto le'issur.*
2) *Muktzah machmat chisaron kis.*
3) *Muktzah machmat gufo.*
4) *Bassis le'davar* forbidden.

Today's learning has been dedicated for the continued Hatzlacha and Bracha of Reuven Zarabian and family.

A Utensil that is Used for Issur

3 A *kli she'melachto le'issur* is an object that is used in order to perform a *melachah* which is forbidden. Examples of this are a pen to write with, scissors to cut with, etc. The *din* is that one may move such an object for non-*melachah* needs, e.g. taking a hammer to break open nuts. As well, one may move this type of *muktzah* object if he needs the place where it is resting.

○··○

4 Regarding an object with both *issur* and *hetter* uses, if most of its use is for *melachah* which is forbidden then it has the *din* of a *kli she'melachto* le'issur. However, if most of its use is for *melachah* which is allowed on *Shabbat*, or even if it is used equally for both *issur* and *hetter*, then the object has the *din* of *kli she'melachto le'hetter*.

○··○

5 If one uses *kli* whose general use is for *issur* in a permissible way, for example to move it out of his way or for a non-*melachah* action, it is *muttar* for one to put it down anywhere he wants as long as he is still holding it. One need not put it down immediately after he is done using the object or using the area.

Today's learning has been dedicated for the continued Hatzlacha and Bracha of Nuriel Niamehr and family.

It is forbidden to move a *kli* whose general use is for *issur* in order to protect it from getting damaged or stolen. However, if one thinks he will use it, it is *muttar* for him to move the item even if his initial intentions were to move it in order that the object would not get ruined or stolen.

○⋯⋯⋯⋯⋯⋯⋯⋯⋯⋯○

When it comes to *tefillin*, the *din* is like that of a *kli she'melachto le'issur*, that they are forbidden to move unless to use the space they occupy or one is worried that they will get ruined or stolen. One may certainly pick them up if they fell. *Le'chatechilah,* one should be careful to remove his *tallit* from the bag in which he keeps his *tefillin* before *Shabbat*. If he forgot to do so, it is *muttar* for him to move them off the *tallit*. However, if he is able to pull out the *tallit* without moving the *tefillin* by hand then he should not move the tefillin, but rather just take out the *tallit*.

Today's learning has been dedicated by Rodney Hakimi, for the continued Hatzlacha and Bracha of the Hakimi family.

∾ᴄᴏ∾
• Day 312 •
ᴄᴏ∾

∾ᴄᴏ∾
• יז' תמוז •
ᴄᴏ∾

8 A *kli* which is widely accepted as having a forbidden *melachah* as its main use (e.g. pen, hammer, matches) is considered a *kli she'melachto le'issur* even if he never used the item for a *melachah* of *issur*. On the other hand, a *kli* that is not recognized as such (e.g. a bowl set aside to light an oil candle or a wallet set aside to hold money) is not considered a *kli she'melachto le'issur* from what one sets it aside for, but rather through using it to perform an *issur*.

9 Matches, a wallet with no money inside, an oil lamp which was not lit from before *Shabbat*, a ruler, a comb, a nail, cigarettes, and laundry supplies, are all considered a *kli she'melachto le'issur*. When one needs the space where these items rest, one is allowed to move them. Similarly, one may open an empty wallet to retrieve a key from it. However, when it comes to scissors that are used for *hetter*, e.g. to cut food or to open a bag of milk, they are not in this category and their *din* is like that of a regular knife.

∾ᴄᴏ∾
Today's learning has been dedicated for the continued Hatzlacha and Bracha of Dr. and Mrs. Ezra Nourmand and family.

Muktzah Because of Monetary Loss

10 Any object which is used for performing an *issur* on *Shabbat* and the owner is meticulous that no one ruins it (for example a knife for *milah* or *shechitah*, a radio, a camera or any other expensive device) are in the category of *muktzah machmat chisaron kis* and are forbidden to move on *Shabbat*, even for a permitted usage or its space.

11 Bills, commercial letters, checks, money documents, securities, or any other documents that one is careful to keep safe, or a bus pass or the like, are all under the category of *muktzah machmat chisaron kis* and are forbidden to move on *Shabbat*.

12 Utensils which are specific to commerce that one is *makpid* not to use otherwise so that they don't get ruined, have the *din* of *muktzah machmat chisaron kis*. However, if he is not meticulous about them then one may move them, even if they are specific to trade and stored away.

Today's learning has been dedicated for the continued Hatzlacha and Bracha of Yehuda Shnidman and family.

13 Dates, almonds or other foods, are *muttar* to move and eat on *Shabbat* even if they are merchandise. This is because no (detached) food that is ready to be eaten which is considered *muktzah* on *Shabbat*, but rather they are considered prepared. However, if the food is not ready for consumption, like an *etrog* that is waiting to be sold before *chag Sukkot*, then its *din* is that of *muktzah machmat chisaron kis* and it is forbidden to move. The same applies to *matzah* of *mitzvah* on *erev Pesach* that falls on *Shabbat*.

○·······················○

14 Some say people's objects, or a house's expensive and important objects, which one is *makpid* not to move lest they get ruined and instead have a specific place to be placed (e.g. an artistic picture affixed to a wall) are generally considered *muktzah machmat chisaron kis* and are forbidden to move.

Therefore, if a guest comes over to one's house on *Shabbat*, it is forbidden to take down the picture from the wall in order to show it to the guest up close.

○·······················○

15 Calendars that remind one to say *Mashiv Ha'ruach, Tal U'mattar, Ya'aleh Ve'yavo* or the like, which are affixed to the wall of a *bet hakenesset*, are not considered *muktzah* and may be moved since they are made to be put up and taken down based on whatever is required.

Today's learning has been dedicated for the continued Hatzlacha and Bracha of Mr and Mrs. Rafi Agalar and family.

∼⦁∼
• Day 315 •
∼⦁∼

∼⦁∼
• כ' תמוז •
∼⦁∼

16 A large and very heavy item, even though it is not normally carried at all because of its size and heaviness, is still *muttar* to carry on *Shabbat* like any other item that is carried and it does not lose its "*kli*" status. However, if the utensil is only used in a specific place and is not moved from there in order to prevent it from breaking, it is forbidden to move it on *Shabbat* because it is considered *muktzah machmat chisaron kis*. However, one may use the item where it lies.

17 An item that is *muktzah machmat chisaron kis* that one set aside before *Shabbat* for a non-*melachah* usage, is *muttar* to be moved on *Shabbat* like any item which is *melachto le'hetter*. One may even set it aside by mere thought, without doing so verbally.

○···○

18 An item which is *muktzah machmat chisaron kis* that broke on *Shabbat*, and subsequently the owner is not *makpid* to not use it for other things, is still forbidden to be moved.

Today's learning has been dedicated for the continued Hatzlacha and Bracha of Mr. and Mrs. Daniel Katibian and family.

Muktzah Because of Itself

19 Any item that is not a *kli*, and is not fit to be eaten by man or animal (e.g. rocks or sand) is *muktzah* and is forbidden to move. This *muktzah* is called *muktzah machmat gufo* or *muktzah de'lo chazi le'midi* (as it has no use).

din also applies to bones that are really hard that are not even fit for a dog to eat. However, if there is some meat still left on the bones then it is *muttar* to move them.

20 Bones or peels that are not fit to be eaten by an animal, like the shell of a walnut or an egg, are forbidden to move. This

21 Bones that contain marrow are not considered *muktzah* even if the bone surrounds the marrow and the marrow is totally concealed.

Today's learning has been dedicated for the continued Hatzlacha and Bracha of Mr. and Mrs. Amiel Taban and family.

22 If one would like to remove bones or peels that are not fit for an animal's consumption from his table, he should shake the *tavlah* (a paper placed on the table in order to put down bread on it) to cause them to fall. The same *din* applies by tablecloth that one may shake the tablecloth. If there is bread on the table, then it is *muttar* to pick up the *tavlah* or tablecloth and move it in the regular fashion because the bones are considered *batel* to the bread. Similarly, if one needs the space where the bones are, he may move them with something else; for example, one may drag them with a knife from the tablecloth. If it is disgusting for him to leave the peels on the table, it is *muttar* for him to remove them by hand because they are then considered *graf shel ray'ee*.

23 The best method of dealing with bones and peels that are not fit for animal consumption is to place them on a plate, because it is *muttar* to move the plate and throw the refuse into the garbage. There are some who are careful to place a piece of bread onto the plate, so that it is *muttar* to move the plate with the peels even though he's not moving the plate for its place.

24 Bones that are fit to be eaten by a dog, peels that are fit to be eaten by an animal, or crumbs that do not add up to a *kezayit* are *muttar* to move from the table, even with one's hands.

Today's learning has been dedicated for the continued Hatzlacha and Bracha of Hillel ben Oshra and Hadar bat Oshra.

25 Foods that are not fit for consumption unless they are cooked or baked, such as flour, beans or potatoes, are *muktzah* and are forbidden to move.

◦·····································◦

26 Uncooked meat which is hard like that of an animal, is *muktzah*. In a pressing situation, where one forgot to put the meat in a cold place or the such, since it is vital, he may move it. When it comes to uncooked chicken, one may be lenient that it is not *muktzah* in a scenario of need. Frozen meat in a freezer has the same *din* as uncooked meat. Therefore, if one's freezer breaks on *Shabbat*, it is *muttar* to move the meat from one freezer to another.

27 Herring is *muttar* to move. However, unsalted fish (which is uncooked) is forbidden to move since it is not fit for consumption. In any event, if the fridge stopped working on *Shabbat* and there is a large amount of fish which would render a big loss by becoming spoiled, it is *muttar* to move it to another fridge.

◦·····································◦

28 Pills for one that is healthy, which are prohibited to swallow on *Shabbat*, are *muktzeh* and are forbidden to move. Pills that are permitted to take are not *muktzeh*.

Today's learning has been dedicated by the Author, for the continued Hatzlacha and Bracha of my dear sister-in-law, Miriam bat Elana.

Animals

29 A fish seller who keeps the fish in pools and some of the fish died, and by not removing the dead fish he will suffer a big loss to the whole pool, may remove those dead fish in a way that will not be *borer*.

30 An aquarium is *muktzah* and is forbidden to move on *Shabbat* from one place to another. The same *din* applies to a bird cage. In any event, if the sun is shining on them and causing *tza'ar ba'alei chaim*, it is *muttar* to move it out of the sun to the shade.

31 One may lead any animal or bird, big or small, for a walk in its courtyard by holding it around its neck or sides, if the animal needs the walk. This is specifically where one does not pick up the animal into the air, since they are *muktzah* and forbidden to move.

Today's learning has been dedicated for the continued
Hatzlacha and Bracha of Mr. Daniel Golfeiz and family.

A Support for Something Forbidden

32 A *bassis le'davar assur* is a *kli* of *hetter* where something *muktzah* is placed on top of it. This *kli* is forbidden to be moved just like the *muktzah* item on top of it. Even if one removed the *muktzah* from on top of it on *Shabbat*, it is forbidden to move the item if something of *muktzah* was on top of it from the beginning of *Shabbat*, throughout all of *ben hashemashot*.

○·························○

33 If one forgot money on a pillow, he should move the pillow to let the money fall. This applies specifically when he needs the pillow to sleep on. However, if he does not need it, rather he is worried the money might be stolen, it is forbidden to move the pillow. However, if he pushes the pillow off with his body and not his hand, it is *muttar*.

○·························○

34 If he placed the money there with the intention that the money should stay there going into *Shabbat*, it is forbidden to move the money since the pillow became a *bassis le'davar assur*.

○···················○

Today's learning has been dedicated for the continued Hatzlacha and Bracha of Rabbi and Mrs Hersel Gholian and family.

35 Anything which is forbidden to move is also forbidden to place a utensil beneath it to let the item fall into it. This is because he is making the item under it forbidden to move. However, it is *muttar* to cover the *muktzah* item with a *kli* if it doesn't touch the *muktzah* item.

○·····································○

36 A bed that had money on it during *ben hashemashot* is forbidden to move because since it was set aside to hold *muktzah* at *ben hashemashot*, it remains *muktzah* for the whole *Shabbat*. It is forbidden to move it even to use the bed or the space it occupies. This *din* applies to all permissible objects which have *muktzah* on them. If there is currently no money lying on it, and there wasn't money on it at *ben hashemashot*, it is *muttar* to move.

This applies even if he set aside the money and placed it on top of the bed before *Shabbat* because he removed the money before *ben hashemashot*.

Today's learning has been dedicated for the continued Hatzlacha and Bracha of Mr. and Mrs. Moshe Chaim Gholian and family.

37 A candle which was lit close to the start of *Shabbat* is forbidden to move on *Shabbat* even after it goes out, no matter if one wishes to use it in a permissible way or to move it for the space it occupies. Since it was *muktzah* at *ben hashemashot* it remains *muktzah* the whole *Shabbat*. It is permitted to make a condition before *Shabbat* to move the candles after they go out, as making this condition permits him to do so. One may make this condition one time for the whole year. Ashkenazim are *machmir* not to move the candles even with a verbal condition. This *din* also applies to candlesticks that people place wax candles inside of.

38 If someone removed a *muktzah* item from the pocket of the clothing he was wearing on *Shabbat*, he need not worry about the *din* of *bassis* for his clothing or his pocket. This is because it definitely wasn't his intention for the *muktzah* item to be there on *Shabbat*. If possible, he should shake out the *muktzah* item from his pocket immediately after he realizes it. However, if he is worried that the item will get ruined or lost if he shakes it out where he is standing, or he is embarrassed to do such a thing in front of people, it is *muttar* to move the clothing item (where there is an *eruv*) while the *muktzah* is in the pocket and shake it out wherever possible.

Today's learning has been dedicated for the continued Hatzlacha and Bracha of Mr. and Mrs. Refael Nakhon and family.

Unusual Laws Pertaining to the Halachot of Muktzah

39 A pocketknife that contains scissors or a nail file with other tools, even if he is *makpid* not to use them for anything else, is *muttar* for him to move it in order to use the knife inside. This is *muttar* only if he does not open the other tools that are forbidden to use.

40 A key ring that has a nail clipper or the like attached to it may be moved on *Shabbat*, but it is better to remove the keys before *Shabbat*. Likewise, if one has *muktzah* keys on the ring, he should remove them before *Shabbat*.

Today's learning has been dedicated Leilui Nishmat Aziz ben Binyamin, may his Neshama have an Aliyah.

41 An empty notebook is *muktzah*. However, if a notebook is partially filled and the writing is important to him that he occasionally reads from it, the blank pages do not make it forbidden to move. In any event, he should hold himself back from flipping through the empty pages. However, if the pages in the notebook have no significance at all to him and he does not read them, he should not move the notebook at all.

42 A button that fell from one's clothes is not *muktzah*. However, it is better to be *machmir* regarding this since it can't be used for anything. However, a new button which has never been sewn to any clothing is *muktzah*.

43 Feathers, hair or any other trash found on one's clothes are not *muktzah* and may be removed from the clothing. However, after one takes them off he should be *machmir* not to move them.

Today's learning has been dedicated for the continued Hatzlacha and Bracha of Mikey Hecht and family.

THIS MONTH'S LEARNING HAS BEEN DEDICATED
Leilui Nishmat Mordechai ben Daniel, Daniel ben
Mordechai and Rachel bat Eliyahu, may their
Neshamot have and Aliyah.

44 A new utensil that has not yet been brought to the *mikvah* is not *muktzah*. A dusting pan is not *muktzah* nor are the dust and dirt while they are being gathered and thrown out. However, after they are discarded it is forbidden to move them.

45 An umbrella is a *kli she'melachto le'issur* and is forbidden to move.

46 A *kli She'melachto le'hetter*, or even a *kli* which is both *le'issur* and *le'hetter*, is *muttar* to move for any reason. It is *muttar* whether he moves it for immediate use or in order for it to be ready for a later time, whether he moves it for the space which it occupies or he moves it for its own. Similarly, it is *muttar* to move it when he gets pleasure from simply moving and engaging with the *kli*, even without a productive purpose. However, it is forbidden to move it if he has no need for it. On the other hand, when it comes to *sifrei kodesh*, food items or jewelry, the *din* of *muktzah* does not apply and one may move them even if he has no need to.

47 One who would like to take an item from his weekday clothing but is unsure whether there is money, or other *muktzah* items in the pocket, if he is in equal doubt whether there is *muktzah machmat gufo*, it is forbidden for him to stick his hand in the pocket. However, if he is leaning more towards doubting that there is *muktzah*, or he thinks there is only *muktzah machmat issur*, then it is *muttar* for him to stick his hand into the pocket.

o...o

48 If a baby took something that is *muktzah*, the father should not just tell the child to put it down in a safe place but rather the father should tell him, "How could you pick up something that is prohibited? Go and put it down in this specific place."

Today's learning has been dedicated for the continued Hatzlacha and Bracha of Mr. and Mrs. Yitzchak Yair Balakhane and family.

Chapter 45	The Laws Pertaining to One who is Sick without Danger

1 A person who is sick but not in danger can have his needs taken care of by a non-Jew. We do this by directly instructing the non-Jew what to do. This includes cooking and baking for the sick person. However, one is not *mechalel Shabbat* by doing *issurei deorayta* even if it puts a limb at risk.

2 If a doctor states that not curing his limb will lead to *pikuach nefesh*, his *din* is like that of a *choleh* that is in imminent danger. Nowadays, doctors say there is practically no limb-threatening condition that does not endanger the rest of the body as well. Therefore, we are *mechalel Shabbat* even through a Jew by doing an *issur* from the *Torah* for a *choleh* in this situation.

3 Regarding a *choleh* with strong pains that as a result weaken his body, or if he fell to bed rest even absent *sakanah*, it is *muttar* to administer treatment which does not involve *melachah*. It is *muttar* to give this person drugs such as pills, syrup or drops. It is also *muttar* to mix peroxide into water for him to gargle.

Today's learning has been dedicated by the Author, for the continued Hatzlacha and Bracha of my dear sister, Ariella bat Rivka Chaya.

4 Even when it is permitted for a *choleh she'ein bo sakanah* to take medicine, it remains forbidden for him to take other medications for other issues in his body. For example, if one is suffering from the flu, he may not take a pill for a toothache.

o···o

5 For one who has minimal pain and is able to walk and function like a healthy person, it is forbidden to make medicine for him and it is forbidden for him to take any medicine.

6 One who started taking a doctor-prescribed medication which must be taken for several days including *Shabbat*, if there is worry that skipping the medicine will be detrimental (for example antibiotics which need to be taken for many days in a row to take effect) it is *muttar* for him to continue and take the medication on *Shabbat*. There are those who are lenient by all medication that one started taking before *Shabbat* and will cause him pain beyond the boundaries of worry or will cause him anguish if he does not take it.

Today's learning has been dedicated for the continued Hatzlacha and Bracha of Danny Farzan and family.

7 One who is habituated to take daily vitamins as substitute for food in order to hold himself back from eating and not gain weight, or if he takes them as a result of his frailty to strengthen his well-being or to cure an ailment, may take these vitamins on *Shabbat*.

8 For sedatives that do not cure any physical issue and work merely to calm the nerves and tension, there is room to be lenient in taking them on *Shabbat*.

9 One who has a headache but is strong enough to carry on like a healthy person and does not have a temperature higher than normal, may not take any medicine. However, if he feels unable to stand on his feet, it is *muttar* for him to take medicine. Similarly, it is *muttar* for one to take medicine to bring down his fever.

Today's learning has been dedicated by Dara and Chana Abaei, for the continued Hatzlacha and Bracha for Shlomo Abaei.

10 One who is in much pain due to lack of sleep, is allowed to take sleeping pills. Likewise, if one knows that lack of sleep will cause his body to become weak, and certainly will cause him to catch a sickness, he may take sleeping pills all in accordance to the judgement of the *posek*.

11 If one has slight stomach pains and he is strong enough to carry on like one who is healthy, it is forbidden for him to take medicine for his bowels. Examples of this are castor oil, paraffin oil, and epsom salts. It is likewise forbidden to eat coal balls or to set up an enema for him. However, it is *muttar* for him to drink tea with lemon or eat fruit which will loosen his bowels, since they are foods for healthy people as well. On the other hand, if he has strong stomach pains which cause him to fall to bed rest or which weaken his whole body, it is *muttar* for him to take any of the aforementioned medicines. It is best to take the medicine orally as opposed to taking them through an enema or the like, since these methods may cause a number of *issurim* to be transgressed.

Today's learning has been dedicated for the continued Hatzlacha and Bracha of Mr. and Mrs. Elisha Loloyan and family.

∾ର∾
• Day 331 •
∾ର∾

∾ର∾
• ז' אב •
∾ର∾

12 A *choleh she'ein bo sakanah* may take medicine for diarrhea. A healthy person may take the medicine as well if the need is great. A baby who is suffering from strong diarrhea is considered a *choleh she'yeish bo sakanah,* and one should consult doctor immediately.

∘···∘

13 One who has an intestinal illness to the point that he is unable to eat a full meal at once, but rather drop by drop, and he must take a medication in order to eat a meal normally to digest the food (in some situations this medicine is taken after eating) it is *muttar* for him to do the *mitzvah* of *oneg Shabbat* to eat and drink as usual, even if this requires taking the medicine.

∘···∘

14 A woman who is on birth control (given that it was done with the permission of a *Rav*) may take the pills on *Shabbat* as well since there is so sickness here and there is no *issur* if there is no sickness.

Today's learning has been dedicated for the continued Hatzlacha and Bracha of Shlomo Shemtov and family.

15 It is forbidden for one who is suffering from a runny nose or cough to do anything to treat himself, such as using nose drops or to take pills or cough drops. However, if it is strong enough that it weakens his whole body or drives him to bed rest, it is then *muttar* to take drops or other medicine.

16 If one is suffering from a strong runny nose that is blocking his breathing channels, we may allow him to utilize a smelling ointment called Vicks. This is because it doesn't heal him, rather it temporarily stops the nose from running.

17 One who has a small toothache should not take a pill to numb the pain. However, it is *muttar* for him to drink a sharp drink that healthy people drink, like brandy or whiskey. One must be careful to drink it at once and not swish it around his mouth and spit it out. It is forbidden to let it sit in one's mouth for a while before swallowing. However, if the toothache causes much anguish and weakens his whole body, he may take pills to soothe the pain.

Today's learning has been dedicated for the continued Hatzlacha and Bracha of Mr. and Mrs. Moshe Nourmand and family.

18 A serious eye disease is under the category of *piku'ach nefesh*.

∘·····················∘

19 If one has a small pain in his eye, he may not do anything to treat himself. However, if it is a more intense pain in his eye or an eye inflammation, he may use eye drops.

20 It is *muttar* for one who has asthma to use a non-electric breathing machine with medicinal ingredients inside to make it easier for him to breathe. If there is a worry of *sakanat nefashot* then he may even use an electric breathing machine.

Today's learning has been dedicated for the rebuilding of the Beit Hamikdash speedily in our days.

Injections on Shabbat

21 It is *muttar* to give an injection to a *choleh she'ein bo sakanah* on *Shabbat* and one should not be *machmir* at all regarding this.

22 If one has diabetes and takes an injection before every meal in order to lower the amount of sugar in his blood, it is *muttar* to give him this injection on *Shabbat*.

Thermometers

23 It is *muttar* for a *choleh* to take his temperature on *Shabbat* even if he is not on bed rest nor is his whole body weakened, but rather he is a worried to the point that disturbs his *menuchat Shabbat*. It is *muttar* to shake and lower the line of sight of the mercury thermometer and one need not prepare this before *Shabbat*.

24 One should not rub the thermometer with an ointment because this transgresses the *issur* of *memare'ach*. If necessary, he should immerse the thermometer in oil. However, if he does not have oil, he may immerse the thermometer in an ointment without applying it.

Today's learning has been dedicated for the continued Hatzlacha and Bracha of Yossi Cohen and family.

25 It is *muttar* for one to use a thermometer that portrays pictures on *Shabbat*, in which if the *choleh* has a temperature it displays letters and when removed from the sick person's mouth the letters fade away, as there is no problem of writing or erasing. It is very clear that it is forbidden to use a digital thermometer, since that type runs on electricity.

○···○

26 It is forbidden for one to measure his temperature on *Shabbat* unless he is sick and needs to know his temperature.

Bleeding and Wounds

27 If one suffers a minor skin abrasion and is bleeding, he must first rinse the area off with water so the blood can't be seen and only afterwards bandage the area with a piece of cloth. It is forbidden to smear ointment on the abrasion or the bandage. If the wound continues to bleed even after rinsing it with water, it is *muttar* to bandage the area with a red bandage or white bandage even though the bandage will become discolored by the blood. There is no issue of *tzove'ah* in doing this.

○···○

28 It is *muttar* to disperse a yellow powder (Dermatol) on the abrasion to stop the bleeding. Similarly, it is *muttar* to put any disinfectant on the abrasion in order to prevent infection. However, one should use a synthetic applicator and not cotton in order to avoid issues of *sechitah*.

Today's learning has been dedicated for the continued Hatzlacha and Bracha of Mordy Spero and family.

∽৶৹
• Day 336 •
৵৶৺

∽৶৹
• יב' אב •
৵৶৺

29 If one suffers from nose bleeds regularly and it is sometimes difficult to stem the bleeding, one may be lenient and place cotton in his nose in order to stop the bleeding.

○···○

30 It is *muttar* to use a band-aid on *Shabbat* in order to bandage a wound, a cut, or the like.

However, if the band-aid is too long, it is forbidden to cut it into smaller pieces. Rather, one should cut it to the right size before *Shabbat*.

○···○

31 If a band-aid was cut before *Shabbat* in a particular way (e.g. in a butterfly form) it is *muttar* to stick it to one's body in order to close up the wound.

○························∽৶৹∽························○
Today's learning has been dedicated for the continued
Hatzlacha and Bracha of Yael Yehoshua and family.

32 It is *muttar* to take off a band-aid that is stuck to one's body hair, when necessary, even if the bandage will pull out hairs while being removed.

∽⦿∾
• Day 337 •
∽⦿∾

∽⦿∾
• יג׳ אב •
∽⦿∾

....

33 It is *muttar* to pull off a scab with one's hand on *Shabbat*. However, if the wound will positively bleed as a result of pulling off the scab, it is forbidden to do so.

34 If one burned himself with fire or boiling water and is in tremendous pain, it is *muttar* for him to disperse Dermatol on the burn. As well, it is *muttar* to remove ointment from its container and place it upon the burn. If the ointment is hard, he may not spread it around, but if the ointment is loose then he may spread it if there is risk to the limb. If the ointment is very loose, one may spread it on the burn if his whole body is in pain.

∽⦿∾

Today's learning has been dedicated for the continued Hatzlacha and Bracha of Marc Ward and family.

Smearing Oils and Dispersing Powder

35 It is *muttar* to smear a baby with oil, even on places where there is a skin irritation due to a wet diaper. When one smears the oil, he should pour the oil on the body of the baby and smear it with one's hand or a piece of cotton. However, one should not pour the oil onto the cotton in order to smear it onto the body of the baby since this causes issues of *sechitah*. This *issur* applies to a synthetic sponge material as well.

36 It is *muttar* to give a child any medicine, whether it be drops for the nose, ears, or eyes. This also includes any pills or syrups that are needed for his recovery. It is even *muttar* to crush and dissolve the pills into water.

37 If one is suffering from dry or cracked lips, it is forbidden for him to smear his lips with chap stick or any other type of substance because this violates the *issur* of *memare'ach*. One may not smear oil either. This *din* applies to dry or cracked hands as well.

38 If one sweats excessively, it is *muttar* for him to disperse plain talcum powder (which does not contain medicinal additives) in the places where this occurs since the talcum powder is not healing him, but rather it merely stems the perspiration temporarily.

○○○

Today's learning has been dedicated for the continued Hatzlacha and Bracha of Mr. and Mrs. Nissan Ommatyar and family.

THIS CHAG'S LEARNING HAS BEEN DEDICATED
for the continued Hatzlacha and Bracha of
Mr. and Mrs. Isaac Zarabian.

Medicine for One Who is Healthy

39 A healthy person who does not have any health concerns can eat and drink any food or drink he pleases, even foods intended specifically for sick people, like medicines. The *hetter* for this, according to *Maran Shulchan Aruch*, even applies if he eats or drinks for his health to strengthen his temperament.

Exercise

40 One may not exercise on *Shabbat*. Therefore, it is forbidden to exercise with an elastic band in order to strengthen the body's muscles. However, it is *muttar* to exercise one's hands and fingers with a small elastic band since this does not tire him nor does it induce perspiration.

41 One may not give a massage on *Shabbat* in order to help one gain strength back and take away tiredness.

42 One should not do physical therapy on *Shabbat* unless he has the status of *choleh she'ein bo sakanah*.

Chapter 46 — Laws Pertaining to One Who is Sick with a Danger

1 If one has a critical sickness, it is a *mitzvah* to break the *Shabbat* for him. One who is swift and hurries to break the *Shabbat* in such a scenario, is considered praiseworthy. One who delays to ask if he should break the *Shabbat* causes blood to be shed. That is to say, one who is over-pious and afraid to break the *Shabbat* without Rabbinic direction causes bloodshed because as he delays to ask for permission, the *choleh* gets weaker and the danger grows. This refers only to cases where delaying any amount of time increases the risk (or even if it is a *safek sakanah*). However, if the danger is not to this degree then one is required to ask a halachic authority.

2 The words of the Rambam are: "When we do these things (to break the *Shabbat* for the sake of a *choleh she'yesh bo sakanah*) we do not do it by the hands of a non-Jew, nor a child, a servant or a woman, so that the *Shabbat* does not become lightened in their eyes. Rather, we follow the hands of *gedolei Yisrael* and their wisdom. It is forbidden to procrastinate in the *chilul* of *Shabbat* for a *choleh* who is in *sakanah* for it states "*Asher ya'aseh otam ha'adam ve'chai ba'hem,*"– and not for one to die by them. This teaches us that the laws of the *Torah* are not vengeful but rather *rachamim, chessed, and shalom* in the world.

Today's learning has been dedicated for the continued Hatzlacha and Bracha of Rabbi and Rebbetzin Shlomo Shoub and family.

3 For a *choleh* who is in danger that one breaks the *Shabbat* for, the *Shabbat* gets pushed aside because of *pikuach nefesh* and it is *muttar* to do any *melachah* for him even to lessen his degree of pain and suffering as long as it constitutes minor necessity for the *choleh*. This is true even if there is no concern of danger of withholding it, and one should not be *machmir* about this at all.

....

4 One is *mechalel* the *Shabbat* for a *choleh* who is in danger, even if the action he performs only saves the person for another hour. This *din* applies also for someone on their deathbed.

Today's learning has been dedicated for the continued Hatzlacha and Bracha of Rabbi and Rebbetzin Daniel Shaliachtzibur and family.

5 If one broke the *Shabbat* for a *pikuach nefesh* and later found out that there was no need for him to do what he did, for example the situation of the *choleh* improved or another person did whatever needed to be done, despite this he still performed a *mitzvah*. He also gains a good reward from *Hashem Yitbarach* because of his good intentions.

○···○

6 One who makes a phone call for the sake of *pikuach nefesh* should try to pick up the phone in a way different than what he does during the week if he can. For example, if he's able to pick it up with his elbow, it would be better to do that than two people picking up the phone together.

○···○

7 If one calls for the sake of a *pikuach nefesh* and suspects he will get a call back from the hospital or other emergency servies, he should pick up the phone on *Shabbat* for the *pikuach nefesh*. It is *muttar* to return the phone back to its place afterwards because if he does not, then the doctor will not be able to call others and make arrangements when necessary. Similarly, it is *muttar* for the one receiving the call to return the phone to its place. Whatever the case, it is proper for him to put it back by way of a *shinuy*.

Today's learning has been dedicated by Avichai and Chagit Samimi, in honor of their Wedding Anniversary.

8 It is *muttar* to travel to a doctor for a *choleh* who is in danger, even if there is a doubt if the doctor is home (e.g. he went away for vacation and one is unsure if he returned home). There is no *issur* in doing so and anyone who is swift to travel in order to save *choleh* is praiseworthy.

9 It is *muttar* to turn to a doctor who is not *shomer Shabbat* or is a non-Jew if he is more of an expert. This applies even if there is a religious doctor present or if he knows that the non-*shomer Shabbat* doctor would break the *Shabbat* unnecessarily (for example, he would drive to the hospital even despite his house being in close proximity, or he would light a cigarette on the way, etc.).

Today's learning has been dedicated for the continued Hatzlacha and Bracha of Rabbi and Rebbetzin Reuben Khaver and family.

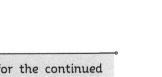

10 If one goes to a doctor's house in order to have the *choleh che'yesh bo sakanah* examined, it is *muttar* for him to travel with the doctor to the hospital in a car since we are worried that the doctor will not be in such a hurry or he will get delayed along the way with another matter if he travels alone.

·····

11 It is *muttar* for a close family member or anyone who takes care of the *choleh*, to travel together with the *choleh* to accompany him to the hospital. It is *muttar* to do this even if there is someone else in the car that can help the *choleh* with what he needs. The reason this is *muttar* is that we are worried the *choleh* will become distraught if one does not accompany him to the hospital, and *Chazal* give permission to do so even if the *choleh* does not request it.

Today's learning has been dedicated for the continued Hatzlacha and Bracha of Rabbi and Rebbetzin Avraham Cohen and family.

12 If one accompanies a *choleh sheyesh bo sakanah* on *Shabbat* to the hospital in another city, he must say *tefillat haderech* just like he would during the week. There is no issue of making personal requests on *Shabbat* in doing this since they need the success in their travels to help the *choleh* and his condition allowed them to travel and traveling is considered a *sakanah*.

13 The driver who drove the *choleh she'yesh bo sakanah* to the hospital and the one who accompanied the *choleh* are forbidden to return to their homes with their car on *Shabbat*. Similarly, it is forbidden for the doctor to return home with a car after he visits the *choleh* (unless there is concern that he will be needed at home for another *choleh* in danger). However, one may lenient to allow them to return to their homes in a car if the driver is a non-Jew and the house is within the *techum Shabbat* (two thousand *amot*) from where they currently find themselves.

Today's learning has been dedicated for the continued Hatzlacha and Bracha of Dr. and Mrs. Babak Imanoel and family.

Guidelines of a Sick Person in Danger

14 One may treat a *choleh she'yesh bo sakanah* with the following symptoms even before he is judged as such by a doctor.

1) High fever with a bad feeling, before the cause is determined.

2) A temperature, even slight, if it comes as a result of a sickness in the lungs or any other internal organ, and people are regularly a bit concerned of danger.

Today's learning has been dedicated for the continued Hatzlacha and Bracha of Ahavat Shalom Congregation Baltimore, Maryland.

Wounds or Fractures

3) Internal wounds, meaning from the teeth inwards, internal bleeding, or a strong internal pain with the cause unknown, which then stimulates concern for a serious disease.

4) An arterial or venous hemorrhage.

5) An open fracture or a fracture in which the movement of the ends of the broken bone are in the longer bones, even if only suspected; a skull fracture; a spine fracture, or any other break inside the body.

6) A blow to the back of the hand or the back of a foot, when there is concern for damage to the blood vessels.

∽✅✅✅∽

Today's learning has been dedicated for the continued Hatzlacha and Bracha of Yoel Kamyabfar and family.

7) A deep wound or cut which came as a result of a knife or any other iron utensil; a hard blow from an iron implement; a cut from anything contaminated; a wound contaminated by soil or anything else that if contaminated will put one in a danger if not addressed appropriately.

8) A wound which is infected and swollen, or that causes inflammation in the lymph nodes around the neck, armpits, groin or the neck

9) A wound with a red line coming out of it and one is concerned for blood poisoning.

10) A large boil, or even a small one on one's lips; a disease in one of the body's limbs, if there is a concern that it could develop a danger to the whole body.

Today's learning has been dedicated for the continued Hatzlacha and Bracha of Elazar Kahen and family.

Thorns, Heat Strokes and Stings

11) A thorn or splinter that penetrated underneath the nail.

12) Heat or sun stroke.

13) A wasp or bee sting or the like to a person who suffers from a sensitivity to such a sting.

Bites and Poisoning

14) A bite by a rabid dog, snake, scorpion or any other animal, like a horse or donkey, in which it is established that there is a concern for danger, and so too a cat's scratch.

15) Swallowing poison or a poisonous substance such as a detergent or pill; swallowing a needle or any other item.

16) Loss of consciousness; trauma; or a concern of shock as a result of something falling on him or because of severe pain.

Today's learning has been dedicated for the continued Hatzlacha and Bracha of Mr. and Mrs. Ari Jager and family.

∽ઈબ
• Day 350 •
ઈબ∾

∽ઈબ
• כו' אב •
ઈબ∾

Chapter 47	The Laws Pertaining to a Woman Whom Recently Gave Birth, and Nursing on *Shabbat*

1 A woman who recently gave birth is considered a *choleh she'yesh bo sakanah* and it is *muttar* to break the *Shabbat* for her for anything she requires. In any event, we strive to do them through a *shinuy* when possible.

2 Since the pain of birth is a natural phenomenon, the *Chachamim* went *le'chumrah* and said that when one does an *issur* for the *yoledet*, he should change the way he does it from the way he would do it during the week.

3 When a woman who reaches her ninth month of pregnancy, it is proper for her to prepare the things she may need for the birth before *Shabbat* to save her from any unnecessary *chilul Shabbat*, since she may go into labor on *Shabbat*. For example, one should write her name and personal details on two pieces of paper so that one may be given to the ambulance, if she needs to travel, and the other to the hospital when she is admitted. Nevertheless, certainly *bediavad* these things are not necessary and it is *muttar* for her to travel in any way necessary. Similarly, it is *muttar* for her to enter the hospital on *Shabbat* even if they will write her name on *Shabbat*.

○ ○ ○

Today's learning has been dedicated by David Akva, Leilui Nishmat David ben Massoud and Yosef ben Yichya, may their Neshamot have an Aliyah.

4 From the moment a woman feels it's time for her to give birth, like when she feels the labor regularly, and even if she isn't quite sure, it is *muttar* to call the ambulance and she may ride in it to the hospital. She may even go to a hospital further away when there is one closer if she is unsure if the closer hospital will admit her or if the further hospital has more expertise or the like.

5 It is *muttar* for the husband of the *yoledet*, or the one accompanying the *yoledet*, to travel together with her to the hospital to escort her in order to prevent her from becoming agitated and come to a *sakanah*.

6 If a *yoledet* needs to travel to a hospital on *Shabbat* and the husband has his own car, it is better for him to travel with the ambulance, even if one has to call the ambulance to come on *Shabbat*. This is obviously referring to a case where they can wait for an ambulance. If they cannot wait for it then he should drive.

Today's learning has been dedicated for the continued Hatzlacha and Bracha of Mr. and Mrs. Yossi Soleymani and family.

∾ଐଚ
• Day 352 •
ଐଚ∾

∾ଐଚ
• כח' אב •
ଐଚ∾

7 Things that are able to be pushed off, one may not do them until the moment the womb opens or until the moment the blood or fluids starts to drip. Therefore, even though it is permitted for one to bring the woman to the hospital, one should not turn on the lights for her so she can see, for example, until one of these things occur.

∘⋯⋯⋯⋯⋯⋯⋯⋯⋯⋯⋯⋯∘

8 If a woman came to the hospital to give birth but it became clear that the time is not yet and she was dismissed from the hospital, it is forbidden for her return home with a car driven by a *yehudi*. If she does not have a place to wait near the hospital until *motza'e Shabbat* and she is pained to wait on the street, there is room to be lenient and allow her to return home in a car driven by a non-Jew, as long as her house is in the *techum*.

○ ○ ○

Today's learning has been dedicated by the Author, for the continued Hatzlacha and Bracha of my dear father, Elazar ben Atta.

9   During the first three days after the childbirth, regarding things that are done for all women following childbirth, we break the *Shabbat* for her even if she says, "I don't need…". From the third day to the seventh day, if she says, "I don't need…" then we do not break the *Shabbat*. After that point, even if she says, "I need…," we do not break the *Shabbat*. Nevertheless, in the first thirty days she is considered like a *choleh she'ein bo sakanah*.

10   The days mentioned above are calculated by the hour, meaning to say that the 'first three days' is seventy-two hours from the birth, and we do not say that part of the day is like the whole day. The same applies by the first seven days as well.

○···○

11   If the *yoledet* has a complication even after the seven days, and there is concern of danger to her, she has the *din* of a *choleh she'yesh bo sakanah*.

Today's learning has been dedicated by the Beroukhim Family, Leilui Nishmat Rakhamim ben Moshe, may his Neshama have an Aliyah.

Nursing

12 If a nursing mother has a surplus of milk (on account of her baby nursing less due to sickness) that causes her pain, it is *muttar* for her to express the milk by hand in such a fashion that the milk is immediately ruined. For example. She can express the milk directly into a sink or onto the floor. However, it is forbidden to express the milk into a *kli*. On the other hand, it is *muttar* for the mother to direct some of the milk into the baby's mouth to cause the baby to latch on.

13 If a baby is not nursing because of sickness, or if the baby was premature and is to be kept in an incubator for an extended period of time to heal, and the mother needs to pump her milk and store it to feed the baby later on, one should arrange for another woman to help her while she nurses into the container.

14 A nursing woman may use a synthetic material to disinfectant and cleanse before nursing However, she should not use a cotton cloth for this use because of issues of *sechitah*.

O O O

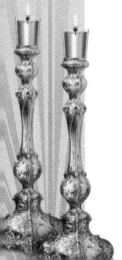

Today's learning has been dedicated for the continued Hatzlacha and Bracha of Mr. and Mrs. Faramarz Lavaei and family.